DEDICATION

For Simon and Callum (known as Jack).......
and the family and friends we left behind.

ACKNOWLEDGEMENTS

Our grateful thanks to all who helped us,
before, during and after, our travels.

Our congratulations to the Lonely Planet
Publications and their Guide to Mediterranean Europe,
which helped to steer our course

— and I emphasise that the views and opinions expressed
in this book are purely personal, based on our experiences.

Front cover designed by Noel Wilford

ABOUT THE AUTHOR

Hazel Jackson was born in Cheltenham, England in 1950 and moved with her family to rural Herefordshire to do 'The Good Life' in 1987. In 2003, having finished renovating their home, and with three sons grown and flown the nest, they sold up and with their youngest son, set off to explore Europe. She now lives with her husband and son, on the Welsh borders.

Simon Jackson has travelled extensively in the past and spent a year on the desert island of Cocos, off Costa Rica, as one of the original members of Gerry Kingsland's first 'Castaway' group.

FREE PHOTOGRAPHIC WEB SITE

To view photographs of the countries visited in this book, please go to the free web site at geocities.com/h.hdj@btinternet.com

Europe in a Motorhome

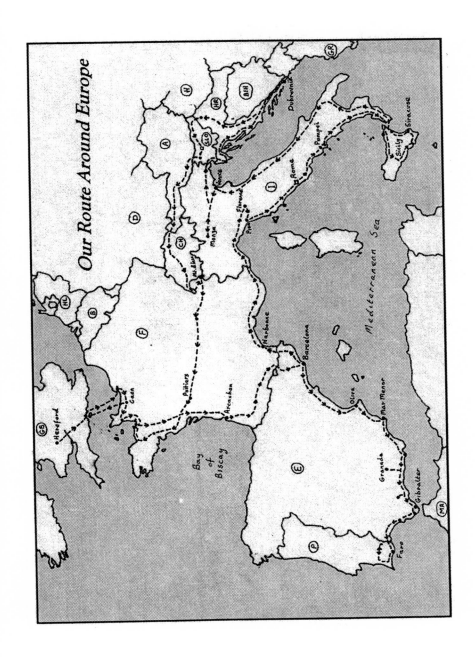

Our Route Around Europe

Casting Off

Decisions, decisions. I want to keep that, and that, and those pictures my mother gave us, and that rug from Ken and please let me store those chairs.

Simon's eyebrows went up yet again as he struggled to cram my latest 'keeps' into the small van that was supposed to hold everything that wasn't going to auction.

Men don't need possessions, men don't need nick-knacks, men don't need objets d'art – ....well, my man doesn't. In fact he doesn't even need a home really. A wooden hut on a beach would suit my man, plus a raft to fish from – as he had once lived for a year on a desert island.

What we did need was a change – not a short break in Paris for two type change, ...more a life change.

At our age this put us well into the category of mid life crisis – we could see it writ large on familiar faces. We could have bought a motorbike or a powerful sports car, but instead – we made ourselves homeless. We pulled the rug from under our own feet and stepped out into a void. Our strange idea was to sell home and possessions, and move into a thirty-three foot, luxury, All American Motor Home, to be referred to from now on as The Beast. Some friends looked horrified, but others thought that to be taking our son out of school, to leave the rat-race behind and travel Europe for a year in a motorhome, had a certain appeal. All that the three of us would need was, in theory, on board the Beast. Our house on wheels, with the usual facilities, plus books, games, music, maps etc and the contents of our old pantry. We three would live and travel in her; wash, sleep and eat, on the move, with a new view almost every morning. We wanted the luxury of independent travel and we wanted to share it with Jack, our thirteen-year-old son. This book must be dedicated to him for being a constant, patient and brilliantly funny travelling companion for my husband Simon and myself. It was the icing and the cherry on the cake that we would share the year and all that we did, with him.

So, have you planned your route?

No, we're just going south.

Won't you miss everything, and how are you going to get on for a year, all together in a motor home?

We don't know, but we want to go and see.

Ok, there were good times, there were bad times and sometimes there were downright ugly times, but do we regret it now? No way...... it was an amazing experience.

Would we do it again?...... You bet.

Our policy throughout was going to be 'here and now'. We had a big motorhome and a limited budget, but we decided that if we found ourselves somewhere with the opportunity to do or see something new, then we would do it and hang the expense. Who knows if we would ever pass that way again? Some people we met on our travels were on a very tight budget, and others had money to burn, everyone does it differently......but it doesn't matter.... you must travel to suit you. So, waving goodbye to our past life, we rolled out of our home county of Herefordshire, one bright September morning and with Cold Play singing away in our well appointed mobile home, we left family and friends for a year to travel Europe – the great escape was finally going to happen. We headed down to Portsmouth for our first overnight stop and our last night in the UK. Tomorrow we would be catching the early morning ferry to France.

Parked at the docks that afternoon, so near and yet so far from all that had ever been my security, I have no doubt that the hollow feeling that dwelt in the pit of my stomach was sheer, unadulterated panic. Oh my God, what have we done?

It really felt as if we were stepping out into a big, black hole that was at once completely terrifying and wildly exciting. We knew that it would do our nerves no good to sit around for the rest of the afternoon waiting for our early morning crossing next day, so with time to kill we invoked our 'here and now policy' straight away. This would be the first of many, many such trips of discovery, which we would take over the coming year, from our quite amazing motorhome.

So, we asked ourselves, (making a guilty start on Jack's extra-curricula education), what did we know about Portsmouth... well, besides the ferry terminals and a University, not a lot, and our first discovery was that there was plenty to keep us busy, especially at the historic dockyards. We could view the treasures of The Mary Rose, which was painstakingly raised from the bed of the Solent in 1982; tour the Guild Hall, or hire a headset and follow a historic ramble through 'old' Portsmouth and the Gun Wharf Keys, – and all with a French translation if desired. But we decided to spend our last afternoon in the UK on board the Royal Navy's most famous war ship and the worlds oldest commissioned ship. Lord Horatio Nelson's flagship at the battle of Trafalgar which, 199 years ago almost to the day, had sailed into battle against the combined fleets of the French and Spanish, who we were just off to visit. Yes, HMS Victory.

It didn't really sink in at this point, (no pun intended there) that I was going to be travelling with two males for a year and, with no other female company, we would be doing slightly male orientated things. Of course six months down the road as I was being dragged past the exquisite and totally irresistible shops in Venice's St Marks Square, pressing my nose for the briefest moment to the glass to view the shimmering and desirable objects on display, before being rushed on to find an exhibition of Leonardo da Vinci's inventions, it clicked that this was going to be a bit of a boysy tour. I'm not a great shopper anyway, so it was no hardship really, but there were times when I did yearn for a day in a full-blown, take no prisoners type shopping arcade, with another female. Just to touch base with those little gee-gaws and totally unessential items that us girls like to fondle. But England expects that every man shall do his duty, and this was day one of our year out and no time for a mutiny, so The Victory it was.

And it was good; very good in fact. Jack loved it and absorbed every detail, or at least the guns and cannons. Staring up through the mass of ropes and rigging you couldn't help but wonder at how physically hard life was in those days, and when we scrambled below and took part in the explosive reconstruction on the gun decks you realised how dangerous life down there had been. Everything made of wood, so if a cannon ball didn't get you then a huge wooden splinter probably would, and the crude surgeon's tools were hardly something to be thankful for. Still, there was always the tot of rum or brandy at the end of the day, although poor Nelson made his final voyage home in a barrel of brandy; not quite what he'd planned I guess.

We passed the afternoon on a merry high, feeling as if we'd all been let out of school early for a special treat. As evening fell, it was time to go home. Home? But our old home, our beautiful old home of sixteen years was gone, sold. The commitment was made to travel for a year – there was no going back. So we bade farewell to Nelson, with a new understanding of how he and his sailors must have felt when they left England, not knowing what would be in store for them or if they would see those shores again, and we ambled back to the Beast.

The autumn weather was kind to us that night. Parked up at the docks in our cosy motorhome we watched the no-nonsense, industrious dockland take on its evening cloak as cars arrived and work continued under a clear starlit sky. This was our last night in the UK for a year and our thoughts were a mixture of excitement and sadness. We had no real route planned ….. we would go South, and then where the wind would take us. We didn't know then that we would meet some wonderful people on our travels, or see so many interesting places, or sometimes be so scared or sometimes be so happy. We just knew that we were doing something that we had never done before. So, our son Jack made up his bed on the pull down sofa, snuggled under his duvet and got stuck into the complete trilogy of Hitch Hikers Guide to the Galaxy. We pulled down the blinds and tried to get to sleep in our big double bed in the back. It was probably helpful not to know that the next night, which would be our first night in France, we were going to be totally exhausted and trying to sleep in the corner of a dirty old car park by a disused factory on an old industrial estate. Not quite the free wheeling cosmopolitan scenario that we planned, but hilariously funny at the time.

A sense of humour is absolutely essential when travelling, along with plenty of sleep, good walking shoes and in our case, a satellite navigation system. Any traveller will tell you that you are going to get into some difficulty or other fairly frequently and although you may be mouthing obscenities at each other or someone else at the time, the important thing is to have a good laugh about it when it's all over. Our first day in France is one that we can look back on and laugh like mad dogs about. What did we think we were doing! We were emotionally and physically exhausted – after all, our house had sold in record time leaving us just four weeks to buy a motorhome, move into it, sell most of our possessions, organise all the paperwork and say our goodbyes. So it's hardly surprising that after a sleepless night and a dawn crossing we landed at Le Havre feeling excited – but just a little weary.

We had decided to wait until we were in France before we filled up the Beast with diesel and LPG gas on the understanding that it would be cheaper. The motorhome had a huge LPG gas tank, which could run the generator, heating, cooking, hot water and fridge. Some of these could also run on electricity when hooked up to power at a camp site. The joy of the Beast was that we could be totally independent for up to three or four weeks as all of her tanks, i.e. fresh water and grey water were huge. A large fridge, good size freezer, shower and toilet made her exceptionally easy to live in. She was already fitted with a TV, DVD and Video player and her storage lockers were enormous. As we travelled throughout the year we met people in every different combination of accommodation on wheels and although some purists may frown at dragging your mobile bungalow along the highways, we felt that because we had a growing teenager with us, we would last longer in something like a Winnebago, and she was left hand drive which was fairly essential. The important thing is just to travel. The downside to having such a large vehicle is that you can't always get where you want to go ….. as we learnt on our first day in France.

So, not quite at our best, we rolled off the ferry onto the right hand side of the road and drove off looking for LPG gas and diesel. Maybe we were just dazzled by the spectacular sweeping bridges that the French weave at great heights and lengths over their varying countryside, or maybe we just missed the turning because we hadn't yet had time to master the satellite navigation system and we were relying on my appalling map reading, but we soon found ourselves trundling off in the completely wrong direction towards Paris when we really wanted to be going the other way, towards Caen. How many people have done this; you roll off the ferry, get confused and head off the wrong way. No problem in a small car but not so easy when you have to find somewhere to turn the motorhome around in. So, some kilometres later we turned around to try again and at last after several attempts, we found a garage selling both diesel and LPG gas.

So now, never daunted although it's getting towards the afternoon and we were already quite tired, we decided that it would be a good idea to do a huge food shop and fill up the food storage lockers so that we were totally equipped with everything we needed for a while. At this point we stopped and programmed the satellite navigation system to take us to Caen and to find us the shopping area, and we also decided that it was time to give this amazing sat. nav. system a name. For those who have not tried one, I can tell you that when you have programmed in your final destination, it will direct you there by giving you advanced directions, and if you miss the correct turning you will get the familiar message of " at the next opportunity, make a U turn!" Our sat. nav. gave us directions in a choice of voices, male or female, and we decided on a very calming female voice that we promptly named Maisy. To be fair, once Simon and Jack had spent some time getting to grips with Maisy, she guided us beautifully across Europe with hardly a falter. Without her, I fear that divorce if not murder may have ensued due to my total lack of understanding of maps. I'm the type who turns them upside down so that they are pointing the way we are going and has to keep putting her reading glasses on and off to read them.

Totally frustrating to the driver who needs advanced warning and instant decisions when faced with mad Italian drivers at unsigned junctions.

Undeterred, we headed for Caen and the shopping area, and following Maisie's dulcet tones we proceeded into the town centre. If you have visited central Caen you will know that it's a fairly busy place and we hit it at rush hour, in the dark, in the rain and in a very large American motorhome. Not good. Things began to get sticky when we entered a one way system of gradually diminishing roads and, as they turned into one lane streets congested with darting French motorists trying to get home from work, we really started to fret. Did I say *fret*; I should have said *sweat*. Dismissing poor Maisy as being a fairly stupid female as she was constantly advising us to 'make a U turn', we launched down a side street and came very swiftly into a pedestrianised area with a two meter high tunnel as the only exit. We were three and a half metres tall. Disaster.

With no way forward, we are now reversing up this narrow street with the greatest of difficulty, with all the other cars behind reversing too because we've totally blocked it. This is where you go and hide in the toilet until it's all over, but worse was yet to come when, in a desperate attempt to get out of this horrendous shopping area, we then swung down another street only to arrive in a small parking square with the road ending in three black bollards. To be absolutely fair, the French were so patient with our efforts that I shall feel eternally grateful to them for not hooting their horns at us and making us feel even worse than we did. I jumped out at this point and did my best to impersonate a French policeman, (all five foot of me), as I halted traffic and waved my arms trying to look efficient and as if I had a clue about what I was doing, directing Simon as he made a twelve point turn to extract us from our miserable position. The French looked on bemused by our English antics and our son, bless him, determinedly put his head set on and did the only sensible thing, which was to listen to the Red Hot Chilli Peppers and pretend that he wasn't really with us.

We laugh about it now and of course this happens to everyone at some point, but at the time you really want the floor to swallow you up and beam you off to a desert island. But at last, we found the right road out and once again, headed off. By now we had that really over-tired feeling, where the slightest wrong word gets a fairly snappy retort followed by a grumbled apology and, we were still looking for a supermarket which might have a car park big enough for us to get into or at least somewhere for us to park close by. Two hours later, exhausted, red eyed and feeling weak at the knees, we were dragging our trolley loads (plural) of food and wine across car parks and roads, in the dark, to load into the Beast, with mission impossible almost accomplished. Sensibly we decided that we could go no further and didn't care where we slept the night, so we drove into an adjacent industrial estate and eventually crept into the far corner of a dark, empty, rubbish strewn car park. We closed our curtains, put some music on, I cooked up a meal, and we gulped down the red wine (not necessarily in that order) – and there we hid for the night. Son Jack was fairly convinced that we would be surrounded by baton wielding French factory workers in the morning, so we decided that we would be up and away by 6 am! He named it Operation Hasty Exit. We had quite a few 'operation hasty exits' over the coming year and we can laugh about them all, but we really can't believe how we managed to make such a mess of our first day in France.

Freefall into Europe

Next morning at the crack of doom we headed away from Caen. It had all been too much too soon. We needed a few days rest, just to familiarise ourselves with the Beast and to catch up on some much needed sleep. The Manche area on the western coast of Normandy looked inviting and we quickly settled at a very quiet campsite in a small town called Barneville-Carteret. This pleasant, unspoilt peninsular, named after the English Channel, (La Manche), is a land of contrasts. With spectacular granite cliffs in the north and sheltered resorts and long sandy beaches as you head south, it is a favourite holiday place for those who like walking and nature. Offshore is the French island of Chausey, and the Channel Islands of Jersey and Sark, and of course the infamous Le Mont St Michel is just down the coast. Inland you can explore the Cotetin and Bessin Marshlands or walk the delightful bocage (hedgerow country), filling up with excellent local seafood dishes at restaurants along the way. In early October though, when the days were shortening and the weather was cooling, it was almost deserted and we had the place pretty much to ourselves. Our bikes were strapped to the back of the Beast, so we spent several days here just cycling along the quiet coast roads, through peaceful towns and villages, past shuttered holiday homes and wandering on the empty beaches collecting shells. It was a good place to chill out and start to plan the first part of our trip, which, we decided, was to see the World War Two sites in Normandy, 'here and now,' before we headed South for the winter months.

With our batteries re-charged we headed for La Cambe first. The route through the historical area of the Battle of Normandy is a great attraction, but don't let the latest invasion of tourists and the accompanying circus of fast food, floss and fancy fake mementoes prevent you from visiting it, and, if you can, go out of season when it will be less busy. We were armed, not with guns and bombs, but with endless amounts of literature gathered from the local tourist information point. We had all seen Saving Private Ryan and various guns and glory films depicting the most famous battles and campaigns of the last war, and some of them seem more realistic than others, but nothing really prepares you for the war cemeteries. At La Cambe, almost twenty two thousand memorials are laid out in small groups, each group marked by five heavy, stone crosses, under which lie the bodies of German soldiers who fell during the fighting in 1944. This was a real-life history lesson for Jack. Just one of many such cemeteries, dedicated to the various nationalities involved in the fighting here, and they would all be very moving to visit, none less so than the next one on our list, which was at Colleville-Sur-Mer.

The sky was a crystal clear blue with a gentle autumn sun and the sea was flat and perfectly calm as we stood and gazed down at Bloody Omaha, the nickname given to the notorious Omaha Beach. Behind us, in the cemetery, lay the bodies of the American soldiers who had fought and died there on June 6th 1944 in Operation Overlord. It was not difficult to imagine the scene when they spilled from their landing craft to wade through the sea and face the barrage of fire which had rained down on them from where we were stood above the beach. The noise, the smell, the fear and the fighting. It must have seemed like a small piece of hell, on earth. We turned from the beach and entered the cemetery, a monument in itself to the graceful beauty that man can create and the clumsy ugliness of war. I defy anyone to walk through this cemetery amongst the ghosts and not be moved by the sight of over nine thousand perfectly aligned, smooth as silk, white marble crosses. Laid out in serried row after row, as if still standing to attention and ready to march, most crosses engraved with name, rank and hometown. I couldn't help but envisage them all as young men, stood tall and strong, but now all dead; buried below the soft, green, beautifully tended lawns which cushion this 170 acre area. You can walk the tree-lined paths or walk between the graves or just sit and think. We three talked and walked, and read the names and wondered at man's inhumanity to man. A small piece of world history brought to life for Jack and somewhere that we would never forget.

That evening we found a great little *aire municipal* (municipal parking area for motor homes and caravans), tucked into the centre of the small fishing village of Port en Bessin, and after our evening meal we wrapped up in gloves, hats and warm jackets and strolled down to the harbour. The tide was full out and small white fishing boats balanced their bottoms on the mud. Along the harbour wall above them, a line of wild-camping motor homers were parked up for the night, opening their local wine and having their evening meal while they watched the shadows lengthen over the incoming tide. The French are great accommodators of motor homes, it seems almost a national pastime anyway, you see so many on the roads. Their motorways have excellent *aires de services*, which are free and usually have good facilities. Most towns and villages also have municipal aires where you can stay overnight and pay just a few euros to the man who comes round each evening collecting the money. They also tolerate wild camping, so long as you are not obscuring or obstructing anyone, although in season you would be expected to stay at a campsite if there was one nearby. We managed to squeeze our big American butt into some fairly small places, thanks to the excellent driving skills and determination of Simon, and we wild-camped and used aires and campsites throughout the year in many different countries with varying degrees of success.

The highlight of the next day was a visit to Arromanches and the D Day Landing Museum. On the way, we had stopped off at the Point du Hoc, a large and strategic German gun emplacement which had controlled the whole area where the allied landings were going to take place. Wrapped in our warm winter clothes, against a cold, damp autumn mist, we clambered through the fortified bunkers and bomb craters, on this vital piece of headland which had been so pivotal in the control of the coastline. A small group of intrepid rangers had bravely scaled the towering sea cliffs early on June 6th 1944, to capture this position, which had allowed the D Day landing to proceed.

At Arromanches museum we began to fully understand the enormity of Operation Overlord and what had been required on this Normandy coast for the landing to be successful. In the absence of a large port in the area to unload the heavy machinery and equipment required, an artificial harbour the size of Dover was constructed at Arromanches in a matter of days. The planning and building of it all, had gone on for months beforehand in England in total secrecy. Over one hundred enormous concrete pontoons were sunk on the Calvados reefs, along with seventeen old ships, and this formed a four-mile long breakwater, one and a half miles from the shore. Floating platforms made of steel created 2,300 feet of pier-heads, which were then linked to the shore by four floating roads of concrete and metal pontoons each one about 4,000 feet long. These were for unloading everything required for the invasion, from light vehicles such as ambulances, command cars and jeeps, to heavier tanks, bulldozers, cranes and various cargoes. And all of this material had to be first constructed in England and then towed across the channel in complete secrecy. The statistics are amazing and it was a great accomplishment that by June 12th, six days after the beach landings, it had not only been built but 326,000 men, 54,000 vehicles and 110,000 tons of supplies had been disembarked. This was the allied push into occupied France.

There was plenty to see here, but we were already one week into our year and we still hadn't left Normandy; we had our own push to make, and we also wanted to return to Caen. This was not to the ill-fated shopping area again, but, having become fascinated with the history of this area, we wanted to visit a museum there, before we moved on. Maisy, behaving perfectly this time, took us straight to the museum, and as darkness settled, we spotted an overflow car park situated on a piece of flat land close by. It still felt strange to simply turn off the engine, cook a meal and go to bed wherever we had stopped and we felt rather vulnerable in the centre of the busy, built up town with main roads on all sides of us, but the French just didn't bat an eyelid. It was obviously not such a strange thing to see a motor home parked in the middle of the neighbourhood on a dark October evening. As usual in France, people were out strolling and the evening was busy, even though there was a chill winter feel to the air. The beautifully flood-lit building was something we hadn't expected and it has remained one of those great memories...... strolling around gardens, fountains and a stunning building, in the middle of Caen, on a clear, dark autumn night.

The Caen Memorial, a Museum for Peace, is a building designed by Jacques Millet. From the moment you walk up the steps to the front doors you will understand that this is not a normal museum. It is neither a War Museum nor a conventional museum and its purpose is not just to display collected exhibits. The Memorial aims to take you through the history that shaped the conflicts of the 20th Century and to understand the fragile but essential requirement of Peace. Architecturally, it's a wonderful building. We arrived there at 9.0 am the next morning with our ready-made sandwiches and essential chocolate, and studied the massive white limestone façade. This smooth, cream coloured building is literally cut through the middle by a narrow, jagged vertical gash of dark glass and mirrors. This is the entrance doorway. It symbolises the allied sword cut that opened the Atlantic wall, breaking down the German sea defences along France's coastline. Inside is spacious, with modern unusual architecture and materials, used to direct and display information. Once inside you have free access to a media library, the usual bookshop and restaurant and even a childminding service for under ten's.

We started our visit with a journey into history that began in 1919 and which is displayed as a continuous trip down an ever descending and ever darkening, spiral walkway. At first the display walls are smooth and light and bright, but as you go further down the passage of time and information, you realise that they have gradually become very dark and rough in texture ..... you are descending into an abyss of war. I didn't realise how much the design of this had affected me until I suddenly felt very trapped and claustrophobic and felt I wanted to escape from such a depressing atmosphere. I was suddenly, desperately, looking for exit signs. I then realised that I had reached the dark years of occupied France and the holocaust. Here the walls, the dim lights and the very air was dark and oppressive, as was the feeling in Europe at that time. As you move out of these years and on to liberation and eventual freedom, the walls, lights and colours return and you walk up a spiral to ground level and fresh air again.

There is far more to this interesting museum and we, true to our usual style, completely overdid it and stayed there for six hours. You can be overloaded with facts and I would advise anyone visiting to get information beforehand so that you really understand the building and its displays. It is well worth a trip if you are in the area. We staggered out boondoggled and returned to the Beast exhausted, but pleased that we had decided to go there, and even more pleased that we had plenty of wine and good French food for our supper. We slept like logs. This time Caen had been good to us.

Two hours down the motorway was our next stop. The famous and ever popular tourist destination of, Le Mont St Michel. There is no sneaking up on this place, as you will get your first captivating glimpses of the turreted and spired islet from across the perfectly flat coastland as you drive towards it. And it is difficult not to be impressed. What you may not be impressed with is the sheer number of us tourists that are there year round, although once again, at the end of October when we visited for the first time, it was not too bad. (When we called in on our way home, at the end of our trip, it was September and it was a wonder that the rock didn't capsize beneath the weight of camera snapping, jostling, pushing and shoving people). However, it is amazing. The Mont of St Michel sits like a granite castle floating in the sea; surrounded by deep water at high tide and bare, muddy, sand flats at low tide. It is approached by a 900 meter causeway.

We drove towards it with the morning sun catching the huge gilded statue of St Michael, slayer of devils and dragons, who stands majestically above the massive Benedictine Abbey which is built at the very summit of this rocky island. Simon swung the Beast into the large car park and there we stopped for the next twenty-four hours, along with literally hundreds of other motor homers, while we explored the island. Jack led the way up through the massive wooden gates, into the ancient and pedestrian-only town; his biggest hope being that there would be shops selling swords - and of course there were. The cobbled streets are steep and sometimes incredibly narrow and the houses of the ancient town cling like a family of limpets around the base of the rock. Ramparts, fortifications and spires of stone, huge doorways and impregnable walls reminded me of the buildings in Lord of the Rings and on top of it all sits a massive Abbey. Simon and I shared a headset to walk around the Abbey, (a desperate measure of economy), while Jack had his own headphones. Take our advice and don't ever try to share headsets. With one ear-piece each we had to walk joined at the hip for the next few hours, and were reduced to much frustrated tut-tutting as we negotiated stairs or changed direction, especially as he wanted to spend longer on some things and I on others. In the end, I was gripped smartly by the elbow and told not to move in any direction other than his. Being a truly obedient wife I took my ear-phone off, let him have the lot and stomped off, only to get totally lost. No matter though, we saw it all. The Abbey is a unique confusion of a building, added to and destroyed many times during its long history, its plan unlike any other due to the pyramidal shape of the mount. Wrapped around the rock, the abbey church sits at the top, supported by crypts, and atop the church in gilded glory is the golden statue of the head of heavenly militia, Saint Michael.

We slept in the car park that night with a wonderful view of the floodlit town. The grey, stone buildings floodlit against the black sea and sky, a golden winged figure shining aloft. Next morning we went back very early; the sun was hardly up and the crowds had not yet arrived. Then it was even better as we could freely tour the ramparts of the town walls that weave amongst wooden shingled roofs, and explore the near vertical alleys that descended to the main thoroughfare. Jack bought his sword by the way and it travelled with us all round Europe, hidden under his bed. Life size and real metal, it now hangs on his bedroom wall. But hey – here and now – he will never forget Le Mont St Michel.

We decided that we'd had enough culture for a while, (that's just how fickle you can be when the world's your lobster), so we headed straight down the west coast of France to the Gironde region, and to somewhere that we hadn't visited for nearly twenty years – The Dunes of Pylat. Robbie Williams was now our singing companion in the motor home, so with Jack feeling glad that his mates couldn't hear him singing along to such music, we headed off, all in full song along the French highways. Jack was thirteen, and a joy to travel with. He is the youngest of four sons, the others having grown and flown, and we had just a one year gap before he started his GCSE syllabus. He grew so much in every way during this year and it was of no detriment to his education, in fact we feel it was of great benefit. We discussed all subjects as we went. Simon good at some and me, at others. Geography, religion, history, languages, maths, cultures, science..... there were endless opportunities to cover all of these subjects as we moved from country to country, landscape to landscape, town to town. How was that fortress built? Why did they have that war? What is this insect? How do you ask for a coffee? What is this festival celebrating? How did this glacier evolve? What stars are we looking at? If you are interested in life then you can learn anywhere, and his next lesson 'on the road' was going to be Geography.

We had visited the Dunes of Pylat before in 1984 when camping in France with the three other boys, when they were young, before Jack was even a twinkle in our eyes. We have photographs of us all standing on the wind blown top in the baking sun and sand. Now we wanted to show them to him. Situated just below Arcachon and almost opposite Cap Ferret in the Bay of Biscay, these are the largest sand dunes in Europe, standing 117 meters high and 3 kilometres long. A strange freak of winds, tides and nature. We arrived just before dark at the end of October and again it was quiet, although still warm in the daytime now that we were further south. We parked up and went for a quick walk up the dunes before it got dark. Actually, it's almost impossible to go for a 'quick' walk up the dunes unless you're an Olympic athlete, and most people go for a long slow climb up the dunes, stopping many times to get your breath back. When we eventually reached the long, wide summit we could only stand and gaze; the views all around were still just as amazing as we had remembered. In front of us was the huge darkening sea of the Bay of Biscay, stretching for miles and miles to the thin line of the horizon; to either side the fine pale sand of the flat-topped dunes, an endless windblown surface of streaking, ghost-like, abrasive grit. Behind us, inland, as far as the eye could see extended a vast, green tree-top canopy of maritime pines, part of this huge forested area.

A 360 degree view, from our wind-blown eerie; as if we were sea birds in the sky. You may think that you have seen sand dunes but you will not have seen sand dunes like these unless you have been to the deserts. We played all the next day on the dunes, with Simon and I mostly laying in the sun or paddling in the sea or flying kites and Jack racing down the moving dune sides, swimming in the sea or finding bronze backed beetles and tiny sand insects. It had been a sizzling hot day, but that night the wind blew hard and as we lay in our beds, in our sheltered campsite under the trees, we listened to the roar of wind and sea, in the Bay on the other side of the dunes.

We stayed five days at the Dunes. Sometimes playing and walking on them, but also exploring this area on our bikes. Our three bikes were invaluable during the year and we cycled at almost every stop. More often than not we found designated cycle lanes. There had been an excellent cycle path both ways along the coast at Arcachon and when that had disappeared, even the main roads were quiet. We now cycled through Pylat sur Mer and La Teste, past shuttered holiday homes and closed cafes and campsites, and explored for far too long, ending up at strange places where our shortcuts had misled us.

We always went too far because we just wanted to see what was round the next bend. Coming back after one of our cycling forays we saw another motor home parked up by ours – with a GB sticker on the back. We had been the only ones in the pinewood parking area by the dunes, so this was a pleasant surprise. The motor home was owned by Gerry and his fair haired, long legged companion Figgy….. a gorgeous golden Labrador. Gerry and dog were travelling for a year too and that night they joined us for supper; a big bowl of pasta and tuna. Gerry was the first of many people that we met on the road over the year, all of them friendly with advice to impart or reading books to swap. He told us of a pretty lake just down the coast, which had a great aire. It sounded interesting, but we had already decided that we should soon head over the Pyrenees and down into Spain before the winter weather really set in.

That night the wind howled again, and next morning we said our goodbyes and all headed on, our first priority to find a laundrette. I had discovered that when travelling, clothes can vary in degrees of dirtiness. We had been very economical with our clothing, but by now we were glad that we had assigned the port forward locker as the laundry locker, because the laundry bag was beginning to get a bit whiffy! (All the lockers were named as if on a ship. For example Starboard Aft was the spare food and drinks locker. This was because my husband would really like to have travelled in a yacht, not a motor home).

Gerry's pretty lake, Etang de Biscarrosse et Parentis, was at Gastes. Another spacious municipal aire was available to park in, this time a grassy orchard area, next to sun bleached wooden boathouses, a small marina and the lake. Jack swam from the sandy beach and French fishermen sat in their boats and looked on as if he were mad. But then it *was* nearly November; the leaves were off the trees and autumn was turning to winter. It was peaceful here but we couldn't linger long….. pleasant as it was, the winter was catching up with us and we had to keep moving South. We motored on down to Dax and then on to the pretty town of Orthez which sits astride the River Pau. From there we had our first views of the Pyrenees and a few miles further on we stopped for the night in another interesting aire de service called the Aire d'Astronomie. All of the play equipment provided at this motorway car park was designed to educate children and adults about the planets and our solar system. It even had a large, circular astronomical centre with film shows and a café. We spent a happy evening there, wandering through the solar system and playing on the planets, before sleeping peacefully in our home on wheels, – how well the French design their motorway stops. Up with the sun next day we moved on towards Foix, stopping for a quick, but memorable lunch, at St Girons on the way.

St Girons is a town not to be missed on a Saturday morning if you enjoy street markets or if you are in any way inclined to be hippy. Stalls offering anything and everything, of the region or not, lined the streets of the old town and the banks of the Salat, a clear mountain river which tumbles down from the Pyrenees. Hippies were everywhere. We didn't see this anywhere else on our travels and it was like re-visiting the sixties. Rasta hair, sweet heavy perfumes in the air, brightly coloured woven clothes and plenty of beads.

Young and old. Sandals and smoke, babies strapped onto backs, groups of stray dogs having a good time, ... a monkey on an organ grinders shoulder, drunk or stoned beggars loitering on street corners with dogs on string. It was like a time warp and Jack had never seen anything like it. As if the world's hippies had sometime gravitated to St Girons to live, and once there had got cut off from the changing world, some just growing old and grey. We felt quite at odds with it all, even though Simon had been quite hippy when he was young. It was almost embarrassing to be in modern clothes and not sporting a ragged afghan coat or carrying a beaded bag and, it was incredibly busy. The local French were mixed amongst it all, but they didn't look too impressed. It was very strange and we couldn't quite make it out, maybe we had breathed in some of the questionable smoke that was drifting around, but hey peace man, who were we to comment, we were just passing through.

We moved on to find an overnight stop. We wanted to have plenty of time to enjoy the scenery as we crossed over the Pyrenees, which now loomed before us, and so decided to wait until the next morning before starting to make the drive up and over. Our motor home was big, weighing seven and a half tons and we were not going to rush. It was getting late and nearly dark, but luckily we spotted a sign to a village municipal aire and decided to sleep the night there. Unfortunately the aire was nowhere to be seen, but we did notice a small car park surrounded by tall fir trees, next to a sports field, on the edge of town. That looked fine, it was empty and not near any houses so we tucked ourselves quietly in and settled for the night. I cooked chilli-con-carne for supper, we opened the wine and relaxed.

Cosily unperturbed in our dining-cum-lounge area, and half way through our quiet evening meal, the gentle darkness outside was suddenly replaced by a searing light, which starkly illuminated the whole area, including our large American motor home. Quickly pulling up the blinds, we saw that floodlights were on all around us, and, looking like startled diners in a fancy restaurant window, we watched in horror as three referees ran onto the pitch next to us. They were shortly followed by two complete football teams in full strip, who jogged smartly on and started warming up. Supporters started to arrive by the carload, all warmly wrapped for the cold night, and they lined the sidelines next to us shouting 'allez –y' as the game commenced. Can you imagine this happening in England. Surely we would have been asked to move, but not the French. Hardly glancing at us, the spectators cheered, their breathe hanging frosted in the cold night air, and rubbed their hands and stamped their feet to keep themselves warm, while players raced up and down the pitch right next to us, dribbling, spitting and shouting like footballers the world over. We might as well have not been there. We quickly swallowed our embarrassment along with our chilli, opened the windows and cheered too. It was the only thing to do really. Blue and white socks against yellow socks – nothing too technical for us, we cheered for them all. This was Saturday match night in the small village of Les Cabannes. Much later, game over, cars skidded off into the night. No doubt, celebration or commiseration would be discussed over a few bottles of biere or wine in the local bar, but our peaceful darkness returned. We pulled down the blinds and made up Jacks bed. Just the three of us again, sleeping well, before we crossed the mountains and entered Spain; and, as far as we could tell, the 'yellow socks' had won the match.

November

Oranges in Oliva

I was designated to the seat behind the driver's seat for the next part of our journey, for very good reasons. I had been sitting in the front and Jack had been in the rear seat but it was generally thought that my being in the front was not such a good idea and we should swap. The Beast was quite high and sometimes, to me, it was like sitting in the front of a fairground roller coaster. Flyovers that spanned gorges and valleys, on stilts of concrete, had had me clutching the sides of the seat and almost sitting on Simon's lap as he drove. My now familiar saying of "we're awfully close to the edge Si!" in a very high pitched voice, was really rattling him and didn't help one iota. 'Get in the back mother and don't say anything', was basically the format as we wound our way up through the mountains – which was fine by me. The weather was clear but cold on the French side of the mountain range and the autumn colours were as beautiful as you can imagine. Stunning, snow capped peaks came into view now and again, but as the road ground ever upward, with staggering sheer drops beside us, I felt the need to get out a bottle of Pina Colada and swig at it with ever increasing ferocity as we zigzagged up through the hairpin bends to the top. I'm not sure why I suddenly found heights so difficult to deal with. When I was younger I had been a high board diver, but with age had come caution. This was something I had to overcome as we often used cable cars, ski lifts and climbed to the tops of just about everything and anything that we visited. Throughout the year my fear of heights got better, but it was never easy.

Eventually, we reached the top of the pass and stopped at around 6000 feet at Porte Puymorens for a cook up of eggs and beans and to call some friends from the singular, desolate telephone box that huddled at the side of the mucky road. The mist and freezing drizzle hung about at this height, clouding the craggy bare mountain sides. We stared down at the deep valley ahead with apprehension and eventually started down the road of shiny, icy tarmac which twisted and switch-backed its way down into Spain. More Pina Colada was consumed by the lady in the rear seat as she gazed at the amazing scenery: for 'amazing scenery' please read 'scary dizzying drops at the edge of roads which clung impossibly to the sides of mountains!' Through the Tunnel del Cadi and at last we reached level land again on our way towards Barcelona.

We soon realised that Spanish roads in this area were far busier than the ones that we had left behind in France. Catalunya and Barcelona had recently received EU money for massive road building programmes, which was great. However most of that money seemed to be going into digging up and re-laying the ring road around

Barcelona. Weaving our way through convoluted road works, alongside hundreds of speeding lorries and cars was daunting, and we needed to be on our toes. The Spanish in this area also seemed to have an interesting approach to driving; i.e. ignore all rules, white lines, speed restrictions and warning signs. Overtake anything that moves – car, lorry, bird, plane, you name it and they'll overtake it, even if it's on a blind bend and next to a ravine. Also park anywhere at anytime. Our law-abiding, pedantic English adherence to the rulebook was wasted here as we were jostled along the motorway like lemmings on the way to the edge. A fast flowing river of traffic that was impossible to escape from. We decided to return to Barcelona another day and agreed that when we did, we would use the extensive and fast public transport system. For now though, we were still heading south down the coastal road. That night we pulled up in a motorway parking area just north of Valencia. Tremendous thunderstorms and torrential rain had swept across the area during the day, making driving even worse, so we stopped earlier than usual that evening, which turned out to be a blessing in disguise. The car park was fairly empty when we pulled in and we found a good spot to park. Lorries were still hurtling down the motorway but before too long they came screaming into the car park, one after another like racing cars into the pits, searching for a space, until it was almost full. Huge juggernauts gliding up alongside us made us look positively insignificant and we wondered why on earth they all parked so closely together.

We got quite used to sleeping amongst these giants as the year went on and never had any trouble. We were too big for car-sized slots in normal parking areas, so had to bunk down with the big boys. That night we slept ok, and awoke early next morning when the first lorries were starting to head off. Laying in bed, listening to the background noise of revving engines and hawking Spaniards, just beyond our windows, was not quite 'Kings of the Road' material, but if we had thought that the car park was full when we went to sleep, it was nothing to how full it was now. Lorries were jammed nose to tail, side by side, in every possible bit of space. This was another lesson to learn. There really isn't enough space in the Spanish motorway car parks for lorry drivers to park up for the night and if you don't get a space early, you could be driving for a long while before you find somewhere to lay your head.

However, like most Spaniards, the lorry drivers seemed to do everything with a flourish and a passion. Whether it was neck and neck racing down the motorway, sulking and arm waving because they had been pipped at the post for a parking space, cooking up a lunch at the side of their cabs, or even just answering the call of nature. Oh yes; no bashful discreetness for them when nature calls. Out of the cab, down with the flies and straight on with it, often not making it to the grass at the curb, or even a nearby tree. When you've got to go, you've got to go, and anywhere, including the tarmac, will do. Were they just frustrated bullfighters full of macho daring do? Who knows, but this was Spain. So Viva Espagna, Espagna por favour.

Spain is such a huge country, so diverse, so crammed with treasures both natural and man made, with so much to see that you could spend years there and still want more time. So often I was exasperated with Spain. It was a land of opposites for me. It could be so dirty, so noisy, so difficult to deal with but just when I was cursing some illogical, frustrating or maddening situation or some surly unhelpful person, some wonderful festival or event would happen, or some person would behave with such flamboyance, such generosity of spirit or we would see such beauty in land or culture that my previous ideas would be turned on their heads. When we finally left Spain to travel on to Italy, I said I would never go back. But now, I would go back tomorrow, because for all its failings and frustrations, to live in Spain is to live life.

This country has a population of over forty million, drawn from all the many peoples who have settled there over the millennia. Each region will proudly, and I mean proudly, boast of its culture and cuisine. It is surely Europe's most geographically diverse country with landscapes ranging from the lush, green coastal inlets of Galicia, to the sun-baked plains of Castilla-La Mancha: from the mountainous, snow capped Pyrenees and Sierra Nevada to the near desserts of Almeria. Ski in the morning and swim in the Med in the afternoon. Spanish cities will dazzle you – the architecture, the people, the energy, the conversations held at top volume – everyone will listen to a private conversation, shared with much hand waving and tossing of heads – if only we had understood what even half of it was all about. But in the countryside it will be the tiny old ladies dressed in black that will catch your eye, and you'll feel as if you're rudely trespassing as you sneak a look through cool, dark, doorways in silent villages. You may boil over in the summer in Andalusia but you could freeze in the winter in Madrid. There are so many variations. But in general the coast will be mild in the winter and that's where you will find the majority of the 'snowbirds', the huge number of older people, from many different nationalities, who rest the winter there.

We arrived at our coastal campsite, in Oliva, late in the afternoon after a fairly stressful drive. We had tried to go through nearby Gandia instead of around it. That had something to do with the lack of signposts, and it didn't help that it was a madly busy town of small roads and it was school collection time. As usual, parking restrictions were non-existent on anyone's agenda, so parents parked three and four deep in the town centre, with doors open for children to eventually hop in. Traffic piled up, horns blew, heads were tossed and we all got very heated. We imagined this happened on a daily, if not hourly, basis. Eventually we squeezed out of Gandia and reached the campsite, and with light fading fast we wriggled in through the small entrance and into a space in what we would later call, the British quarter. With neck muscles seized and too tired to cook a meal we slurped some red wine and headed for the camp restaurant. This was situated on the long beachfront and had a great seating area outdoors, under a big canvas roof. It seemed strange to us that no one else was eating there, but we thought that maybe we were too early, although it was now dark. The bored waitresses regarded our dishevelled and weary appearance with some surprise and offered us seats indoors, probably trying to hide us in a corner. Oh no thank you…. We want to sit outdoors under the canopy.

And so we did…..totally alone in the restaurant for the whole evening, Jack being very impressed by the personal attention of three waitresses, all to ourselves. We had a wonderful meal of paella, the first of many in Spain, and by far the most expensive too. That would account for the lack of customers. Snowbirds live economically. They live on the excellent, cheap local produce bought at markets and cook it back at camp. They often get incredibly low rates for their six-month winter stays in their caravans or motor homes on the camp sites and they enjoy the mild winter weather in relative peace. In summer of course they leave, and the usual tourists arrive with money to spend and good times to be had in the baking sun. That is a different kind of Spain again.

The next morning we were shattered and didn't even open our curtains until gone eleven o'clock. Curled up in our pyjamas, munching breakfast, wrapped in duvets, we slobbed it and watched a video of Alien 3 on our TV. Well, once in a while you just needed to do that. When we did finally open our door we found ourselves in a pleasant corner of the site, with parakeets flying in the trees about us and curious neighbours on either side; Graham and dog, avoiding a long English winter, and Gerald and Lizzie (French) who had literally ground to a natural halt when their back axle had broken. A little further on were a young London couple who were also travelling in a big American motor home on a two year gap. Their passion was to ski and sail and they had not only brought their skis with them but had a collapsible catamaran sailing boat on board the motor home too. The majority of the rest of the large campsite were German. 'Morgans' as we called them. Our 'good morning' replied to by a gruff 'morgan'. We were amazed at how many Germans were over-wintering on the Spanish Coast. Like the Brits, they too were leading a double life of boules and card games in the warm winter, just returning to home for the summer months.

Before long our bikes were oiled, tyres pumped up and we had found the easy cycle route into town, past purple flowering bougainvillea and swathes of heavily scented flowers that I shamefully did not know the names of. Over little bridges crossing channels of water running down to the sea, past the local indoor swimming pool and up through the broad avenue of wide topped plane trees that shaded Oliva's main promenade. We locked our bikes at the big town square where children played and the elderly sat and chatted, then walked up to the 'old town' area to explore the steep winding streets, preserved churches and white washed houses. Up to the top of the castle remains, and a wonderful view across Oliva's tiled roof tops to the sea. Then down again until we eventually staggered wearily back to the square and flopped on to a bench.

Overheard conversations in English had been repeatedly caught on the wind and a British-run Internet café and shop, selling everything from baked beans to Christmas puddings, soon reminded us of home. We had been away from England for nearly four weeks – not long really, although Jack now admitted that he was missing his mates. Guilt seems to come as part of the parenting package and we now felt very guilty that he was stuck with us for so much of the time. (These feelings disappeared quite quickly as the year went by and we all fell into slightly different roles.) Anyway, as there was obviously an English community in Oliva, we decided to try to find some friends for Jack. The owner of the Internet café gave us an idea.

"All the English kids meet in the town square on a Saturday night", he promised, as he filled our rucksacks with good old English salad cream, the only thing that Simon ever missed, and as the next day was a Saturday, we had a plan. Jack was a little sceptical but prepared to go along with it. We spent the morning exploring on our bikes but headed home early and had a siesta. It's not that easy to go to sleep at four o'clock in the afternoon if you're not used to it, but we struggled on until we could get up again at around six. Showered and dressed in the smartest clothes we had, we headed into town on our bikes, ready for a great night out. You know that saying about the greatest plans of mice and men…. well, we walked the town in search of the elusive English teenagers, but they were all obviously having a rare, quiet night in. Maybe there was something good on the telly, whatever. Those quiet streets echoed with our footsteps until we eventually gave up and stopped for a drink at an empty bar in the old quarter. One other couple sat there, also looking forlorn, and although they were English, they were not teenagers. Allan and Cath were on a fact-finding mission, and thinking of moving to Spain, so we sat outdoors with them and chatted and tried to ignore the fact that the weather had by now changed from a pleasant night to one that had a distinctly colder, wetter feel. By ten thirty the rain was beginning in earnest and we were ready to give up.

Dashing back through the town to our bikes, in sandals and shirts and pouring rain, we headed for home. The weather was about the only English thing we had found! We peddled like crazed hamsters against the driving wind and torrential downpour, completely soaked, with no bike lights, (really getting into the Spanish way now) in our mud splattered Sunday best. A short-cut alongside an old canal, in pitch black, past big barking dogs and pushing our bikes through muddy, long wet grass eventually led us to within meters of the camp site…. if only the marina hadn't been in the way…. so back the same way again, past the barking dogs and through the long wet grass, and then the long way round on the pitch-black roads. We certainly know how to have a good Saturday night out. Like dripping water rats we crept back into the motor home. With a wisdom born only from experience, Jack tactfully suggested, "Let's stick to the cup of cocoa and early nights in future, I think I'd rather find my own friends thanks" Poor lad, with parents like us what hope did he have.

The bad weather continued on and off, for five more days. Quite unusual for the area and time of year, but everywhere we travelled during the year, people complained of unusual weather. During this time we got to know Gerald and Lizzie well, and cycled daily, between the showers, finding the excellent 14 kilometre cycle track which joins the towns of Oliva and Gandia. This flat, wide, peaceful track which takes you through endless groves of orange trees, was used by young and old alike for commuting on cycles or just strolling. Littered with oranges fallen from the trees, our thirsts could easily be quenched. Jack will always remember this as the place he learned to ride 'no handed' and I shall never forget him speeding off ahead of us, weaving between walkers, with his hands casually clasped behind his head, thoroughly chuffed with himself. At Gandia another road led us off to the coast and more stretches of sandy beach, while behind us the rocky sierras were outlined against a blue sky. When the weather settled again, we decided that to really see what the area was like, we would hire a car and explore the white washed villages, which we could see nestled up in the folds of the mountains.

Our first car trip was not however to the mountains but along the road to probably the best-known place on the Costa coast, poor besmirched Benidorm. Who can ever remember what the village of Benidorm had originally looked like? It's been a package holiday tourist town for so long, that it has changed beyond all recognition. We expected the worst but ended up quite pleasantly surprised. Of course, it was 'out of season' which makes a huge difference. Benidorm does have a sea front of towering hotels and an enormous number of tacky tourist shops, but it's been cleaning up its act over the past few years and it shows. There are also designer shops now, many classy shoe shops, expensive restaurants and spacious open squares. The clean blue sea and beautiful sandy beaches are edged by a pleasant promenade that follows the cliff face and of course the weather in late November was very warm. And it's not all chips and ice cream, because we did find a locals café, tucked up a side street, where we had an excellent three-course lunch of salad, paella, then meatballs or fish, for eight euros a head. Benidorm may not appeal to everyone, but in winter, it obviously appeals to thousands of older people….. and why not. We sat by a cooling fountain under shady palm trees and watched an endless parade of white haired couples in shorts or tracksuits taking a walk along the beach and promenade, sporting tanned faces and looking relaxed. Who is to say that they would be happier battling against the cold winter rain and frantic traffic of England. Why not wear shorts at eighty, even if you are on a zimmer frame, and why not spend your winters in the warm? I only hope I have the sense to do the same at that age. So, maybe not for us right now, but definitely good for others. What it's like in August of course, I dread to think.

We took other car trips with Gerald and Lizzie because, besides enjoying their company, Lizzie knew the area well as she had lived in nearby Denia for a while. Squashing all five of us into the little Seat Ibiza, we drove the switch back roads up into the hills, past clusters of new developments and amazing scenery, squeezing through tiny quiet villages whose roads were really only meant for donkeys, and passing dark open doorways that invited a peek, with the mouth-watering smell of fideua coming from dim kitchens within. On past orange and olive groves, stopping quickly to pick lemons straight from the trees, which, if you rubbed their warm skins gave you the sharp strong smell of sherbet. Then to Parcent, and on to Altea, the delightful village on the coast, whose famous white washed houses line the cobbled streets, which led us up to the great white church on the hill. That evening, as the light was falling, a large well-dressed congregation with many important dignitaries were gathered in the square before the church and a full choir could be heard through the open doors. Children played in the square and adults chatted, it was obviously a special occasion, but the lady who caught my eye was an old flower seller. Small and stooped, she was dressed all in black, her thick stockings wrinkled around her ankles and her tired grey hair escaping from its grips. She wandered through the crowd, but very few wanted to buy her flowers and most turned their back when she approached them. I was trying to get to her, to buy a flower, but she had moved on by the time I reached the church. Many times on our travels we saw people begging by church doors, often with children, but when the well-heeled and expensively dressed congregation came out they more often than not gave them a cold look or simply ignored them. It always seemed very sad to me and somewhat hypocritical.

The opulent, glamorous interior of Spanish churches sometimes comes as quite a shock when it is set against a poor neighbourhood. In Altea the church façade is plain, but when you push open the huge, brass studied door you enter a glittering, brilliantly lit interior of white and gold. Statues, domes, cornices and ceilings, all adorned with rich paints and skilfully lit with soft warm lighting, make this church most inviting. It was a church that they were proud of. When the joyful singing of the choir finally faded, we went for a beer in the café overlooking the floodlit square and listened to the next musical offering of the evening, which came from the local brass band. They were all quite young, and cheerfully struck up with a swinging rendition of Abba's much murdered 'Dancing Queen'... and a following medley of their best known hits. It was obviously going to be a party night in Altea but not for us, as we wanted to move on to Denia, for supper in one of Lizzies' favourite restaurants. Denia, again on the coast, had plenty to offer the tourist, with wide streets shaded by acacia trees, pretty squares adorned by crimson bougainvillea and a long sea front and harbour. Fishermen's houses were still low level, with few high rise blocks of apartments. Picture postcard working and pleasure boats, faded and worn, coloured this small, busy port with blues, reds and yellows and the seafood restaurants were a treat. Lizzie knew of one; a small family-run affair used by the locals and there we feasted on tasty tapas, fresh fish dishes and of course paella. I never, ever tired of eating paella. We had a charming waiter whose face I can remember quite clearly. He was French Algerian and had features that looked almost sculpted from smooth, dark coloured stone; beautiful almond eyes and full perfect lips and a very unassuming and gentle manner. It's strange how you can remember some people so well from your travels. I can picture him now as he stood with his hands behind his back, quietly looking out of the window to the dark sea, while he patiently waited for us to finish eating. We ended our feast with a rich Musquadet liqueur, on the house – with a non- alcoholic apple liqueur for Jack. Gerald and our waiter talked into the night about Algeria, their homeland. A fascinating conversation, which we were just glad to sit and absorb.

The history of this area, like all of Spain, is as undulating as the landscape. Five centuries of Moorish rule has ensured a legacy of rich culture. Castles, culinary delights and carnivals owe much to the Arabic influence. Countless villages and place names beginning with "Beni" (meaning 'son of' in Arabic), confirms that for centuries this land was peopled by the Moors. It was also influenced by Majorcan families who arrived in the 17th Century to re-populate the area, and that added another layer of culture. Dominated by impressive Sierras, this mountainous area is full of tiny villages and historical sites to visit.

We spent a few more days visiting local markets and beaches and then went back to the mountains in search of the impressive, El Castell de Guadalest, the hidden jewel that sits high on the edge of the Sierra d'Aitana. This old Moorish fort was built on a craggy outcrop, 500 meters above the Guadalest valley. From the fortified town we peered over the walls and down to the Guadalest River and the blue green waters of a large, deep reservoir, way, way below. Opposite was the scrubby rock face of the Sierra de la Xorta, and all around the endless mountains and valleys fenced us in. Guadalest is listed as a national heritage site and has a fascinating centre of old houses and steep cobbled streets, but the real treat comes when you discover the hidden entrance to the old town and the castle of San Jose. Created through a triangular, natural rock tunnel, the entrance, with its smoothly worn steps, leads you up through cool solid stone and into the old town. Carved into and around the jagged peninsular, the houses grow into the rock faces, and although they are now mostly used as museums and tourist shops, it is still a much 'lived in' town. The castle perches above it all on the very edge of the steep cliff face, with staggering panoramic views down and across the valley.

Up to this point we had been going along pretty much according to plan and I guess we should have known that behind every silver lining, there is a big black cloud just waiting to rain on you. Well, our next big black cloud was just rolling into view at this time. We had one place that we still wanted to visit in this area, while we still had the car. That was Les Fonts d'Algar, otherwise known as the Algar Springs. So, making an early start on a morning filled with sunshine and blue skies, we packed a picnic and headed back into those mountains for one last time. It was just the three of us that day, as Lizzie and Gerald were busy, so we reverted to singing our personal anthem of the trip – "just the three of us, we can make it if we try"!

We headed straight to the high point of Pego, from where six mountain roads fan out across the countryside. From there we worked our way through the mountains to Planes, then back to Castell de Castell and then down to Callosa. The mountains looked fantastic in the sun that day. Endless tiers of olive trees on steeply terraced slopes, almond trees along the road side and plenty of orange groves to tempt us. The huge leaves of the regions medlar trees casting welcome shade, and limes and lemons too. We stopped at peaceful, pristine villages, where languid dogs stretched out in the shade too lazy to move, and round old ladies gossiped in dark doorways. A few children played, but mostly the villages were silent and quiet in the warm November sun. We parked and explored them, feeling not for the first time like the three cowboys in The Good, The Bad and The Ugly as we walked abreast down the hot, empty streets with camera loaded, ready to shoot. When we stopped for our picnic on a grassy verge, high above a valley, it seemed that even the insects were having a siesta and you could have heard a pin drop in the valley next door.

We finally got to the Font d'Algar by mid afternoon. This is a big tourist attraction normally, but at this quiet time of year it was almost deserted. Set in a small, lush valley the impressive waterfalls and series of cool pools are fed by the Algar River, and can be explored on foot by way of designated paths. Taking off our shoes at a shallow ford, we cooled our feet in the mountain water, before we followed the path which took us literally climbing and walking up steps built into the lush, green covered rocks and cascading river. It should have been a pleasant afternoon and a great end to our day trip but I had made a few fatal errors at the car park earlier, which would have a miserable effect on us all.

When we had arrived at the falls, we had pulled into the almost empty car park and as we arrived, a car with a young man in, pulled up next to us. Feeling relaxed and full of bon ami, we smiled at him, and then gaily opened our car boot and threw in our rucksacks, jackets and my shoulder bag – for once I didn't want to carry it. Then, as we walked up to the entrance kiosk we practically accosted three other young men who were walking down to the car park to meet their friend and asked them if the falls were open.

"Oh, Si, Si", they chimed in unison, looking particularly happy to be asked. What nice young men, thought I! Of course, I might just as well have said to this group of four dodgy looking lads….. "We're just going for a long walk up to the falls; we'll be gone for several hours, all our stuff is in the boot, help yourselves why don't you!"

Yes, on returning to the car after our wonderful walk, we found the back window smashed in, glass everywhere and everything gone from the boot. If our curses at that point ever became effective then those four lads would have suffered badly, but of course, our ranting was useless, and in the end Jack and I huddled by the car feeling miserable, while Simon strode up to the nearby restaurant, with murder in mind, to discover where the nearest police station was. The owner was most kind and had actually noted their car number plate earlier as he thought the lads looked suspicious, so we did at least have that. (Be warned, apparently it was a prime spot for thieves). He then kindly jumped in his car and led us to the nearest Guardia Civil and wished us luck

— we'd need it. We had reached the Guardia Civil just as they were locking up for the afternoon, so it was with some reluctance and a look that plainly said, 'damned tourists, that's my paella ruined again', that the unimpressed policeman unlocked the door and let us in. It was a futile effort really, but we felt better for struggling on and making a statement, albeit in broken Spanish, and as it was a hire car, we needed to make it official anyway. An hour later we left, fairly depressed, and, having made phone calls to stop bank cards and my mobile, we headed home with the wind blowing a hooley through the broken window and glittering glass all around the inside of the car. Another Spanish experience, but of course, it could happen anywhere in the world.

My shoulder bags are never costly affairs and it is known in the family that to put your hand in one takes courage, as you could find anything in there. Nappy pins and dummies were a long time favourite, but that progressed to bananas and lego bits as the kids grew, and now it is mostly broken pens, string, bits of paper and old receipts. There is invariably very little money. The most annoying thing was the loss of a very old address book and the most expensive thing turned out to be the loss of the only spare set of keys to the motor home. This was a big, big problem. Unprepared to travel on through Europe with only one set, Simon had to spend the next day trying to get new keys cut, (an impossibility as no one had American sized blank keys and the Spanish locksmiths were all in cahoots against us anyway), so when that failed he had to get a new lock and keys sent out from England, to our camp site in Spain.

That night we were predictably rash with the red wine and our spirits sank to an all time low as we realised that we would be delayed for at least a week while this was sorted out. That may not sound very long, but we had been at Oliva for longer than we had planned already and we really wanted to move on now. We only had one year and we had a long way to go. We were champing at the bit. As fellow travellers will know, irrational as it is, when you are ready to move on, you just hate getting stuck somewhere, but sometimes it just turns out that way.

On looking back at this experience I remembered one good thing that came from it. Before we left England, a very close friend had given us a bag of individually wrapped presents, to open when we felt the need. We felt the need on the night of the robbery and after some sneaky shaking and rattling, we decided to open just three presents, one for each of us, (after all, we might have more catastrophes in the future so we thought we had better save some). Jack opened a yummy box of chocolates, which we ate to console ourselves. Simon opened a great card game set, which meant that we could try something other than the usual gin-rummy that we habitually played, and when I opened mine it was a new handbag. How could she have known I would need one so soon? How lucky we are to have friends like that.

You may wonder what we did with ourselves while we waited for the spares from the UK to arrive. But with our bikes we could still explore, and one of the benefits of staying in a place for longer, is that you see more of the real life of the country. To me, the more I saw, the more Spain remained a land of opposites. We would round a corner and smell the sweet heavy fragrance of burgeoning flowers or we would smell a smell which would send most Englishmen running for their drain rods. Rubbish would be strewn down the most beautiful hillside or dry river bed. Attractive houses and gardens would have fierce guard dogs chained behind heavy gates, canaries in cages sang sweetly from endless balconies, hoopoes sat on telegraph poles, parakeets ate the dates in the palm trees and dogs fouled everywhere. Children played safely in the streets until mid-night, driving seemed crazy and yet they were considerate of cyclists. It always kept me guessing. Maybe it was the unpredictability that I enjoyed in the end.

Well we did eventually receive the spare parts from England and with the door lock changed and our new keys hanging in their rightful place, we said fond farewells to our friends at Oliva and pulled out of the campsite. We were on the road again, heading down the sunny coast towards the peninsular of La Manga at Mar Menor and then on to Granada city with its wonderful Alhambra Palace. It was good to be moving again, watching the ever-changing scenery as we trundled along; not knowing what was in store and not knowing that when we reached Granada, there would be a great opportunity waiting for us — which we just couldn't say no to.

November

How do you make a Spaniard smile?

The flat area of coastline in Murcia had many campsites, again full of all nationalities over-wintering in the sun. We pitched up at quite a large site, with a full range of facilities: swimming, tennis, supermarket, laundrette etc. As usual the boules games and siestas came to a halt when we trundled in and tried to wriggle ourselves onto a pitch. With many a 'dah' and a 'yah' and a 'left hand down a bit mate' we got into our position…….. everyone likes to be involved in getting you parked up, with at least three people at the back seeing you into position and two either side to help you avoid low branches or the roof of the toilet block. It was a good way to meet people, although it was sometimes more confusing than helpful. I guess for some, it's a bit of excitement to help while away those long, lazy days.

Mar Menor has, as usual, plenty of history and plenty to offer the traveller. It is, in effect, a huge, sandy bay of clear shallow salt water, no more than seven meters deep, which is cut off from the Mediterranean sea by a long thin peninsular, called La Manga. The peninsular would enclose it completely but for a few channels, which keep it open to the sea. It is the largest saltwater lake in Europe. Palaeolithic finds have helped to date the area but it was the Romans who really established themselves here when they developed an important salt industry. They, and later the Arabs, were also quick to make use of the healing qualities of the salt water and the therapeutic qualities of the mud and clay in the lagoon. Many people are still attracted by the opportunity to ease rheumatic or arthritic joints, or to de-toxify the system and relax in the almost perpetually warm weather. The average annual temperature in this micro – climate area is 17 degrees Celsius, with winter months not falling below 10 degrees. With hardly any rain and a boasted 320 days of sunshine per year, it's a wonderfully dry area for those who suffer in damp climates.

La Manga del Mar Menor, is a narrow strip of land 21 kilometres long which divides the lagoon of Mar Menor, from the Mediterranean Sea. Until 1863 it belonged to the state, but then was sold by public auction to raise money. Most of it is now taken up with tourism; apartments, hotels, restaurants, sailing facilities, villas and discos, but the last few kilometres are quieter and in a more natural state. The great attraction for us, out of season, was that we could ride our bikes for the whole day, down this peninsular and back up again, along cycle paths and a very quiet central road, with the sea waves rolling onto the Mediterranean coast on one side and the quiet beaches of the lagoon on the other. At most points we were only yards from either. The temperature was around 70 degrees, and we were in shorts and t-shirts in late November now.

By lunch time we had cycled and explored for three hours, and were glad to find a restaurant at the edge of the lake where we collapsed, alongside the local Spanish diners, to eat tasty pizzas covered in fresh anchovies and huge prawns. We still had to cycle all the way back and unfortunately Simon's bike saddle was un-padded and un-sprung, so for him it was about as comfortable as sitting on a fence rail. We continually tried to find a comfortable saddle for his bike, but never did throughout the whole trip and it still has the secret instrument of torture to this day. We noticed that Dutch and German cyclists had much more comfortable bicycles, with huge padded seats that could accommodate soft ample rears and 'sit up and beg' handle bars that meant you weren't bent over the front, aggravating your bad back. I really don't know why we British have to indulge in the painful purgatory of balancing on bike saddles that are only an inch wide and made of 'hard as nails' plastic. Whatever happened to the good old, fully sprung variety, which gently bounced you over bumps in the road. Suffice it to say that with Simon's bottom getting quite a lot of abuse, we didn't cycle every day.

We'd planned only a short stay here, but on reading through the guide books of this area, we could see that again, we could have seen more if we had wanted. Nature Parks boasting flamingos, herons, storks and avocets, cycle routes around the lake and old gold mining regions up in the hills, particularly appealed to Jack. Plus the exceptional summit of Cabezo de la Fuente, which offers the best view of the Mar Menor and its unusual geographical situation – never mind, another day maybe? For now though, the friendly male drivers on the campsite assisted us in extracting ourselves from our pitch and we headed off south-west towards Almerimar, which sits at the entrance to the Coast of Sun….. better known to most as the Costa del Sol.

So far we had clung to the coast all the way down through Spain, partly because we love the sea but also because we just didn't want to go inland to the colder winter weather. We were being spoilt, avoiding a winter and it was a real treat. We drove along the motorway between Murcia and Almeria, amazed by the way the barren hills and mountains of pale unyielding rock had been literally sliced through to enable the road to continue its way to the farthest corner of Spain. At Almeria we swung off the motorway and headed down to the coast to Almerimar. Here we were again amazed, but this time it was the acre after acre after acre of plastic-covered land that surprised us. This is veggie growing country, big time, although you won't actually see the vegetables unless you stop and peer into one of the dirty, grey, scruffy plastic greenhouses that are usually blowing themselves apart in the wind. These stand cheek by jowl and nose to tail, over an enormous area of land, stretching from just behind the coast, to right back into the lowest hills of the Sierra de Gador. Small dusty service tracks run between them all, and all other landscape has been obliterated to make way for more and more intensive agriculture.

The lure of work has attracted thousands of young Spaniards, and others, from poorer regions but we got the feeling that this was cheap labour for someone. As we approached the sea, the land dropped down from this un-natural agricultural plateau to a long flat coastal strip containing fishing harbours, yacht moorings, campsites and holiday complexes. Rather like an old film set, it was all front. Yes, there was a pleasant coastline and behind us in the distance, was our first wonderful view of the snowy peaks of the Sierra Nevada, but in between was just ugliness. We didn't get off to a good start at this campsite either, as our electrical connection (hook-up), wouldn't work here. Camp site electrics are often a bit of a mystery depending on the whim of the owners and the amount of electricity available.

That night we had a rare, heavy downpour and next morning our large awning was holding a small lake, hanging dangerously low and looking for all the world as if it was about to split asunder. All ready to catch the first bus into town, to find the elusive electrical connections needed, we decided to let the water out of the awning first. Of course we were rushing to catch the bus and it was difficult to lower one side of the awning without causing it to rip, which is probably why the whole lot emptied neatly but unfortunately onto our heads soaking us completely. Strange how something like that can colour your day isn't it?

Something I have learned from our travels is that although you may thoroughly enjoy visiting somewhere, someone else may have a completely different experience and hate the place. It could be the weather, or a surly guide or you may have a good row about something totally unimportant....... but it all colours the day. I found that traipsing around Spanish ironmonger shops, (known as ferreterias or as we called them Ferrets Rears), looking for elusive electrical connections, to be particularly uninspiring that day. Especially as the assistants serving behind the counter were completely uninterested in our problem and had not a glimmer of a smile between them. I wrote in my diary that night, that it would be my mission in life to make a Spaniard smile. My memories of El Ejido are definitely coloured, but maybe someone else will have a great time there, and if you do, please let me know!

Now we needed to gird our loins and make the most of the following days before we headed for Granada, which was to be our next stop. Jack felt convinced that his loins were girded enough, thank you, and spent a quiet day at camp on his own. We all needed our own space once in a while; me to do a little domestic goddess stuff or shave my legs in peace. Simon to read, or mend bike tyres or plan ahead, and Jack to read, watch Euro news or a video, or his favourite method of relaxation, which was to draw. Spending a year together in a motor home required give and take between us all. But, the next day we got our act together again and cycled along the coast, past glossy yachts and smart but empty holiday villas. The sea really was crystal clear and perfectly clean in the marina, with shoals of large, very edible looking fish, swimming lazily in the warm surface water. As we cycled ever onward to see what was just around the next bend, we discovered the marshland nature reserve of Punta Entinas Sabinar, which, according to the brochures, promised sightings of flamingos.

Certified as a *nature landscape* by the Andalucian government, this sixteen kilometre long coastal strip, of marshland, lagoons and virgin beach, is home to numerous species of birds – some endangered and some using it as a stop over whilst migrating. We were hoping to see the flamingos, but on first inspection, as we skidded and bumped along the narrow sandy paths, we had no luck. Then Simon spotted one of the unmistakable long necked, gangly-legged birds flying over the park and dropping down to land about half a mile away. We peddled furiously to the point in the distance where we had seen it land and as we got closer, heard their strange goose–like honking call.

They were quite far away, tiptoeing daintily on spindly legs, with heads down, sifting the water of a shallow lagoon. With our binoculars, we could see them well, these exotic, Alice in Wonderland creatures, that moved as one or slept calmly on a single, wiry leg. We wandered further under the hot mid-day sun, and Jack soon spotted the crested head of a Hoopoe, searching the long dry grass for insects and lizards. Dropping our bikes we crept low and close, like a trio of David Attenboroughs, until we were only yards away and were able to view his salmon pink body and startling black and white striped wings. Skylarks were plentiful singing high in the sky and Kites soared past a rocky cliff face, Little Egrets searched the waters edge for small fish and aquatic insects and Buzzards circled far above us. But, the loudest wings of all, and by far the most numerous and painfully over friendly were those of the insatiable mosquitoes. Unfortunately, they were out in force and we only escaped them when we clambered up into a cool cave to open our rucksacks and eat our lunch.

One of the great things about travelling is that you do eat your lunch with a different view every day. When we were on the move, we often picked lay-bys or car parks that were next to beaches, so that we could swim too. Those little things, like looking out over a bay or mountain range while eating fresh sardines, salad, and local bread, with addictive anchovy-stuffed olives, are some of the moments that I will always remember. They were as important as visiting the Alhambra......... yes, Granada was next on the list. Even though we were country mice at heart, we all loved visiting big cities. Granada was great, although our favourite came later when we thoroughly enjoyed the delights of Barcelona. At Granada there was a really good camp site situated just down the road from the main bus station, not far from the centre of the city, (called Camping Nevada). We pulled in easily this time and there was plenty of room, it was after all, 'out of season'. Having said that, this was a great time of year to visit Granada; the weather was warm, but not hot, and there were far fewer crowds than in summer.

Granada sits a mere sixty kilometres inland from the Costa coast and nestles at 2,200 feet above sea level, in the foothills of the Sierra Nevada Mountains. It is in a great position. You really could swim in the morning and ski in the afternoon, should you have the energy left over from a wild night on the town. The city itself has plenty to offer but we were mainly interested in the Alhambra, so the day after we had arrived, we walked up to the bus station and caught the number thirty two bus to the Cathedral and then the number two bus to the Alhambra, this last bus driven at crazy speeds through a narrow, cobbled one way system of tiny streets in the old town.

What can I say about the Alhambra that hasn't already been said a million times over… except that you should visit it at least once. It sits on a hill above Granada, the Hill of Gold, and is the finest example of Islamic architecture in the western world. Reading from the guide books you will find names such as The Alcazaba Citadel, The Nasrid Palaces, The Mauror Hill, The Vermillion Towers and the gate called Bab al-Sari'a, all of which conjure up a time of sultans and emirs, spices and trade, prayers and poetry. I would not try to fully explain the complicated history of this intricate collection of buildings, even if I understood it myself. The Alhambra was a palace, a citadel, a fortress and home of the Moorish Nasrid sultans and their entourages. It had a complete city within its walls, with houses, schools, stables, mosques, baths and cemeteries, some of which have thankfully survived invasions and earthquakes. We bought our tickets at the incredibly good value of eight euros each and, following the guide books, passed through heavily carved, arched gateways, massive iron bound doors and cobbled roads, on our way through the old Medina and up to the Alcazaba (the military area of the city). From here we wandered around gardens and towers, enjoying fabulous views down on to Granada, and across to the snow capped mountains and surrounding countryside. Moving on, we entered the heavily ornamented, open air rooms of the Nasrid Palaces. What struck us most about the architecture of these rooms was that they appeared almost weightless. What were solid, heavy beams and walls, looked lighter than balsa wood, due to the intricate carving which covered all stonework. Slender pillars supported high, domed, carved ceilings: arched carved windows offered classic eastern views – there were walls like lace work, ceilings of stars, floors of mosaics and view beyond view through Moorish doorways to reflections of buildings in mirroring pools. Water is the other element which makes the Alhambra so special. Golden coloured, sun drenched stone reflected in endless pools; fountains of cooling, tinkling, life-giving water in elongated water channels, leading you from one paradise to the next. I can't wait to visit it again, it was stunningly beautiful.

We moved on to The Generalife, the private home of the sultan, where he relaxed away from his court, with the aid of his harem, and yet was still within distance should he be required. The land around the Generalife was always cultivated to a very high standard, to be both productive and ornamental and it is still a gardeners delight to visit. Re-established gardens and original orchard terraces have been once again brought to life by the addition of fountains and waterways, which weave through gardens paved with mosaic floors, surrounded by arched walkways. Every wall carved like lacework. Intricate 3D patterns on warm stone for you to trace with your fingers: small birds bathing in fountains; avenues of cypress trees; stray cats drinking from pools. We spent a long, long day there and eventually walked back down the hill, through old and new Granada, to the bus stop. Exhausted as usual, with our poor feet aching and our senses overwhelmed.

That evening we had a stroke of luck. A British couple had turned up at camp for just a short stay and they told us about the opportunity to drive the Beast up to the ski resort in the Sierra Nevada Mountains, where a car park was reserved for motor homes. This sounded like a great opportunity to go skiing and although Jack and I had never skied before, we were keen to have a go. Three cheap ski suits, gloves and hats were quickly purchased from the handy supermarket over the road, along with a small fake Christmas tree with lights and some tinsel and baubles to decorate the Beast. We shall never forget the endless, horrendous Christmas tune that was being played on a continuous loop at top volume in that heaving Spanish supermarket in late December; I've only got to think of it now, to get a headache.

Leaving the camp site next morning, we headed off up the excellent A 395, a road which had good passing areas for those who wanted to overtake our lumbering home as we climbed 6000 feet in 35 kilometres. Luckily, going up, we were on the side of the road next to the rock face..... coming down those switch back bends later in the week was something else. Up and up we drove, enjoying far-reaching fantastic views all around because we were now in the snow covered mountain range. We zig-zagged the final stretch with Simon doing his usual brilliant driving, (although it had been a difficult drive in the Beast and he was looking a little stressed), until we came at last to the ski village of Pradollano – and two ridiculously small, snow covered mini roundabouts. The signs to motor home parking directed us round the roundabouts, but there was no way that we would get our big American Beast around them very easily. The ground was very icy here and jovial skiers were mindlessly milling about in groups, quite unconcerned about the fact that we might at any minute, uncontrollably mow them down. Cars had come up behind us, so we were back in that whisky-swigging situation, of manoeuvring the Beast in dire circumstances. At this point the reverse gear also decided to play up. Isn't it always the way - that this kind of thing happens just when you don't need it. So, in trepidation, we started going round the first roundabout, but we're too long and need to shunt. So we try to get reverse gear, which jams and engages the auto park brake. Now we have to do a series of leap-frog type manoeuvres, jumping our eight ton, thirty foot motor home, back and forth between a stone wall and a ten foot drop, with milling skiers trying to dash between the gaps, and all on thick ice. Need I say more? No. Except that we had to repeat this at the second roundabout, although by this time the steering wheel was slippy with sweat, I was searching for the Pina Colada again and Jack had his head under a cushion. We got to the motor home parking place of course, high above the village...... (you always get there in the end)..... and we stood outside the Beast, toasting the glorious view with an extremely large whisky.

This parking area up above the ski village was excellent and Jack was out of the door in seconds, rolling in the snow like an overgrown puppy. A convenient hopper bus called every twenty minutes to collect or drop skiers and took you straight down into the ski village of Pradollano. It cost just five euros a night to stay there and it was equipped with a 'grey water' emptying point. The views were to die for. I adore mountains anyway. They have such serenity and calmness, and we were at a height where we could look right across the snowy range of the Sierra Nevada, and down onto Granada. In the evenings the frozen land turned a cold violet blue as the sun dropped, lighting up the undersides of whispy clouds with yellow and orange streaks. Mount Valeta stood alongside us, and the valley of the ski runs was lit at night by moving beams of light from piste-bashers and skiers who were preparing the slopes for the next morning. It was so peaceful and calm, it was another world, but we were glad to have heating because it was very, very cold.

Next day, with ski equipment hired, we were down in the village ready for the nine o'clock lift up from Pradollano, to the slopes at Borreguiles. I was fifty four years old (or young, which ever way you look at it) and had never skied before, Jack hadn't either, but Simon had been a good skier twenty years earlier. We arranged to have some lessons to get us started and our instructor was José; kind and cheerful and very patient, he spoke very good English and soon had us doing snow ploughs and turns. Simon quickly got into the swing of it again and rapidly moved on to harder slopes, but Jack and I stayed on the nursery slopes all day and practised falling over and getting up again, until we were really proficient at it. But it was exhilarating and although exhausted and red faced, we had loved it and couldn't wait to do it again tomorrow. At the end of the day, we clumped our way back through the village, in awkward ski boots with skis casually slung over our shoulders, almost like regular accomplished skiers. Except that, being short and round, I had a problem looking casual and trendy, in my bulbous cheap ski suit, clumpy boots and skis which seemed to have a mind of their own. I felt more like a Michelin man. How do these people make it look so cool and elegant? Do you really have to be six foot four, slim as a rake and wearing the latest one-piece suit, to look as if you were born to ski? If so, I shall never make it.

Trying to get up early again the next day was more of a problem as our leg muscles had seized like greaseless pistons. But we forced our feet back into the ski boots and clumped down to the village again. José gently moved us on to the first runs and Jack especially, did really well. I did ok too and thoroughly enjoyed confidently skiing down the green runs. That was where I was happy and I spent the following two days just playing there in absolute bliss. Jack had two more one-to-one lessons with José, to smarten up his technique and by the last day he was able to ski with Simon, from the top of a high blue run, way up on the Valeta slopes, right down through Borreguiles and all the way down the valley to Pradollano. I was waiting at the bottom to watch him ski down the last part and it brought tears to my eyes. I know that I can be a bit

emotional sometimes where my kids are concerned, but seeing him ski down with all
the other skiers, Christmas carols playing behind me, with the clear blue sky just deepening to early dusk, gave me such a good feeling. I felt so proud of him: it had all been
worth it. He absolutely loved skiing and was so chuffed that he had done so well. Ever
after he has wanted to be a ski instructor. Maybe he will be, he could do a lot worse,
but I think he may change his mind a few times yet.

As the Christmas holiday season got under way, the slopes became busier and busier. With wall-to-wall sunshine every day, the mountains shone and glistened, sparkling
white against a blue sky and when I needed a coffee break at one of the balcony cafes, it
was fun just to people-watch. All ages, and in all colours of the rainbow, they swished
across the slopes, sending crystal sprays up into the air as they twisted and turned.
Lines of tiny children in puffy, brightly coloured suits followed their instructors like
ducklings in a line. They were so confidant and at ease as they weaved along, arms
out sideways, supple little legs and backs bending like willows. Teams of husky dogs
rolled in the snow while they waited to give jingling sleigh rides and the ski lifts worked
overtime to get the people up the slopes. For me, the ski lifts were daunting, and at first
I studiously avoided looking down and gripped the rail convinced that I would be the
one who would fall off. I can't say that I ever enjoyed going up on them but, if you want
to come down you've got to go up, so that was that. We had five wonderful days on the
Sierra Nevada pistes. On our last day we called at the ski office, left a bottle of bubbly
for kind José and negotiated a good price to buy our boots and skis from the hire shop.
We were sure that we would ski again, so they would come with us in the Beast. It was
Christmas Eve. Pradollano was now very busy, and it was time that we headed back
down the mountain, to spend Christmas in Granada.

Back at the campsite again we soon got parked up and then made another quick
shopping raid to the supermarket. Christmas wouldn't be Christmas without big fresh
prawns, salmon, stuffed chicken, wine, chocolate, and a Christmas pudding that I had
brought with us from England. While Jack decorated the motor home and Si got the
Christmas tree lights to work, I hid in the back bedroom and wrapped stocking fillers
and presents. We were only buying token Christmas gifts for each other, and in fact
we had already decided to have a new tennis racquet each, which again, we bought
from the supermarket. Our old racquets were made of wood, and were thirty years old
and as most camp sites had tennis courts we were playing quite often as we travelled
around.

We had some surprises tucked away for Jack; a few new books, a beautiful marque-
try box from the Alhambra and little things I had collected from some of the places
we had visited. I'm afraid we didn't go out and sample the delights of Granada on
Christmas Eve as we probably should have, but instead we snuggled up in the Beast,
with chocolate and liqueurs and watched The English Patient on a DVD. How boring
is that! But after all the skiing, it was just about all we could manage.

Christmas Day arrived and Jack, in his pull out sofa bed, had his stocking open, the chocolate eaten and was well into a new book before 8.30 am. We lazed over a breakfast of champagne, smoked salmon and scrambled eggs before phoning family back home and then heading for the camp tennis courts, all the while being vaguely aware of a violin being played somewhere close by. A small igloo tent had appeared over-night in the campsite, with a forlorn looking young couple sitting outside, practising lively music on their fiddles while they waited for their kettle to boil on their very small primus stove. Even if it hadn't been Christmas day I think that we would have invited them in.......but it was an extra bonus that we met Nick and Becky, who were back packing and busking their way around Europe. Mulled Sangria wine, games of cards and far too much Christmas dinner, finishing with Christmas pudding and a huge, heavily decorated Spanish cake, left us all stuffed. We ate too much, drank too much, went to bed too late, and had too much fun. Fellow motor homers at the site probably wondered what was happening as we floundered our way through Christmas carols and then sang our very own version to the tune of 'We Three Kings'.

We three Brits of Herefordshar ?
Looking for culture, near and far,
Pyrenees mountains, Alhambra fountains,
Why didn't we come in a car!
Chorus... OH, cycling hear and driving there,
Grid locked fear, but we don't care,
Maisies leading, we're proceeding,
God knows why and God knows where.

Normandy sites, we've seen our fair share,
Mont St Michel, was never more fair,
Pylat, Arrachon, but in Caen we went wrong,
French signposts drive us to despair.........Chorus

The Costa Coast had little to boast,
High rise apartments and urbanised coast,
Geriatric Germans all hiding their Sherman's
The British enjoying their roast.........Chorus

At ten thousand feet, the skiing was neat,
What is that smell, I think it's your feet,
The genny is stalling, Granada is calling,
So Christmas on mains is a treat.........Chorus.

Well it took us a while to make this up and if you consider the copious amount of Spanish wine and champagne that we got through, I think it could be worse. Jack remained sober of course and was the only one of the party who didn't wake up in the morning with a head that felt as if a jackhammer was destroying it from the inside. He was also the one who discovered that we had managed to completely flood the toilet carpet with the entire contents of the fresh water tank. During our revels the water pump had got jammed on, but we hadn't heard it running due to the volume of our music and singing. What a good job Christmas only comes once a year.

December

Auld Lang Syne

Boxing Day was bright and sunny with a clear blue sky, but we didn't stir before ten o'clock. More motor homes arrived: a Dutch group, some Spanish and Germans, all on their Christmas holidays. We recovered at camp and while Simon dried out the sodden carpets and re-filled the water tank, I sat on the motor home steps in the quiet sunshine and watched the campsite come to life. Birds competed with their usual sing -song in the trees around us. Spanish children, dressed in new clothes, rode their shiny Christmas bikes along the road behind the camp site, with parents arm in arm, strolling behind. I could almost smell roast beef and Yorkshire pudding cooking in the oven. Some things are the same the world over.

The following day was a Saturday and we caught the bus into town again, this time to visit the cathedral. Spain is full of fabulous churches and cathedrals but you can become blasé if you view too many. Granada Cathedral is definitely worth seeing though, if only for it's richly ornate Spanish Renaissance architecture and it's spectacular altar. It took nearly two hundred years to complete the Cathedral and the flamboyant Royal Chapel situated behind, where Queen Isabella and King Ferdinand are buried in an extravaganza of architecture. Originally this Cathedral was destined to be of the old gothic style, however when a young Flemish architect joined the team in 1528 he persuaded Charles V that a Renaissance design would improve it both architecturally and ideologically.

The result was a new concept of space, with the interior pillars rising to double their original height and light cascading in through high windows, giving a wonderful luminosity. Elaborately carved, white domed ceilings, soaring fluted pillars and gold-embellished Corinthian capitals, lead you processional from the square body of the church to the circular main chapel. Stained glass windows, high around the chapel dome give bright colour relief, and help to throw light into the elaborate alcoves reserved for the Saints. It would be easy to mock the excessive grandeur here but you would have to applaud the achievement of building this complicated structure. Of course there are other religious buildings in the area that are well worth seeing, like the Monastery of San Jeronimo and the Carthusian Monastery, but to see them all may be a little like eating a whole Spanish gateaux at once, a bit too rich. Better I think to just take one slice, and of course having taken your slice of culture, you then need to go and eat something a little less weighty. We left the Cathedral and worked our way through narrow cobbled streets of tiny colourful, touristy shops, to the Plaza De Bib Rambla, where we found an empty table outside one of the many cafes which edge this busy square. It was Saturday again and Christmas was only two days past, so for the Spanish it was a day for shopping, strolling and wearing your best finery and furs. Suited gentlemen with polished shoes and camel coloured overcoats escorted their families to lunch, with wives well wrapped in costly clothes and wearing their best gold jewellery. Flower stalls spilled across the square, live music entertained the crowds, craft and food stalls offered their wares, and central to it all a fountain carved with strange gothic creatures, poured water from their mouths. Yes, there is plenty to see in Granada and one day we may go back for more.

The next day Nick and Becky were leaving, so we said fond farewells and swapped addresses before they walked up to the bus station, with their worldly goods carried on their backs and their violins tucked under the arms. Little did we know that we would bump into them twice more on our travels and they would remain good friends when we all returned to England. But we were ready to move on as well. Back down to the coast and on towards our next destination of Ronda, which we had been told we mustn't miss. However, New Years Eve would have to happen first.

We left Granada taking the scenic road to Motril, then turned left for Nerja and Malaga. This was a pleasant coastline 'out of season'. Beautiful low sierras rolled almost into the sea, but they stopped just short, and we found a good coast road alongside sandy coves and beaches. Further back was the motorway which runs from Nerja to Algerciras; the holiday route, passing Malaga, Torremolinas, Marbella and down to Gibraltar. Small touristy towns along the way catered for the thousands of English residents, motor-homers were wild camping by the empty beaches and we met quite a few people who were travelling or looking for property to buy. Avocado pears were growing on the trees and fresh fish was in the markets. Yes, I am talking about the Costa del Sol here; in summer this must be an incredibly busy area, but at the end of December it was quite quiet, warm and very pleasant. We visited the cathedral-like caves at Nerja, with their dripping stalactites and stalagmites, and wild camped for the night alongside the beach at a small village called Benajarafe. (If that seems hard to pronounce, I should explain that all 'j's are pronounced as 'h', so it is said as Bena-harafe'.)

We loved wild camping by the sea. There was nothing nicer than to listen to the ocean as we lay in our beds, or to sit on a beach at night and watch the moon rising over the water, reflecting a silver path right to our door step. To wake and step out of the door bare foot onto the cold sand and walk along a virgin beach at dawn was magic. We constantly collected 'beach bits'; white twisted driftwood, perfect shells, crab claws and little, smoothed pieces of coloured glass, which we used to play the old desert game of Mancala. With heads down we would wander the beaches, stuffing our pockets with treasure.

Well, the next day was New Years Eve and we awoke to a million dollar sunrise. I opened the blind and sat in our bed with a cup of sweet tea. Jack laid in his bed opposite the open 'front' door and we watched it unfold. The sea was a mass of dark moving shapes, with just an edge of white where it ran onto the grey sand. The sky, at first inky dark, gradually lightened as the earth turned towards the sun, and a golden light hinted at another dawning. Black silhouettes of sea birds moved silently across the sky and then a small brilliant dot showed on the edge of the horizon as the sun peaked over. One small, dark, thin strip of cloud hovered above the horizon and as the sun slowly rose it gave us an ever changing display, under-lighting the cloud through a spectrum from deep red to a glimmering yellow. Within two minutes the earth had turned enough to reveal the full sun. The sea gradually lost its sinister moving mass and became the deep blue friend that we knew. The sky changed colours from grey to orange to green to pale blue and I could quite understand how ancient peoples had worshiped a sun god. It's the most joyous sight – here comes the sun – reliable warmth and light. Another day had begun.

New Years Eve was spent exploring inland and cycling along the coast on our bikes. Fishermen pulled in their nets early and then rested their boats on the beach. The small village on the hill behind us enjoyed a quiet holiday with families gathering for a feast and children played in the streets with their Christmas toys. The odd banger exploded somewhere in anticipation. We collected driftwood for our barbecue and were just setting up our outdoor table for our own New Years Eve feast, when a car pulled up next to us and someone banged hard on the side of the motor home. A cheerful face came into view and we met Adrian, a retired Brit, who many years ago had bought a small apartment overlooking the sea and was now inviting us to his New Years Eve party. It would be a mixed bunch he said, and we would be very welcome. So, that night, we three kings of the road, had our own candle lit dinner on the beach and toasted all back home with champagne, before taking ourselves over to Adrian's house and joining his party. We all joined hands and sang Auld Lang Syne at midnight, an international chorus of old and young. We three returned to the Beast in the early hours, but they did much better and continued until six in the morning.

New Years Day and breakfast on the beach, after another glorious sunrise. We said our goodbyes again to kind people. Who said this was a lonely planet? Then we moved on down the coast, skirted around Malaga and through the unabated tourist developments to Torremolinos. We felt that we should visit this area just once, just briefly, just to know if it's reputation was justified. Who would believe that only forty years ago, Torremolinos was a tiny coastal village with one main street and few houses. Since that time, with the gold rush approach to tourism, this small fishing community has become a notorious holiday spot, worldwide. Torre means tower and molinos means mills, hence Torremolinos derives its name from the old watch tower, which still sits above Bajondillo beach, and once protected the water-fed flour mills. During the 1960's uninhibited development allowed a concrete jungle to spread and most original buildings and landmarks were swamped by towering hotels, apartments, pubs, clubs and everything else required for a cheap, good time in the sun, as this coastline careered at full speed into endless holiday brochures. And if that's what you're after, then it has it all. Maybe the Andalucians paid a high price when they traded their poor but quiet way of life for better work prospects and a chance to earn big money, and with central government hungry for foreign investment it must have seemed like a good idea at the time. Now, there is growing recognition that the environment must be protected, infrastructure improved and speculators curbed. So what did we think? We parked in a huge wild camp area along with other motor homes, at the Parador del Golf, unhitched our bikes, and took a 16 kilometre cycle ride, weaving through the strolling Spanish and the wandering English, past endless tourism outlets along a coast that, beneath the tat, was beautiful. But the tat was there and it was probably the most un-natural place we had ever been. We only heard one English family swearing crudely at the tops of their voices, but that was one too many for us, so we ticked that box and headed off for Ronda.

The road to Ronda, the excellent A376, clings to the side of the Sierra Palmitera by it's fingernails and if you like a scary ride, with great scenery, and twists and turns all the way, then this is the one for you. So you know where I was sitting! Before this road was upgraded, Ronda must have been much more difficult to access which may be why it was a notorious stronghold for bandits and smugglers. Perched on the end of a high ridge, with sheer cliffs dropping away on three sides, it guards a fertile interior plain which is fed by the Guadalevin River. Close by is the natural park of the Grazalema Range, which shelters the unique Spanish Fir tree and, twenty kilometres south, the third deepest chasm in the world lies in The Nieves Range. However, Ronda is a treasure in itself.

We laboured our way up to it's dizzying heights, 2,300 feet above sea level in the Serrania de Ronda Mountains and found the only camp site in the area, situated just outside the town. It was a small, pleasant, well run site with each pitch having its fair share of gnarled old olive trees. We weren't too sure about the rather long list of do's and don'ts here as most of them seemed to fall into the *don't* category. No music, no television no playing games, no hot water for washing dishes, clothes or bodies, and not too many welcoming smiles. Maybe we just arrived on an off day. Anyway, we had a quick bowl of soup for lunch and as usual, couldn't wait to investigate the town.

The Moorish 'old' town ranges along the edge of the cliff tops, in some cases clinging precariously close to the 500 foot drop into the Tajo (sheer drop) gorge. Carved deep and narrow by the flow of the Guadelevin river, this tremendous gorge cuts straight through the old peninsular of Ronda and would cut the town off completely were it not for the amazing Puente Nuevo bridge. Most of the old town is situated south of the gorge, but there is still plenty to see north of the bridge including a large new town, which has spread itself out there. We walked down to the old town, entered through the 16th century Renaissance gate and walked up through the uneven streets and past the fortress-like Church of the Holy Spirit. Twisting alleyways, with Moorish style houses, plazas, palaces and minarets, tempted us to linger but we were on a quick recce that day, so we continued on to the bridge itself.

The New Bridge (Puento Nuevo) is a majestic wedge of pale, golden stone which blocks the Tajo gorge, joining the older northern side to the more modern southern side. It has three graceful arches, which rise 96 meters from the river floor; two smaller ones on the outside and a third larger one in the centre. In the upper section of the central arch, a chamber was once used as a very effective prison. It dates from 1793 and was the third attempt at building a suitable bridge over the river Guadalevin. The river flows through the bottom of the canyon, between the bridge pillars, over huge boulders. The top of the bridge is quite wide, with walled paths either side of it's main road and it provides a great viewing point from which to watch the busy comings and goings of the town.

We spent the afternoon exploring the 13th century Banos Arabes (Moorish Baths), the two other ancient bridges and a garden walkway, which all gave fabulous views down into the gorge. Eventually, we trekked back up to the camp site and decided to have a drink at the bar before cooking supper. There were very few other people staying at the site but we had noticed two other vehicles with GB stickers. It almost became the first thing you looked for when a new vehicle rolled into any campsite or wild camp area. Is it a GB or a D or an F or an NL; sometimes it would be a B - or an I, but they were not so numerous in Spain. Anyway, the owners of the two English vehicles were in the bar and we soon got to know Barry and Eileen, and Keith and Brenda. Barry and Eileen were regular travellers who aimed to take six months off every year. They didn't appear particularly wealthy, but had simply arranged their lives that way. They were travelling in a small, well-adapted van with a motorbike in tow. They had been to this area before and knew it well. Keith and Brenda had a motor home and were taking one year out, the same as us. We swapped stories and information and, as usual with people we met on our travels, we enjoyed their company over the next few days, whilst we all shared the campsite. We also swapped books. This was often a good icebreaker and most people did it. We all seemed to be avid readers and were carrying many books with us, so book swapping was as important as information about campsites and areas to visit. It also meant that we all got to read books that we would not normally have bought and Jack at his age, read everything we read.

They also told us that the site restaurant was very reasonable, popular with the locals and had a 'special' on the menu - whole roast leg of mountain lamb. Not having cooked roast lamb in four months we couldn't resist this, so that night we decided to give it a try. It was so delicious that I would almost go all the way back there just to eat it again.

We still say, 'do you remember that mountain lamb we had in Ronda' and our mouths water. What we hadn't realised was that we were getting a whole leg each! Our stomachs groaned that night as we rolled on our backs like stuffed lions.

Next morning, we returned to Ronda and took another look at some of the interesting places that we had skipped the day before . The Mondragon Palace, home of previous rulers, has delightful Alhambran style courtyards with arched doorways leading to intimate areas of fountains and flowers. The bullring, the oldest in Spain, where all spectators are seated under cover in arched galleries of smooth stone, was the birthplace of bull fighting and the accompanying museum displays costumes, which you would normally see in paintings by Goya and which are so slight and svelte, that you can hardly imagine a man fitting into them. And then, close to the bullring, the peaceful, shady park called the Alameda del Tajo. From here you can stroll to the Paseo de Blas Infante where you must cross the tiled plaza to the single, wrought iron balcony which extends way out over a sheer drop and allows you the most spectacular views over the rolling landscape around Ronda.

Once again after a long day, we walked back home, Jack itching to open two new airfix models that he had bought in town and us itching for a beer. The camp bar was open and we were just about to go in when we heard our names being shouted by someone walking up behind us. Looking back we saw two figures struggling up the hill with heads down, carrying heavy backpacks, violins tucked under their arms. Nick and Becky shouted and waved ……. we lined up the beers in anticipation. They ate with us again that night, a much more sober meal though, and it was great to catch up with news. They slept in their igloo tent, but found it very cold on the ground. We were at over 2000 feet and it was January so, although it was dry and sunny during the day, it was still very cold at night.

When you're travelling it's generally regarded as a good idea to learn some of the local language. However, if used incorrectly it can get you into embarrassing situations as I discovered the following day, which was a Sunday. I managed to completely fall out with the owners' son before we had even had breakfast, due to a misunderstanding that I had with his mother the day before. I'm not sure if it was my Spanish or her English but our wires definitely got crossed somewhere along the international line. I thought that on the previous day, I had ordered some bread for Sunday, from the mother, by writing my requirements on the bread list by the office. So, I pottered off to collect it on Sunday morning, and was about to say the customary 'Ola' as I entered the office, when instead of meeting the mother again, I saw the son standing behind the counter. It threw me I guess, (it doesn't take a lot), so instead of 'Ola' I mistakenly said "Good morning". This probably offended him, because I sensed a fairly frosty reception and he didn't bother to look up from his paper for about five minutes. I politely said that I had ordered bread for today.

"No, you haven't", said the son who I shall not name in case we ever return there.

"Yes I have", said I, "I did it yesterday".

"No…. you can't have", said frosty son, going back to his paper.

I was beginning to lose it then. I don't mind someone disagreeing with me, but a smile would have gone a long, long way at this point and all I was getting was hostile stares and short sharp replies in between his reading of the paper.

"But I wrote it on the bread list as your mother showed me", I said to the top of his head.

"You can't have", said son doggedly, not looking up.

Now, I may be getting older but dementia has not quite set in yet and I knew that his mother had shown me where and what to write, in order to get bread for the following day.

"But I did", said I, feeling that this conversation is getting absolutely no-where but I'm going to stand my ground.

"Okay" he said, folding his paper angrily and stepping out from behind the counter, "I will show you, that you are wrong".

And with that he frog marched me out of the office and into the lobby where the bread list lived, and stood me in front of the list like a disobedient school girl. But there on the list, is my order for bread for today.........

I seethingly pointed this out to him as I am now at boiling point.

"Hah" said son, "you have filled it in correctly but you can't have bread today".

"Why not", I gasped, almost close to tears.

"Because the baker does not bake bread on a Sunday!" he smugly concluded.

Aaghhhh, why didn't you tell me that at the beginning, you stupid Spaniard and why couldn't you say it with a smile! I eventually left with two stale loaves of yesterday's bread and it was tempting to whack him round the head with them. I stomped back to the motor home and ranted hysterically as I hacked the bread into edible pieces, looking for all the world like an axe murderer as I did it. Of course it was all just a misunderstanding. He spoke good English and although we always tried to speak the language of the country as much as possible, I didn't always do too well at it. Maybe his mother had the same problem. I think it was just the sullen attitude that I sometimes encountered in Spain that made me constantly wonder, 'what makes a Spaniard smile?'

Well, of course, the next day my disgruntled feelings were turned on their head, and we saw just what makes Spanish people happy. We had heard that there would be a festival in town that evening, but because the Ronda area looked so interesting we decided to hire another car and go exploring that day, returning in time for the fun of the carnival. We gave Becky and Nick a lift into town to do a little busking and then headed off along a small mountain road on a circuitous tour, which took us through high bare mountain passes and down lush river valleys. White washed villages, the Pueblos Blancos, were scattered like snowflakes amongst the sierras. We drove through forests of cork oak, and stopped to feel smooth trunks, where the bark had been harvested to make wine bottle corks for the sherry trade. Almond trees with tiny, pinky-white flowers edged the roads and beautiful mini narcissus of pale yellow hid in the grass. Gryphon vultures circled overhead waiting for us to get totally lost, but we safely reached the amazing pass at Gaucin and enjoyed the spectacular view across to Gibraltar and the Atlas Mountains in Morocco. We went too far, got back late and went straight into Ronda for the festival.

It was January 5th and on that day in Spain everyone celebrates the Festival of the Three Kings. This was traditionally their equivalent to Christmas Eve, but the more continental custom of giving gifts on December 25th, has encroached somewhat on this tradition. By the time we arrived back from our day trip hundreds of people were already out on the streets, where brightly lit decorations bathed everything in a soft warm light. We walked up through the busy town to find ourselves a good position amongst the growing crowds of revellers, and it was smiles-all-round at last. As time went on more families arrived, all jostling for a good position, but there was still no sign of the carnival. Then the strains of an approaching band drifted towards us on the warm night air and we could see the headlights of a lorry in the distance.

Slowly, oh so slowly the music got louder as the lorry inched its way towards us, spewing out imitation snow from a machine on its trailer, until it had covered us in gooey white fluff and passed on by, followed by the rest of the carnival. Floats of theme-dressed children, brightly clothed adults, marching bands, and individuals imitating everyone from Father Christmas to turbaned sultans made their leisurely way down the street, hurling toys and sweets at the yelling people. Music blared and horns hooted, and still more sweets were hurled into the swaying crowds. A ten foot chicken waddled by and three huge inflatable, plastic eggs were bounced high, bobbing over everyone's heads as out-stretched hands pushed them on down the street. Then, amongst this cacophonous parade, three live camels came sedately swaying along laden with presents, their lowered eyelids and haughty looks saying that, without a doubt, they thought the whole thing was completely crazy and that they were only there under sufferance. When it had all passed by, everyone rushed to the bottom of the street and waited for the parade to go around the block and come by again. It lasted for hours. When the parade had eventually passed by for the last time it was almost midnight, but children still scoured the streets for more sweets and adults chatted around sleeping babies in pushchairs. The place was alive but we were starving by now, so we headed for a busy Chinese restaurant and had a great meal amongst celebrating Spaniards, understanding at last, that that's what makes a Spaniard smile.

We tried to get up early next day but failed miserably – so a little late but with picnic made, we drove the hire car north to Setenil, a village hewn from a hillside of solid rock. Then up to the larger town of Olvera which rises from the ground like a pyramid of white houses, topped by the 12th Century fort, part of the defensive lines of the Nazari kingdom of Granada, and the church of San Jose with its unmistakably slim, twin towers. Every village in this area seemed to have its own church, castle or Roman remains and the deserted countryside was steeped in history.

Becky and Nick had supper with us that evening and we played a few card games. They were finding it really cold in their tent, but were doing well with the busking in Ronda. We could lend them hot water bottles but sleeping on the ground was the real problem. While we all ate, a regular camp visitor came sniffing round the open door, waiting for her scraps of food. Like everyone else on this campsite, we had fallen in love with a gentle, sweet-tempered stray dog. She had been named Carmen by the other campers and was being regularly fed by them. When Brenda and Keith left next day, they gave us their mobile number and handed Jack the job of feeding Carmen. He relished this, having always wanted his own dog and would have happily smuggled her on board if we'd not kept a watchful eye on her. She was just one of many stray dogs that we took to during the year and we could have easily returned with a whole pack.

So that morning, leaving Carmen with a full tummy again, we headed off in the hire car, this time to find the Cueva de la Pileta near Benaojan, about 25 kilometres from Ronda. These caves, discovered in 1905 are situated in the most beautiful, wild area of Sierra de Libar, part of the Serrania de Ronda. More than a mile in length and filled with oddly shaped stalagmites and stalactites, the cave was found to contain five fossilised human and two fossilised animal skeletons. There are also prehistoric paintings depicting animals as well as mysterious symbols. One of the drawings is of a large black seal-like creature about three feet long, and this chamber, in the heart of the cave, has a precipice which drops nearly 250 feet. But you are unable to view these caves alone and although we waited for an hour, along with a young American couple, the guide never showed up, so we never did get to see into the caves.

Never defeated, we travelled on to the 8th Century village called Zahara de la Sierra. This un-changed mountain retreat, with its highly uneven street layout, is situated by the Zahara reservoir at 511 meters above sea level. We parked, as recommended, at the bottom of the road and walked up into the village through zigzagging levels of narrow, incredibly steep streets until we reached the Baroque Church of Santa Maria de Mesa and then staggered higher and higher and higher until we puffed our way up to the 12th Century Castillo Islamico, the castle built on a sheer rocky precipice. I collapsed on a wall, just as our mobile phone rang, and while I talked to an old friend back in England, I was able to describe an incredible birds-eye view across valleys and mountains, and down onto the naturally shaped reservoir of deep, blue water lying in the folds of the foothills.

We walked back down into the village centre and stopped for drinks at a pavement café. As always, the ubiquitous canaries were singing in their cages on wrought iron balconies, and orange trees, still with their fruit, lined the village square. The place had an air of quiet activity. Locals came and went, chit-chatting about some building work that was being undertaken opposite the café; ladies carrying produce plumped down onto benches to have a good gossip and a selection of busy dogs went about their daily rounds of the streets. It was a very pleasant place to sit and watch the world go by. We reluctantly moved on, back to the hire car and took one of our circuitous tours on upwardly spiralling roads to the 1,357 meter high point at the Puerto de las Palomas Pass which provided a great view of the Grazalema National Park and surrounding Sierras. Once again, the almond trees were delicately blossomed and tiny blue irises with their striped yellow centres, bravely flowered in the lush green grass of the valleys. We counted eleven Gryphon vultures circling overhead on thermal currents, and many more drifting lazily around the hot rocky mountain tops in the distance. This whole area is a wonderful vast nature park and would be well worth another visit. The road to Ronda had proved to be yet another great detour and one that we could recommend to anyone.

January

Monkey Business

We left Ronda the next day, heading back down the mountains on the excellent, but scary road which is carved like a groove along the edge of the hill-side. I sat behind Jack again and stuck my head into the 'Teach Yourself Spanish' book for the whole trip down. I didn't learn any Spanish but I didn't scream either. Ok, so I had it stuffed in my mouth for some of the time, which did hinder the learning process, but it kept me quiet. Anyway, next stop was Gibraltar. It didn't take long to reach La Linea (de la Concepcion), the busy coastal town at the end of a peninsular, which links Gibraltar to mainland Spain. We'd been told that there was a good wild camping site for motor homes, right next to the Spanish border post, so we followed all signs for Gibraltar and sure enough, as we approached the rock, we saw a huge car park with many motor homes parked on it. We got a little confused with some of the traffic bollards at one point, which required me to jump out in the middle of the traffic to grapple single-handedly with a large lump of concrete, but before long we were parked up and had the kettle on.

Gibraltar rises out of the sea; a strange, pointed, lump of limestone rock, and it is quite bizarre to think that this uncompromising piece of land, attached to Spain, is still a British colony. Five kilometres long and only one kilometre wide, most of which is vertical, it houses about 30,000 people and about 300 Barbary Apes. Its early history was turbulent but it has remained in British hands, despite some protest during the Franco period, for over two hundred years. Because of its curious geographical and political position, it seemed to me rather confused about what its present culture really is. Gibraltar is internally self-governing and Gibraltarians, many of whom are Genoese or Jewish, determinedly want it to stay that way. You will need to show a passport to enter Gibraltar, although many of the Spaniard's who cross onto the rock every day to work in the tourist and service industries, are well known to the border guards and simply flick their passports up and dash on through.

That night, as we ate our evening meal, we had a superb view of the illuminated Rock through our front windscreen. From the rear window we looked out across the long marina of La Linea, the promenade lights reflecting in the water with blue, green and gold shimmering detail. We would have slept well were it not for the amorous young locals, who spent most of the night tucked right up behind our motor home, smooching and who knows what else. This big car park was obviously a hot spot for ca-noodlers and boy racers, who wanted to impress their young ladies by racing round the edge as close to the water as they could. Back to that old bull-fighting bravado maybe.

It was just a five-minute walk from the motor home to the border crossing, so next morning we showed our passports and followed the path across the airport runway and up into town. You can catch one of the regular buses to and from the border, but on our first day we decided to walk. Gibraltar is a jumble of cultures, religions and fashions, like many places in Spain, but here it is concentrated into a very, very small area. As you walk the streets you will see the working Spanish, English bobbies, Orthodox Jewish boys and men in their fitted black suits and skullcaps, plus the British who have moved there to open pubs and bars, Indian shop owners, Moroccans selling their wares in the town square and even red coated, be-wigged British soldiers carrying muskets over their shoulders as they march along to guard some building that was strategic in the 1700's. Steak and kidney pie, paella, fish and chips, a good curry or a take away meal from Marks and Spencer are all on offer within half a mile of each other.......... It's almost like home.

As we entered the town we passed the old market area, still used on certain days, before moving into the spacious and pleasant, Grand Casement Square, with its shops and street cafes. On up the high street to English stores like Early Learning Centre, M&S, Mothercare, Topshop and Safeways, who all rub shoulders with jewellers, music shops, and general tourist tat. Eating houses abounded, with names like Piccadilly Gardens and the Viceroy of India and English style pubs were everywhere. It was all very bizarre. We walked out of the centre and up into the older part of town. There were the usual steep streets, where children played with remote control cars, (they must have been top of the Christmas list) outside blocks of flats, and up above, liberally hung washing lines decorated the alleyways. Narrow, back streets with dark doorways, looking distinctly like the Arab quarters, shaded groups of older men who gathered to smoke hookahs and drink mint tea. Small, noisy motorbikes whizzed around and booming music from boy-racer cars, ensured that no one was going to get a siesta. There were an incredible number of cars on Gibraltar and parking was obviously a huge problem. Every day we witnessed long queues at the border as residents came and went. It just wasn't built for cars.

Gibraltar is of course famous for its Barbary Macaques, which have lived in the Upper Rock Nature Reserve for years. You can take the footpath up to the reserve but it would be a very long hot climb, so the next day we decided to have a Rock Taxi Tour. Our driver was named Charlie, a native Gibraltan, who knew the island inside out having been a driver for the navy before he became a taxi driver twenty-seven years ago. He explained the problems of the island; it's reliance on tourism and government work and its shortage of fresh water. Against that, he said that it was a very tolerant and relaxed place to live, where most people were happy with their lot and their neighbours, no matter what race or creed. He drove us up to the Apes Den, where the macaques regularly hang around waiting for tourist tit-bits. Charlie had his usual pocket full of macaroni, which he said they preferred, and before long we had the surprisingly heavy, but soft footed apes, climbing all over us. He knew these apes individually, and they knew that he was the man with the food, although even he was careful about how he touched them and we were not allowed to put out our hands to them, as they can give a nasty bite. Up on the summit, along a precipitous road five feet wide with a 300 feet drop either side, only the taxis were allowed, and we understood why when we reached the top and gazed down at the miniature- sized world below us and North Africa far off across the Straits of Gibraltar.

Charlie finally dropped us off at the last interesting place on the tour, which was the Great Siege Tunnels. I had never realised that the rock of Gibraltar, which we know so well from picture postcards, is actually honeycombed with hand-dug tunnels which cover a staggering thirty seven kilometres. They date from the Great Siege of 1779 – 1783, when British soldiers resisted Spanish attempts to wrest the rock into their rule. The tunnels were hewn from the solid rock to make new gun emplacements, along with sleeping quarters, storerooms and ammunition rooms. Quite a feat of engineering. We wanted to see more of this British colony, so instead of taking the taxi back down, we walked down the steep road, past the old Moorish fort and back through the old town again. That evening, Jack and I took a long stroll along the well-lit promenade which edged the marina and beach of La Linea. We walked for about an hour, past night-time fishermen and strolling townsfolk.

It was a beautiful balmy evening and the promenade lights shimmered on the sea. As always on our walks, we talked about everything, subject hopping just as the conversation led us. When we turned back the breeze was behind us, and we could hear cicadas trilling in the flower beds alongside the path. Jack was determined to make contact with these secretive little beetles so after a fair amount of unsuccessful poking in the undergrowth, he took out his mobile phone and scrolled through the ring tones. He found just the right cicada sound and before long we had a cicada in sight, answering his phone as if it was a long lost friend. We got some strange looks as we knelt on the path communicating with nature, which isn't surprising really, but if you ever want to contact a cicada, you now know what to do – just give them a ring!

While we were parked at La Linea, we saw many travellers who were meeting up, before driving on down to Algerciras, to make the crossing to Morocco together. We wanted to go too, but had no insurance cover for that area, so were not sure whether to take the motor home or leave it at a campsite and go to Morocco in a hire car for a couple of weeks. As we were in no rush, we decided to drive on down the coast to Tarifa, which is close to Algerciras, to make further enquires. The road from Algerciras to Tarifa is marked as a scenic route and after you've climbed steeply away from the town you are on one of Europe's most splendid coastal roads, with views of the Straits, Gibraltar and the 'green hills' of Africa on the Moroccan coastline. Lush, green, rolling sierras on one side and the blue Straits on the other, with glimpses of houses in Ceuta and Tangier in the distance. This is the southernmost point of Europe.

Two factors have prevented the over-development of Tarifa's beautiful three mile white beach, the Playa de Lances. Firstly the wind rarely stops blowing and secondly, it is still a Spanish military zone. We had our own interesting brush with the military while we were trying to find a well-known, wild camp area. There is no beach- side development or tourism along this coast, but running parallel to the sea is a long stretch of low, pine wood interspersed by small, camp sites. Narrow roads take you through the woods, down to parking areas by the beach, where travellers often wild camp. Unfortunately, while trying to find this area, we took a wrong turn which led us through the pine woods on a very narrow single-lane road with no turning points. It also had 'No Entrance / Military Zone' warnings half way along it, but we couldn't find anywhere to turn around and were committed to going forward. Ten minutes later, still having had no chance to turn, a military camp came into view, with two heavily booted and heavily armed Spanish soldiers, blocking the way at an entrance barrier. What they were thinking as our big American beast came lumbering into view down this tiny road, I cannot imagine, but they didn't look amused. In fact it was another of those unnerving moments, as we shuddered to a halt in front of them. They didn't move or smile and we felt like those bloody silly, underdressed tourists from hell, again. But at least there was some space here to turn around – just. So, under the gaze of the serious, jackbooted Spanish soldiers, I jumped out, (wishing I was wearing more clothes and looking more athletic), and Simon completed another of those twelve point turns, with me at the rear to ensure we didn't back into military territory and become tomorrows headlines in a compound somewhere, and Jack with his head out of the window to make sure we didn't take the roof off their hut. I clambered back into the Beast and we smiled and waved goodbye, but they remained stony faced, and I can't blame them really. I don't think they saw us three as much of a threat, in our oversized passion wagon, more of a damned nuisance, but we were glad to get out of there. We made another hasty exit and didn't stop until we were clear of the zone, just in case.

That night we found a pleasant campsite by the beach. The manager was friendly and helpful and we soon made the acquaintance of a young, long term, English resident who gave us plenty of information about the area. Tarifa, named after a Moorish military hero called Tarik, claims to have retained more of its Arab character than any other town in Andalucia. It has the usual narrow, cobbled streets and sudden wide open plazas; cafes spilling on to paths and smells of everything from strong disinfectant to tasty soups. Old stone houses, profusions of flowers, palm trees, roaming dogs, children playing and noisy motorbikes. But it had a very different feel to other towns that we visited on the coast. There was much less tourism and no high rise apartments. It had a very Arab feel to it, perhaps due to the large port which linked it to Tangiers, and yet was quite cosmopolitan due to the huge windsurfing scene that dominates this coastline. We liked this small town very much.

This is a wind and kite surfer's paradise. The strong western breezes and long, clear, sandy beaches are unbeatable. It is obviously a Mecca for the enthusiast, with many shops catering for their needs. Everyday, hundreds of kite surfers took to the water – all colours of the rainbow, the kites gently blowing around, high in the sky. The surfers, in black wetsuits, clung to their kite ropes with boards on their feet, and were pulled along at tremendous speeds, while they skimmed the water and practised jumps and turns in the air. There were easily a hundred windsurfers too - like damsel flies with gaily coloured wings – slicing through the water, chasing the wind on high crests. On cloudy days the sea here was often a deep, green colour, with white horses riding waves that were blown up by the constant breeze; but on rare still days the sea was deep blue and the sky had a luminous quality. We remarked on this to Martin, our campsite friend, and he reminded us that this coastline is called the Costa De La Luz or the Coast of Light, because of the wonderful luminescent quality. Jack was keen to surf in this sea but alas disaster struck before he had a chance to try it. Our wooded campsite was situated close to the beach and once we'd settled in, we got the bikes off and Jack went on a few exploratory expeditions. This is a great walking and cycling area, under a canopy of low, round, wind bent pine trees, with grassy forest floors and sandy paths. Dappled shade gives a magical quality to the woodland and glimpses of the beach and sea entice you further, just the kind of place that kids love to explore. We liked to walk along the beach to watch the surfers having fun and on the third day we did this, while Jack rode his bike through the pinewood. We knew that disaster had struck when we saw Jack limping out of the trees towards us, holding his right arm and looking as white as a ghost. He would like to say that he broke his arm while fighting off hoards of invading Orcs, but he was really just going a bit too fast and crashed head first into a ditch.

We could see straight away that it was a nasty break. Simon rapidly made a sling from his jumper while I ran to collect Jacks bike from the ditch and we met up back at the campsite. We had no car to rush him to hospital, but a windsurfer had just re-turned to camp and although still in his wet suit, he immediately offered to run Simon and Jack straight in to the medical centre at Tarifa. Jack was starting to shiver now as the shock hit him, but bravely made no fuss at all. We helped him into the front seat of the Ford Capri, while Simon managed to squeeze into the back, wriggling in to lay be-tween piles of wet surfboards and wet sails. I had to stay at camp as the car could only just get the three of them in, so with great reluctance I waved them goodbye and started to pace up and down the motor home, wringing my hands, as only a parent would.

It turned out that Tarifa medical centre was not sufficiently well equipped to deal with Jacks arm, so with another temporary sling, this time made from an old geograph-ical magazine, they transferred him almost immediately by ambulance to Algerciras, about twenty kilometres back up the coast. Hospital Punta De Europa was as busy as any other hospital in the world and the benches in the A&E department were full to bursting with complete families accompanying their loved ones as they waited to be seen. Simon's reasonably good Spanish, which was based on what he had learnt many years before when living in Costa Rica, was pushed to it's limits as he explained what had happened and made sense of the bureaucratic system of waiting and moving, from one department to the next, while forms and X-rays were completed. At last they were shown in to meet the man who would give them the final verdict about the break and, as they thought, would put the arm into a plaster cast and send them home again. But it was not to be. Their faces fell, as the kind doctor explained that Jack had a compound fracture and unfortunately the bones had not only moved but were also trapping a nerve. Jack would have to be admitted; he would need an operation immediately to re-set the bones by screwing them to a metal plate which would be inserted into his arm. It was absolutely devastating news.

Simon and Jack were shown to a children's ward where Jack was hooked up to a drip and put to bed in a hospital gown, until the operation could go ahead. That evening, Martin, the windsurfer at the campsite, brought the last of his box of chocolates over to me and he sat and talked, to keep me company for a while. So often on this trip, strangers became such kind friends. Simon and I kept in touch by mobile phone and agreed that he would stay the night in hospital and I would take a taxi over to him in the morning, to allow him to come back and get some sleep. At ten o'clock that night, Jack was taken to the operating theatre, and although it was really only a small operation, he was understandably scared. Simon had to leave him at the theatre doors and for him it was very difficult to be unable to stay with Jack all of the time. He fretted and paced the corridor until 1.30am, when at last, Jack came back out and was wheeled again to the ward. Jack was exhausted and fell straight to sleep.

Now of course, looking back on it, we can laugh about the whole experience, which at the time was an endurance test for us all, especially Jack. The rest of that night Simon, now shattered, attempted to get some rest on the black plastic chair, next to Jacks bed. At this hospital, parents were allowed, if not expected, to stay the night next to their children; not only that but they could bring in televisions, or computers for games to be played on, and any notion of a good nights sleep was an idle fancy. It was unbearably hot and stuffy throughout the whole building and Simon had a really tickly cough at this time, so you can imagine that trying to stifle that, in this small stuffy room full of people, as the night wore on, was another form of purgatory. However, he needn't have worried because in the bed next to Jack, separated by a thin curtain, a boy and his mother watched a Spanish game show until 2.30 am, with the volume scarily high. Blaring game contestants had a whale of a time and the whole darkened room heard about it. Opposite Simon, another mother watched over her child, from her black squeaky, plastic chair, and now and then, joined in the game show fun. By dawn Simon had to get out and get some air before he succumbed to a complete nervous breakdown. He walked the empty streets of Algeciras for a while, before returning to some rather sour faced nurses, who seemed surprised that he had deserted his sleeping son. When Jack eventually woke up, Simon helped him to and from the loo, with accompanying drips, while the hospital swung into another day of non-stop action. That morning, I got a taxi over and relieved him. It was my turn to sit with Jack, and Simon went home to collapse into bed. I'm not sure which of them felt the worse at this point.

The hospital was really very good, it's just an added difficulty if you can't communicate too well, but we got by. In Spain, when one person has a problem, it seems that the whole family is involved, and of course this applies to hospitals too. So, when another boy was wheeled in after an operation, the whole extended family came with him. Mum, Dad, Uncles, Aunts, Grannies etc were needed to settle and fuss, until the television went on and they all became engrossed in another game show. Confined as we were in that hot, noisy room, the day seemed never ending. I read to Jack, one of his favourite books at the time, 'One Hit Wonderland' by Tony Hawkes, and in between sleeping, and eating enormous three course meals, three times a day, we got through another twelve hours. In the next bed another lad played merrily on his Play Station and mothers chatted and answered relatives on constantly ringing mobile phones. There was just no peace for the wicked.

Night fell at last and at 9.0 pm Jack had another X-ray; at 11.00 pm the drip was changed and thermometers were put under armpits; at 1.00 am the television at the next bed was turned off and for the rest of the night, us mothers tossed and turned on our plastic chairs in between getting a drink to prevent de-hydration or tip-toeing to the bathroom for a pee. It was a long night. However, the next day, after some assistance from a kind children's teacher who worked in the hospital and spoke good English, Jack was released with all forms signed. We staggered from the hospital, gasped fresh air and caught a taxi back to the Beast, where we all went to bed early, in separate beds, and tried to recover. You just never know what's round the corner do you……..
and sometimes it's just as well.

January

Sanderlings and Strange Customs

The following week was a strange one. Jack needed time to recover and rest quietly and Simon's tickly cough had not improved, in fact he had developed a bad sinus headache that didn't seem to want to budge, so he too wanted to take it easy. We remained at the small campsite under the pine trees, where we were hooked up to electricity, and I spent most of that week walking on the beaches and watching the surfers, while the others stayed at camp. I was feeling a bit restless, but if you had to be restless anywhere, then this was a good place for it, as there was excellent walking along the lengthy coast line. One morning I went down to the beach early to write my diary and as usual I sat on the stone steps that led up to the campsite. The familiar breeze was ruffling the water and the sky was a clear blue. It was January 19th, and although it was sunny, you still needed to keep a warm jumper around your shoulders. The beach was almost deserted; a spotty Dalmatian dog and his German owner being the only ones enjoying the surf. The sand was wide and soft and white, and the sea was a wonderful turquoise-blue colour, with rolling white breakers running up onto the shore. The colours of the day were heavenly, but I had become enchanted by the little bands of Sanderlings, which inhabited this coastline.

Flying fast and low, they would sweep along the edge of the breakers in groups of about eight birds, rapidly calling their high 'twick-twick' song. Then, they would land on the small, weed covered rocks, which were constantly revealed by the ebb and flow of the sea. The water would come in, washing over their feet and splashing their feathers, but the Sanderlings remained balanced stoically on the rocks until the waves retreated back into the sea again. Then they would quickly jump down onto the wet sand and furtively search around the rocks for tiny insects. They moved incredibly fast and when they ran along the sand to find a better area, they looked so light that they hardly seemed to touch the ground at all. Temporary little footprints in the sand were the only proof that they had actually run and not flown. I spent ages trying to get some really sharp photographs of these bright eyed, round headed little birds, with their straight dark beaks and pure white tummies. They were a real pleasure to have around.

There was a restaurant further along this stretch, which I discovered when I went for a long walk one afternoon. As you left the windblown sands and entered the white washed rooms, the heavy, welcoming smell of a log fire greeted you. Long wooden tables and benches were placed all along the wall facing the beach and a huge panoramic window treated you to a landscape of sea and sky as you ate great food. We all went there for a lunch of tasty tapas a few days later, when Simon and Jack were feeling better. That's another place that we would love to return to. We spent a few more days by the beach, this time wild camping, and explored Tarifa and its castle, but before long we all felt ready to move on again. Jack would have to return to Algeciras hospital to have his stitches out in two weeks time, but we wanted a change of scenery, and after consulting the map, we plumped for El Puerto de Santa Maria, about two hours up the coast, for our next stop.

El Puerto de Santa Maria is a large commercial fishing port and historical town that sits quite sheltered in the Bay of Cadiz, at the mouth of the Guadalette river. It is also one of the three corners of the famous sherry triangle, (Jerez and Sanlucar being the other two), and is close to several nature reserves. The region offers low sandy beaches, marshland reserves, excellent wine and fresh seafood, and it is believed to be the birthplace of flamenco, so good entertainment too. We were probably there at the coldest time of the year and we didn't find it too endearing, but it boasts of all I have mentioned, plus a climate apparently so benign that the first botanical garden was installed at El Puerto in the eighteenth century, to acclimatise the plants and seeds, discovered during that great period of global exploration.

We arrived at a fairly large but quiet camp site on a Saturday, and although it was rather basic in some ways, it had a shower block which we voted 'best on the trip!' You can become fairly obsessed with toilets and shower blocks when you're travelling and of course they vary enormously. Some have no hot water, some are dirty, some are clean, some smell terrible and have little privacy and some are fantastic. The shower and toilet block at the site in Granada was all marble, spotlessly clean and had plenty of hot water, so it got a nine out of ten, while certain other ones were fairly disgusting and got a 'nil point'. Simon particularly, gave the shower and toilet block at El Puerto a 'ten out of ten', and I wouldn't have been surprised to find campers living in it, it was so luxurious. Constantly heated in the cooler months, spacious and modern, with moody lighting, indoor plants and reliable hot water, this was a shower block to worship. For Simon, the piece de resistance was the pleasant, loudly piped music, which gave you the opportunity to perform all functions with impunity. Need I say more... I don't think so, as I expect that most men will relate to this important and oft overlooked necessity.

Very soon fellow campers were wandering over to say hello to us new arrivals. Among them were a friendly young couple from London, who were taking eighteen months out to travel, before heading for Australia to settle down again. He was an accountant and she had a law degree. They had an adorable little toddler, who really needed to be on a long piece of elastic to stop him roaming too far, and they were also travelling with a manic little Yorkshire terrier and two cats which had to be separated regularly as they fought like the proverbial; all in a motor home. (The different approaches to travelling never failed to intrigue me.) The next day was a Sunday and we were told that the local roads would be busy because a fiesta would be taking place in the pine woods opposite our camp site. We had no idea what this was going to be about, but wandered over to have a look. Now when we think back to El Puerto, we always associate it with this wonderful day that none of us will ever forget. It was totally unexpected and brilliant fun.

We walked over to the woods that Sunday morning, with mild curiosity, and as we got closer saw people arriving on foot, carrying animal cages, and in cars towing horse-boxes. There was already a large group of people gathered at the edge of the trees and amongst them were many horses and riders. But these were not just horses and the riders were not just Spaniards out for a trot in the woods. These were statuesque Arab / Hispanic horses fresh from Goya paintings, groomed to perfection, with their tails and manes brushed and plaited; heads held impossibly high on almost permanently arched necks. Dappled greys, deep browns and of course the well-known Andalucian white. And then there were the riders. Kitted out in traditional, black, wide rimmed hats, tight bolero type jackets that were broad at the shoulder and ended neatly in at the waist and full leather leg chaps, they sat at ease in high backed saddles, a rolled blanket across the horses flank, while they drank sherry and regaled their friends and acquaintances. We stood at the edge of the rapidly growing crowd of animal owners, horse riders and general lookers on, but before long we were being dragged into the throng and were offered the first of many plastic tumblers of sherry. (I take back all I said about the Spanish ever being miserable).

After much sherry quaffing, a trio of musicians struck up some lively music and people began to clap and sing along. A small horse-drawn cart was being led towards us, completely covered with bright, fresh flowers. Positioned on the cart, surrounded by the flowers, was the wood and plaster statue of St Anton, the patron saint of pets, with a crook in his hand and animals at his feet. This was the 'Festival of St Anton' and the rabbits, canaries, cats, dogs, horses, even a snake and some chipmunks, amongst many other animals, that we saw being carried, ridden or dragged along to the gathering, were there to be blessed by the saint.

Gradually now, the crowd began to move off........ we knew not where, but by this time we had had enough of the excellent local sherry to go with the flow and the flow was heading along a winding path into the woods. The musicians kept up the lively music and as we walked in procession, hands were clapped in time with the beating drum, while horses and riders flanked the edges or rode three and four abreast on the path. Singing and clapping as we went, we slowly followed the saint and his flower decked cart for about twenty minutes; a halt was then called and more copious amounts of sherry were handed round, along with well-stuffed ham rolls. We practised our poor, but increasingly less inhibited Spanish, on friendly fellow walkers, while round hipped ladies with bright coloured scarves broke into spontaneous flamenco as the music increased in volume and tempo. High spirits, high saddles and high kicking; bottles of wine or sherry were constantly being passed between the horse riders, some two-up now, as more and more joined the group, and before long we all set off again in another procession through a bit more of the forest. It all became a bit bizarre really, with over a hundred horses and riders now thundering around us or galloping off into the woods, and the winding procession following the Icon through the misty forest. Another halt for more sherry and ham rolls, more music and dancing and even higher spirits – and then on again to the beating drum and strumming guitar. At length, after two hours of this wonderful excuse for drinking sherry and having a good day out, we arrived at a large clearing in the woods. A huge crowd was gathered there, along with yet more animals of all types, plus food and drink stands and loudspeaker music. The flower-covered horse and cart was led in and pets were lined up to be blessed.

Next on the mysterious agenda were displays of synchronised riding. Teams of six and eight horses and riders, again in traditional clothing, performed intricate patterns, criss-crossing, high stepping, turning and weaving around each other to music, all in an extremely small arena. Of course El Puerto is close to Jerez, the famous horse riding centre, which we visited later that week. When the displays ended, we went back to the pet blessing area and saw yet another strange custom taking place. Young girls were now lining up to throw small stones at the icon of St Anton. We wondered if the sherry had finally taken its toll, but we were told that if you didn't have a boyfriend, you could throw three small stones at St Anton and if you managed to hit his naughty bits you would be married within the year. It seemed to us, a strange way of getting a husband - surely it would be better to throw flowers or something less debilitating, but that's the fun thing about strange customs....... They are very strange.

We decided to see more of the area while we were waiting to return to Algerciras for Jacks' stitches to be removed, so for the next week we used public transport to take a look at El Puerto and Jerez. To be honest, we found El Puerto to be a fairly dismal place: perhaps it was the time of year or maybe we were looking in the wrong areas.

I christened it the land of a thousand dog turds, which was maybe a little excessive, but the dirt, noise and dismalness did not endear it to us although the people were pleasant enough. Jack got many strange looks here and was almost mistaken for Prince Harry by one lady shop assistant. I should explain that there is some resemblance as he has hair the colour of beech leaves in autumn, a wonderful bright auburn and his face and arms are covered in huge fantastic freckles. He was always getting second looks as we walked the streets, wherever we were, but this particular lady who was serving us, dashed into the back of the shop and re-appeared with a copy of Hello magazine, with Harry on the front.

"Si, si, esta Prince Harry".

"If only", we all laughed as Jack went crimson faced.

She had a few gems of wisdom about our royal family, which she went on to share with us, but I'm certainly not going to print them here.

To visit Jerez we used public transport, which was an experience in itself. The bus apparently went every half hour, so following our town map we found the old bull ring and the two bus stops which represented the bus station, and waited. Two hours later, our fellow 'would be' passengers assured us that the bus would arrive although they had no idea when, but knew that it was a green bus, (but all buses that came past were green), so we ate our emergency rations and drank our drinks, more out of boredom than anything else. Twenty minutes later, we were still sitting on the hard metal seats opposite the old bull ring, watching and smelling Spain go by, when at last a green bus came along with Jerez written on the front. No explanation was given, but the bus was clean, smooth and with reclining seats, so it was almost worth the wait, although we were now wondering whether we should just get in the queue for the bus home again, as soon as we reached Jerez.

Jerez in January was pleasant enough, although not exactly the highlight of our year. A pleasant zoo, a guided tour of a local bodega to view the making of sherry, and of course a trip to the famous 'Dancing Horses of Jerez' at the Royal Andalusia Academy of Equestrian Art, helped to pass our time there, before finishing the week off by gloriously stuffing ourselves at Romerijos famous seafood restaurant. Yet another place that we would go back to on our gastronomic re-visiting tour. This family business, established for over fifty years, specialises in shellfish, and distributes them nation wide. With twenty-five varieties of sea foods available, we did our best to choose the widest selection possible and had such mouth-watering delights as deep fried anchovies, hake in a wonderful light batter and delicious shrimp omelettes. It was sold by weight, so you could choose a selection of many different dishes, which were all cooked to order. That was our last treat in El Puerto, before once more going back to Algeciras hospital, for Jack to have his stitches out.

It had rained hard in the night and it didn't really get light until about 8.30 am, but we were up early and got to the hospital in good time for our appointment, parking the motor home in a wide, side road. The hospital was just as hot and busy as before, but this time we had more idea about where to go for the final x-ray and had brought a book each to read while we waited in the long queues. As the morning wore on and the temperature rose, Simon decided to wait outside – he was beginning to feel very claustrophobic again. At last, we were called in for Jack to have the long line of stitches removed although they weren't stitches as such, but were metal staples. He climbed up on the bed and the nurse set to work with her staple remover while I stood alongside holding Jack's free hand in loving support, which would have been fine, had I not come over all faint at the sight of the un-stapling procedure. The nurse took one look at me turning white, sweaty and beginning to sway, and quickly shoved poor Jack off the bed and laid me on it, tilting my feet up into the air. Fanning me with Jacks notes seemed to do the trick though and after about ten minutes of interesting chatter and fanning, she let me get down and re-instated Jack, to remove the rest of his staples!

Poor lad. I did feel sorry for him. All over at last, we said our thanks and goodbyes and returned to the Beast, now desperately keen to leave Spain behind for a while. We were hot-footing it to Portugal as we had just three weeks available before Jack had to return yet again, for his final appointment and last x-ray at the hospital. The Algarve was not far away, another place that we had never visited, so we programmed Maisy, upped the main sail, and headed off.

A Glimpse of Portugal

Portugal is somewhere that we would love to return to; from the very first moment when we crossed the border, we liked the place. Initially because as you drive across the border, a well equipped tourist office with large car park, and all the information you could possibly require for your stay, provided by a smiling, English speaking assistant, is situated at the road side. 'Dix Points,' straightaway to Portugal! When we pulled into the car park and walked over to the tourist office we felt slightly sceptical; surely this would be too good to be true, but the charming assistant couldn't do enough to help us and we left with armfuls of information about the area and suitable camp-sites. We commented that this was an excellent service, which we hadn't found at the borders of Spain, to which she sharply replied, "Portugal is nothing like Spain".

With only three weeks to spend in this beautiful and varied country, we decided to concentrate on the Algarve, which we had never visited before, although we would have loved to see more of the central and northern areas too. It was now January 31st and England would have been gripped in another cold winter, but there on the famous southern coast, mimosa was in flower, arum lilies blossomed by the roadsides and bright blue borage flowers spread like a carpet on the hillsides. We drove along peaceful, wide roads and soon began to feel that the heart of this country beat at a much slower and easier pace. Portugal looked inviting, even the local radio channel played modern sing-along tunes that we knew, and we felt instantly at home. On reading more about the country we realised that it had not always been this way. Despite its past history of invasions, its periods of conquests when, for a while, it had a rich empire spreading from Africa to the Far East; its unrest and coups, earthquakes, and its more recent recessions and unemployment, Portugal still retains its gentle and welcoming feel. In recent years it has had a new period of economic success starting with Expo '98, which attracted eight million visitors and opened the doors to investment in infrastructure and tourism; but this has not in any way changed the friendly, quietly dignified people and their way of life.

Being there out of season of course was a major advantage and it is the time when you will usually see countries at their best. If you enjoy walking and cycling or just touristing, it's good to leave the crowds behind, although with Jack's arm in a sling, we would not be able to cycle in Portugal. We decided to park up at a recommended campsite at Olhau, a small town which boasts a large fishing port, and to then hire a car to explore the whole Algarve area. Once again we would use the Beast as our base camp hotel – she would be too big to drive through the small villages which we wanted to explore. We found the site quite easily and were able to drive straight in and choose a place to park; it was another over wintering place for all nationalities, with a steady stream of short stay visitors too. These sites sometimes had a 'small town' feeling to them, with fenced areas around the more permanent caravans, flowers around the doors and washing on the lines. This site even had a camp newsletter compiled by residents, allowing all nationalities to air their views, and the bar had the usual games evenings. It was quiet, friendly, with a good small supermarket and reasonable shower blocks. You could easily become critical of the different sites which you stay at when touring, but it pays to remember that you are not in England, you are in a foreign land where they do things differently, and that's what you went there for.

Our routine on arrival anywhere was so well practiced by now that within minutes we were all set up. Jack and Simon went through their drill; hooking up the electricity, lowering the levelling jacks, sliding out the awning and patio table, with three folding chairs, and putting up the satellite dish. Meanwhile I quickly pulled cushions from cupboards, sorted out washing to be done, and put a light salad on the table for lunch. That was our home ready to live in again. We were ready to see the sights, so, never able to sit still and relax when we reached a new destination, we took a short walk to the Ria Formosa Natural Park which was situated literally just down the road from the camp site. This flat area of sandbanks juts out of the coastline, offering protection to the leeward beaches of the Algarve and is a haven for bird life. The nature reserve covers about 60 kilometres of coastline and is sheltered from the ocean by partly submerged sand dunes and a network of salt marshes and lagoons. Several times during our stay, we walked along to this nature park and took leisurely strolls along the three kilometre trail, through pine woods and along the quiet shoreline; exploring the old working tidal mill on our way to a freshwater lake. There we could sit in hides, amongst white storks, large grey herons, and the rare purple gallinule, along with thousands of wading and water birds, who use this area as a stop over and feeding ground. There's also a bird hospital here and the main centre for the almost forgotten, web-footed, Portuguese water dogs. These are bouncy, friendly animals with long, curly black hair, like Rasta dogs, whose traditional job was to help fishermen with their catch, by diving into the water and chasing the fish into the nets.

Our first full day looked like a fine one, so after hanging out a pile of washed clothing on our line, tied to the trees around the Beast, we decided to tackle an ongoing problem which we had been having with our LPG gas tank. This gas ran the fridge, cooker, generator and central heating in the motor home. We had been unable to fill up the tank with fresh gas while we were in Spain, as it was simply not allowed. You had to use bottled gas there and we had bought one bottle as an emergency spare supply, although acquiring it from the dragon-like, power crazed old signora who had controlled the triple, rubber-stamped paperwork involved, had been a nightmare. Simon had almost to give blood to get it, and sweat and tears were definitely expected. (He had sat in her boiling office for hours, along with a room full of similarly disgruntled Spaniards, while she grudgingly bestowed gas bottles to the needy.) Now, however, the gas in our main tank was getting low and, we suspected, rather impure judging by the colour of the flame and the performance of some of the appliances. One of the camp site residents had told us of a garage near Olhau where you could fill up your gas tank and where the owner was a specialist at checking the system. To find someone like that, locally, was a bit of a rarity, so we reserved our pitch with well placed chairs and stones and drove off in the Beast to find him.

'Autogas de Laranjeiro' was run by Edmond and his wife, who were friendly, helpful and more than happy for us to park the motor home on the waste ground next to the garage but Edmond was quite busy with previously booked work, so after an initial diagnosis of 'bad French gas' (which was what we soon put any problem down to, including problems which had nothing to do with 'bad French gas'), it was decided that Simon would do most of the work using Edmonds tools when necessary, and Edmond would give advice when Simon needed it. It was agreed that the gas tank should come off and the small amount of remaining gas should be discarded, then the tank cleaned of any sludge, and re-instated to be re-filled. Simon got to work, and although it was quite tricky getting the large gas tank out of its position, he managed to remove it by using the levelling jacks to raise one side of the motor home. We then had a long wait while the small amount of remaining gas dispersed. We have since learnt that should you decide to do it this way in England, you will be breaking the law and will incur a fine of many, many thousands of pounds!

It was a beautiful blue-sky day, quite hot and with no breeze. This is February in Portugal, and as I sit writing this, back in England in December, I long to be there again. Jack and I had little to do whilst Simon worked on the gas tank, so we decided to take a long walk through the surrounding countryside. We found what looked like a rough goat track, leading up through low hills, and we followed it through bright yellow meadow flowers, wild cistus bushes with their papery pink blooms, and gentians that were bluer than the sky above. The meandering track led through ancient olive groves and past scrubby thyme bushes, to a stone ruin where we sat on the hillside in the sun and listened to the ever present crickets as they rubbed their legs together with glee; heavy smells of herbs and flowers scented the warm air. We had one of our wonderful, subject hopping conversations, which led from this topic to that and ranged through everything from the history of Portugal, to women's rights in India. When we began to get peckish, we walked back down and set our chairs up under a shady tree, where we ate rich black olives, fresh bread and goat's cheese, for lunch. Then we all relaxed and read our books while the old gas evaporated from the tank. Edmund eventually gave it the thumbs up and Simon fitted it back in place. Then it was filled with clean gas and we thanked all concerned. The charge was so ridiculously small that Simon gave

Edmund some extra for his trouble and his help. It was a dirty job, but someone had to do it, and the gas has worked perfectly since then.

Our hire car, a fairly new Renault Megane, arrived the next day; it was going to cost us 120 euros for seven days. Our first trip was to the market at Quarteira where you could buy just about everything from African sculptures to pirate DVD's, or lace tablecloths to Peruvian knitwear. Most markets had the same type of goods on offer, however this is a very large market and if you can't resist them, you can spend a few hours at this one, haggling or just people watching. The rest of original Quarteira has been somewhat overwhelmed by developments and tourism, although it does have a very long sandy beach. We moved quickly on to see some of the famous sand stack coves that start at Quartiera and continue westward all along the coast to Lagos.

The Algarve is littered with fabulous and famous beaches and it would be difficult to agree on a favourite. 'In season' you would have to choose by simply finding one which had some room on it, but at the beginning of February, when they were all almost empty and yet it was still warm enough to play on them and even swim in the sea if you were brave enough, they all looked inviting. That afternoon we went no further than Praia Gale, just past Albufeira. All along this coastline you will find perfectly clean, fine pale sand and golden coloured, low rocky cliffs, with grassy paths leading along the top from beach to beach. Isolated, strangely shaped, sand stacks composed of tiny fossils stand like sentinels in the sun, between rocky coves, where Jack could duck through tunnels of rock and jump over the low incoming waves to work his way round to stand inside forty foot tall blow holes shaped like hour glasses. Jack and Simon exhausted themselves playing in the tide, seeing how late they could leave it before they ran up the beach and didn't get a soaking, while I pottered among the sea shells looking for yet more treasure.

Next day we went further, driving straight down the extremely quiet motorway towards Portimao, and then continuing on smaller roads, down to Sagres, which is the peninsular at the southern most tip of Portugal. This wind swept cape was once known as the end of the world, and when we stood on the headland and gazed out to the constantly churning ocean, we could understand why. Sagres is an unspoilt, low-lying town, which attracts surfers and backpackers in summer, but in winter seemed almost empty. The surrounding countryside of low, rolling green hills, appeared to be unchanging, with twisted olive trees, ancient figs, oranges, lemons and almond trees. Herds of goats were shuffled along the roads by smiling, brown skinned Portuguese and the word for 'stress' was obviously not part of anyone's vocabulary. For such a quiet place it has a surprisingly famous history. It was here in the 15th Century, that the school of navigation was founded, gathering together the greatest cartographers, astronomers, mariners and shipbuilders in Europe. New ships were designed here, including Christopher Columbus's caravel, which he used to cross the Atlantic. Vasco da Gama and Ferdinand Magellan studied here and Sir Frances Drake made the unpardonable mistake of burning down the navigation school and its priceless library in 1587. All that remains from this earlier history is a simple chapel and the huge Rosa dos Ventos (Wind Compass), which is a circle on the ground, carved in stone and forty three meters in diameter. Now, a huge 17th century fortress stands on this site.

We explored all of this and watched the tremendous crashing waves of the surging Atlantic as it battered the towering cliffs. The cliff top walk, with its growling blowholes and flattening wind, had us holding our hats on, but standing on the very edge of these 200 feet high, absolutely sheer cliffs were a veritable host of local fishermen. With no safety ropes attached to them, but holding oversized rods out over the cliff tops, they looked extremely precarious. Some men had even clambered down the almost vertical sides of the cliffs to secure more dangerous looking footholds, and we were told that the previous year, four men had died in this sport of 'Extreme Fishing' as Jack called it. We couldn't imagine that what they caught was any different or better than what you could get in the local market, but maybe the thrill was what they were really there for, although the fishermen didn't look like the Portuguese version of Indiana Jones. But then, after watching for a while, we saw that they were regularly hauling up good size sea bass, which has got to be some of the tastiest fish-eating anywhere. Thankfully Jack decided not to add this dangerous looking sport to his list of 'things to do when I'm older' though.

Crossing the headland by car, we travelled up the western coast to Castelejo. Unlike the southern stretches of the Algarve, the west coast, stretching north from Sagres to Odeceixe, is still quite undeveloped. It is constantly exposed to the strong Atlantic winds, the sea is much cooler and swimming is dangerous; but for sheer rugged beauty it is breathtaking and we wrapped up in what warm clothing we had, to stand down on the rocky shores of Praia Castelejo, to watch the wind blow the tops off the huge rolling waves. It was a magnificent, mesmerising sea and we stayed until the sun went down. Then with glowing cheeks and empty stomachs, we drove back to Olhau for supper in a little café we had spotted near the campsite.

Olhau is a pleasant, quiet, unspoilt town and from the bell tower of the seventeenth century parish church, which we climbed for a charge of 1 euro each, you can look out over the white washed houses with their small flat-roofed terraces. The busy fishing port has centuries old links with Morocco and it shows in the architecture and traditions. We frequently went to the fantastic food markets, which were held in two large brick buildings on the harbour side, and were open from the crack of dawn, every day except Sundays. Meat, fruit and vegetables were in one hall and freshly caught fish in the other. Everything looked delicious. The strawberries, olives, nuts, big juicy tomatoes, salad crops and greens were begging to be eaten; and in the fish market, thirty individual marble slabs, slippery with sword fish, eels, tuna, fresh sardines of every size, shell fish, octopus, gleaming eyed mackerel at 1 euro each and much more, were all displayed and sold by the local men who had fished it out of the sea. In Portugal we ate

like kings for next to nothing. On Saturdays, the market extends to the squares outside
the halls where locals and regular traders line the harbour edge, selling everything from
hand reared chickens and rabbits, to surplus flowers and crops from smallholdings. For
several Saturdays running we wandered the stalls, Jack and I stuffing ourselves on nuts
and almond cakes as we went, while Simon searched for the best fish to barbecue. As
was always the way, it was the people who captured my attention, as much as the food.
The typical little old lady, all in black, sitting on an upturned wooden crate next to her
wares, her battered straw hat so big that it completely shaded her tiny, wrinkled face
from the sun. She worked a piece of white lace, with thin brown fingers that moved
independently after decades of practice, her alert searching eyes looking out for a cus-
tomer. She spotted me taking a picture of her, and gave me such a look that I simply
had to buy some of her home grown flowers and a fresh thick lettuce. The fishermen,
still in wellies and waterproof trousers, bantering amongst themselves at their stalls as
they called for someone, anyone, to buy their ink covered squid or choose from their
pile of fresh sardines. The groups of round bellied, tidily dressed men who greeted
each other at the street café in the market square; and the strange young blond woman
that we had noticed before, who talked loudly to herself and marched about the market, trying to make eye contact with the unwary. My camera was always busy.

After one such shopping trip to the market, we went back and cooked some fresh
fish for supper. Then I walked down to the phone box, which was situated near the
camp entrance and called the family back home. After a good chat, I started back up
towards the motor home, but in the dark I could see a familiar figure ahead of me. I
couldn't mistake her gypsy style headscarf and brisk walk and immediately shouted
for Becky to hang on while I caught her up. Yep, that's what so often happens when
you travel. Becky and Nick had not long arrived, their tent was up and of course they
came round to us later that night and sang for their supper, impressing all around us
with their delightful, lively violin music. It was great to see them again and we soon
agreed on a day out in Faro to celebrate. And what did we do in Faro? Did we look at
the interesting architecture, the old town, the beaches, the museums etc….. I'm afraid
not…… we all went to the multi screen cinema, loaded ourselves with pop corn and
watched the latest Lord of The Rings movie. Just brilliant!

Exploring the Algarve

The beaches of the Algarve may be its greatest tourist attraction but once again, on reading more about the area, we were keen to get off the beaten track and explore inland. Up early with the usual picnic packed, we headed off on a tour starting from Portimao, not the most interesting of places, but from there we headed inland across the coastal plain and then into the rolling hills of Serra de Monchique. This volcanic range soaks up the Atlantic mist, and with constantly flowing mountain streams, tumbling through the region on their way to the sea, it is green and verdant. Cork Oaks, Chestnut and Eucalyptus trees grow on wooded hillsides and heavy yellow mimosa and rhododendron edge the roads. However, bounteous as this area looked to us in February, it suffers from long droughts in the summer, with temperatures sometimes reaching 35 degrees and it needs to retain all the water it can. In recent years, summer fires have been known to burn 85% of the Monchique forests with predictably disastrous results. The cork oak is a long-term investment, with a commercial life of about 150 years. The tree has to be about twenty years old before the first bark is removed and used for tanning. The outer bark then re-grows and is ready for stripping again every nine years and each time it is harvested, the quality of the bark improves. We saw many piles of dusty cork bark, stacked by the roadside, waiting to be taken away to processing plants to be turned into insulation panels and wine bottle corks.

In our zippy little car we drove up into this delightful area, swinging off the main road to take in Caldas de Monchique on the way. This small spa village, which was popular with the Romans, was purchased almost in its entirety by the Monchique Termas company in the year 2000. Much of the old village, particularly around the main square, has been systematically restored from some neglect, into a pleasant enough tourist attraction. On to Monchique itself, where we climbed the warm cobbled steps to the 16th century parish church, the Igreja Matriz, with its columns carved as knotted ropes and then up to the atmospheric, ruined monastery, with old gardens of magnolia and lemon trees and great views across the town to the peak of Picota. From Monchique we took the winding, mountain road to the highest summit in the Algarve, the Pico da Foia at 902 meters, where we leant against our car in the warm midday sun and took in the view across the rolling green hills to Portimao, Lagos and Cabo de Sao Vicente. Taking a devious route as always, we stopped at a roadside restaurant and had excellent chicken piri-piri with hunks of fresh bread and olives for lunch, before detouring to find Omega Park. This is a small zoo, spreading naturally through the hills, with enclosures that house rare and unusual animals gathered together over four years by the English owners. Twenty-two endangered species, including the Bamboo Lemur, Pygmy Hippo, Spider Monkey and Cheetah are involved in breeding programmes there.

We were now thoroughly enjoying the gentle Algarve and Jack, with his arm in a sling, was managing to cope quite well with the car travel. So, early next morning we drove into Faro again, and following the town map, we searched out the Capela dos Ossos, or Chapel of Bones. This rather macabre building, constructed entirely from human bones and mortar, is tucked away behind the Igreja do Carmo (church). These types of chapel are scattered throughout Portugal and Jack found it particularly cool that a whole building could be made of bones. "Gruesomely fascinating" was how he described it, as he posed for photographs beside rows of skulls. Thousands of human skeletons, disinterred from the adjacent monk's cemetery – an interesting way of freeing up much needed space – have been separated into tibias, fibulas, vertebrae, skulls and all other parts of the skeleton, to line the interior of this chapel, including altar and roof and all parts in between. Much like a mosaic, intricate patterns were designed around the shapes of small and large individual bones. This small chapel was not highlighted as some great tourist attraction and we seemed to be the only visitors. It had cost us just one euro each to enter, and later in the year when we were marvelling at mosaics in Pompeii, while fighting our way through troops of Japanese tourists, we thought back to this peaceful little place with fond memories.

Whilst we were in Faro, we went on to visit the Ilha de Faro, which is linked to the mainland by a small road. This island is a long thin strip curving out from the mainland and encircling part of the Ria Formosa. It has low, single storey holiday chalets and a small village of permanent homes. The only commercial buildings are a few cafes and souvenir stalls near the small central car park. With next to no roads on it, we parked our car and walked down the narrow pedestrian street which led us through the village and out. From then on we walked on smooth wooden board walks with swinging rope handrails, leading on down the island, over sand dunes peppered with waving grasses. Beside the shore was a long, thin string of shanty style fishermen's homes, each design seemingly ruled by the materials which had been available at the time of construction and then randomly added to when more space was required. Some with families and some with just lone fishermen living an almost desert island existence next to the inland lagoon. Brightly painted boats were anchored out on the water and fishing nets were drying on the beach. As always, friendly dogs lay in the hot sun, just about managing to thump their tails as we stepped around them. Children rode their bikes along the board walks, and then turned off down side tracks to visit each others houses, like little rabbits scooting around the island.

We followed the warm wooden walkways; our hands trailing along thick rope handrails bleached white by the sun and sea. The Mediterranean shores on one side and the quiet lagoon on the other. At the far end we turned around and pottered back, beachcombing the shore line all the way until our pockets were weighed down with smooth, warm shells. It looked like paradise to us, and the only drawback was that in the unlikely event of war, the Portuguese government could commandeer the island for maritime defence. Not too likely we thought.

We had been in Portugal for ten days now and were really enjoying all that it had to offer. The campsite at Olhau was good and it soon became apparent that we were once again in a small British quarter, although this was more by accident than design. We were parked up at the edge of a wide road which led through the site. Close to us were two other English couples, well established with caravans and awnings, one couple there just for the winter and the other while they searched for a suitable property to buy. They had sold up in England and planned to move permanently to the Algarve. Further over was another English couple, who had originally come from our home county of Hereford; they were also wanting to move to Portugal. They were all both kind and helpful, and we enjoyed another unforgettable meal out to celebrate a birthday. This time I tried a fish dish with mango sauce, and Simon and Jack had the speciality which was tender rump steak, which you cooked yourself on hot stones at the table. The meat sizzled on the slabs in front of them, while they turned and cooked it to their own taste, and it was delicious. A glass of Medronho (arbutus-berry liqueur) ended the meal, and yes..... that's another place to return to.

February 11th was another beautiful hot day and we packed our swimsuits and took a drive along the coast eastwards to one of the many islands that are part of the Ria Formosa natural park. The Ria Formosa, covering 60 kilometres of coast, is a system of lagoons formed by rising water levels when the great glaciers retreated. The resulting depression was gradually filled by sediments, creating a coastal barrier of dunes, which run roughly parallel to the mainland. These dunes allow shallow, warm water lagoons, salt marshes, tidal flats and islets to exist. With its unique vegetation, it has become a vital area for migrating and over-wintering birds and is the nursery area for several oceanic species. It has also long provided a living for many of the local population.

With the car packed with our usual array of binoculars, sandwiches, sun cream, hats, surf board etc we took the road to Tavira – we always seem to have a car full of 'stuff' which we might need. We left the car on the mainland and walked across a swaying pontoon bridge and then waited for the little red and black, toy-train, which carried us across the mud flats to the Ilha de Tavira. We were the only people on the train going over, like three little kids sat at the back, the occasional walker coming back the other way, but otherwise it was very quiet. When the train reached the 13 kilometre island of sand, we hopped off and walked to the rather exotic looking café. There, under a colonnaded pergola, we supped cold drinks before spending the afternoon lolling on the long white beach, playing the old Arab game of Mancala in the sand, with small white shells and 'catch the tennis ball in the sea'; this last game always resulting in complete anarchy as we attempted to soak each other by deliberately throwing it too hard and too close, into the rolling waves. The main aim was always to get each other as wet as possible and invariably everyone ended up soaked. It was almost completely deserted on this hot sandy island and was extremely peaceful, with just the warm sea wind and the crashing surf to break the silence. Interesting flotsam and jetsam ended up in our pockets again, well usually my pockets, and long bleached pieces of wood made great drawing sticks in the sand. There's nothing quite like messing about by the sea – and we always did plenty of that.

The other island that we visited during our stay was the Illa da Armona. To get there we caught the midday ferry from the end of the jetty at Olhau, along with about thirty locals, all paying the usual 1 euro each, each way. It was a Saturday and seemed to be the family shopping day, when those living on the island came over to the mainland to stock up on groceries and all other household items. Trolley loads of food were loaded on to the rusty looking ferry, along with brooms, plants, live chickens in cages, new fridges and a shiny new boy's bike. Families helped to heave each others goods on board before the horn was sounded and we all found standing room on the main deck, as we moved off. At the other end, once again everyone helped to get the shopping unloaded, before starting to walk along the only single, sandy road, which led down the centre of the island. The only motors on this island were of the outboard variety, there were no cars or scooters – just hand pulled trolleys. At first the crowd was large, with neighbours chatting as they strolled, carrying or pulling along their latest buys from the town. Gradually people said goodbye as they turned off to their houses, until just the three of us were left quite alone and the 'road' had turned into a sandy track. Quiet had settled again over the island and smells of cooking wafted our way. It was time for lunch and a Saturday afternoon nap for the locals. We drifted on, and once again we picnicked and explored the sandy beach, before catching the last ferry back to Olhau, this time accompanied by teenagers, dressed in their best, for a Saturday night on the town.

I have to say at this point, before I forget, that we found the Portuguese people to be consistently friendly, with ready smiles and an easy relaxed attitude. Wonderfully though, everything seemed to work – buses and boats ran on time, offices, markets and official buildings opened and closed when they said they would and all was achieved with a quiet and simple courteousness and humility sadly lacking in so many other 'developed' countries. Communication wasn't so easy, as the Portuguese language sounded vaguely Russian to us, with a little Spanish and French thrown in. It is actually spoken by more than two million people worldwide, mainly in Brazil, (where it is the official language) and in five African nations. But it is not so well known in Europe. However, they were always keen to help us with pronunciation, or to solve a problem through a mixture of pigeon English and sign language. They seemed to tolerate the latest invasion of foreigners, who were enjoying their wonderful country, and we didn't feel the same abrasive edge that we experienced in Spain. We were 'out of season' of course, and all may seem quite different in the middle of a hot summer with an overdose of tourists, but we felt very at home in Portugal.

But our time was running out. Soon we would have to be heading back into Spain, to the hospital at Algerciras, for Jack's very last X-ray and check up. Then we would be driving across to southern France to start travelling down through Italy. We still weren't sure about visiting Morocco, our year out seemed to be going very fast and we knew that we also wanted to visit Sicily and Croatia. We did have more of a plan now, but could adapt it at any stage. Of course, you know what happens to mice and men when they have a plan...... but the next black cloud was yet to descend on us. For the moment we visited more of the wonderful beaches, including the picture postcard Praia dos Tres Irmaos (the three sisters) and crammed some more day trips in, while we still had the hire car.

We had been told by our English neighbours, who knew the area well, that we should take the route to Alcoutim before we leave, so after a quick bit of map planning, we did just that. Very often on these day trips, we would put Jack in charge of map reading and navigation. He has a logical mind when it comes to looking at contours and landmarks and became proficient at guiding us along. He would also take charge of town maps and lead us through quite complicated city centres to get to places we wanted to see. It was all good practice for him. I, on the other hand, have such an appalling sense of direction that I have to be almost micro chipped just to visit the nearest toilets. I invariably turn right when I leave any building, no matter which way I should be going, and it was Simon and Jack's biggest worry during the year, that I would get lost. As a safety measure, we started the trip with a mobile phone each, but mine was stolen when the car was broken into in Spain. Ever after that I was not allowed to go anywhere alone! I could say that such an attitude was unfair, but to be perfectly honest, I know I have no sense of direction at all. I only got lost once, in Florence, when I was swept along by a crowd of tall Americans and Simon and Jack completely lost sight of me. It was a worrying fifteen minutes for all of us, and we were so relieved when we were reunited that we just had to have a huge bear hug all round. We hadn't realised how close we had all become on this trip until that point.

However, now Jack was map reading for us, on a roundabout route to Alcoutim. We took a road up to the picturesque dam at Beliche; wild cistus bushes abounded with their papery flowers, each petal marked with a black spot and each flower boasting a bright yellow centre. Pine trees, eucalyptus, rosemary and lavender and fabulous views across green wooded valleys and steep mountainsides invited us to stop much too often to admire them all. We then doubled back to find the small road at Foz de Odeleite, where a fast flowing brook flows into the wide, slow moving Guardiana river. A smaller road follows this river valley, sometimes within a few feet and sometimes, when it climbs the valley sides, from a distance; but at almost all times you have the river in view and are travelling through beautiful scenery. We passed smallholdings, flourish-ing in the rich alluvial soil, and a farmer ploughing his field the age-old way with a horse and plough – the river flowing slowly alongside them.

This river is tidal as far as Alcoutim and in the days when the area was rich in copper, iron and manganese ores, it was the main method of transport to the Mediter-ranean for those cargoes. Alcoutim became a prosperous town, providing for the many sailing ships, which waited there for the tide to take them down river. The Guardiana River also forms the border between Portugal and Spain and as you drive alongside it, you can shade your eyes and gaze across to Spanish life on the other bank. Distant cockerels crow, church bells sound the hour and children's voices echo across the river; far-away sounds, which carry on the breeze and only slightly disturb the tranquillity of this perfect river valley. White sailed yachts drift unhurriedly by, sometimes anchoring out for a few days fishing or disembarking at Alcoutim for fresh provisions and lunch in one of the small but excellent restaurants. Alcoutim is a small attractive river port, with no hustle or bustle, and very little obvious tourism. The fourteenth century castle which stands above it, offers fine views of the town and the continuing valley. This whole mountainous area was once much more important when the Greeks, then the Romans, Arabs and Portuguese sought its riches, but it fell into decline when mining became less profitable and peace was settled between Spain and Portugal. Now it is an area that is just beginning to revive.

We were planning to eat out that day and found a village restaurant, popular with the locals. There was only one main course available for lunch, which was a rich lamb stew with thick chunks of fried bread to dunk in the tasty gravy, and a refreshing salad to follow. It was all being prepared and cooked at one end of the bar; the stew smelling good as it bubbled away in a huge pot. At the other end of the bar our cook, cum bar staff, cum waiter, served drinks and chatted to a regular local as he read the daily paper and smoked and ate his way through a leisurely lunch. We couldn't imagine no-smok-ing rules ever reaching this relaxed corner of the world. There was plenty to eat and the price seemed ridiculously reasonable but afterwards we could hardly move and almost had to push each other up the hill, to view the old Moorish fort. Finally, our drive home took us across the high, flat, inland plain to Martim Longo and then down through pine trees and zig-zag roads to Cachopo. Then over the mountains which form the barrier between the coast and inland Algarve, with their deep, tree covered gorges and tumbling streams which led us down to the sea again, through some fabulous scenery.

Becky and Nick headed off the next day, so once more, we said final farewells. They'd made enough money busking in Portugal to allow them to travel back through Spain, and they had to be back in England by April to play at a friends wedding. When we returned to England in September we met up again, and have kept in touch with them since, which has been a real pleasure. We, however, took another trip into the hills, this time to Loule and en route we stopped at Estoi to admire a bit of local architecture.

The pink rococo palace which puts the otherwise sleepy little village of Estoi firmly on the map has a much grander name really. The Palacio do Visconde de Estoi. I fell in love with this crumbling, ornate and totally romantic estate as soon as I saw it. If I were a millionaire I would buy it tomorrow, but it would not be to everyone's taste.

We stepped through the small elaborately carved wrought iron gate, set in a much larger equally elaborate but firmly locked, set of gates. The cobbled driveway led us past bent old palm trees twenty feet tall and overgrown bougainvillea hanging down to our heads with deep pink flowers. Stately stables, which once housed high stepping horses, now stood quiet with doors and windows locked and barred. We walked on up to the big house, passing the prettiest old band stand, still complete with finely curled, slightly rusty, music stands. The palace is a huge building but unfortunately, you can only view the exterior at present. At ground level, curved stone walls are decorated with traditional, blue and white tiles, depicting scenes from nature and voluptuous semi nude ladies. A secretive grotto beneath the balustraded balcony contains the Three Graces, hidden amongst damp ferns and rocks. More elegant statues and cornucopia shell water features surround a rectangular pool, which once had fountains playing amongst the central statues of bare breasted women holding gaping fish, and wide, sweeping, stone staircases with heavy balustrades, lead to a balcony with long views down the carriage driveway and surrounding gardens.

We wandered under the warm sun, sitting here and there on curved stone benches and took our time in this strange deserted place. The Estoi Palace is much neglected, with peeling pink paint and crumbling stonework, overrun gardens and shuttered windows, just waiting to be rescued, although I think it was almost at its most attractive in this weary state. If Sleeping Beauty was going to live anywhere it would have to be here. One day it will be cleaned, repaired and horribly tidied into a municipal hotel...... it just won't be the same. I'm glad we saw it, as it was that day. I have to say that I don't think that Simon and Jack saw it in quite the same light as I did. Maybe pink just isn't their colour and I know that Simon saw a builder's nightmare at every turn and was probably very glad that we could never afford to buy it. But I shall always dream of it.

Loule was next on the list, the 'second' city on the Algarve, and a vibrant and busy place. Our first stop was in one of the great cake shops situated on the very wide, tree lined, main street. We needed pastries to re-charge our energies and Jack and I had a hard time deciding which of the mouth-watering types we should choose. The whole of Loule was preparing for its Carnival celebrations that take place each February before Lent. It is renowned for having the biggest carnival in the country, and it continues throughout the whole weekend. Oversized banners and bunting already trailed from every lamp-post and available support, and a festive feel was in the air.

As usual our noses led us to the interesting neo-Moorish market hall, situated just off the main street, where fresh, and absolutely tempting merchandise, dictated that we wander the stalls in a daze. Well I wandered in a daze. Jack and I drooled over more pastries, fruits, cheeses, and endless types of olives, nuts, hams, and fresh sea-food. But Simon went straight to the meat counters and bought pork chops to cook for supper. He usually despaired of us, wandering about or debating over a piece of smelly cheese that we didn't really need. Invariably, I was the one running behind to catch up and he was the one waiting for me, so that we could move on. Jack was never keen on the smelly cheese anyway, but for quite different reasons. Since he had broken his arm, he had slept in the make-up bed in the dinning area of the Beast because it was more spacious and comfortable. The only trouble was that it was just opposite the fridge, so when Simon made the early morning tea, and opened the fridge door, Jack got the classic smell of strong cheese wafting across his pillow. "Oh my god what's in the fridge?" were the first words he often muttered in the morning. We said that it was his feet making the smell…it never stopped him raiding the fridge when he was hungry though, and at thirteen years of age, that was almost constantly.

We had just a few days left in Portugal before having to return to Algeciras. Jack's arm was healing well and we were looking forward to moving on to Italy. Our plan was made - but you know what happens when you make a plan – someone else may have other ideas.

Behind every silver lining

Well, behind every silver lining is that big black cloud waiting to pour all over you, and our next big black cloud was imminent. Thursday 19th February was not a good day. We were having a lazy afternoon at camp to catch up on clothes washing and writing letters, when at 4.30pm we received an urgent call from Louis, one of my sons back in England. He'd been contacted by Basildon Hospital because his brother, Peter, had been admitted with serious head injuries as a result of an accident at work. From what we could gather, an extremely heavy, oak A frame, had fallen onto his head, crushing it onto another frame that he had been working on. Simon managed to contact the hospital, who confirmed that Peter was in the Intensive Care Unit and that his injuries were very serious.

How quickly everything can change when you hear this kind of news. Everything that you considered important before becomes meaningless and your priorities become absolutely basic – I needed to return to England immediately. We spent the rest of that evening on the telephone gathering information and next morning we drove to Faro airport to book a flight home. Simon and Jack were going to stay with the motor home and continue to Algeciras for Jacks last appointment and I would fly back to be with Peter. Where and when we would see each other again, we did not know.

Early next morning we said goodbye at Faro airport, which was incredibly difficult to do, and for me it would also be goodbye to lovely Portugal. After four months together in the motor home, travelling, eating, sleeping and exploring so much together, I was very sad to be leaving Jack and Simon. We had become a very strong unit and I felt somehow that I would never return, but I was beside myself with worry for Peter. So, as is often the case when you are a parent, I wished I could divide myself in two. The plane left the warm, green Algarve and within a few hours I was landing at cold, grey Stanstead. It seemed like a different world and I felt desolate; but I was not alone. There to meet me at the airport was Stella, Simon's kind sister, or an angel in disguise! She whisked us straight to the hospital and before long we were sitting at Peter's bedside. He was badly hurt and it would be a long haul to a full recovery. He'd suffered cranial fractures, severe concussion, nerve damage which was affecting his eye movement and facial muscles, lacerations and bruising; but he was alive and considering the accident, that was something of a miracle.

I won't dwell on that time in England. Stella and I will never forget our weekend in an Essex motel, (even though we would quite like to!). I will always remember that week when, after she had left, I had lodgings in the nurse's quarters next to the hospital and spent each day sat at Peter's bedside. When he was released from hospital, Stella drove us back to Hereford; Simon's mother offered to have Peter stay with her, while he recovered further, and until he could return to his own flat. I stayed on with him, until he kindly but firmly said that he really didn't need me fussing over him like a mother hen anymore. Now almost a year later he is still not fully recovered but is his old self again. No matter what age your children are, the umbilical cord is never really cut. Leaving him again and leaving all of the family again, was an emotional roller coaster. I cried all the way to the airport in the back of our friends' car. Then they pushed me onto a plane back to Gibraltar, where I was meeting up with Simon and Jack. Once again, I wished that I could divide myself in two and once again I thanked my lucky stars that we had such wonderful friends and family.

I flew back on a late afternoon flight and as we passed over Spain I watched the day end as the sun set through the clouds on the horizon. I felt suspended in a blue sky, with all the time in the world to think, while the sun slowly turned a deep red and sank behind the earth. It was a journey of reflection; of weighing up what life really meant to me and what was important; of facing truths and considering the past. That time which few of us ever get on our busy planet, a time when we can stop and think. As the sun dropped, the landscape below us darkened, each small detail quickly disappearing, and as we banked over the Spanish coast the sea merged with the black land and only the twinkling lights of towns and villages showed us where the difference was. Looking down, as we flew parallel to the shore, I followed the lights of towns that we had driven through, months before, on our way down to Portugal. Now I was flying over it all. You just never know what life has in store for you. Eventually, Gibraltar appeared in the distance, jutting out and up into the blackness, alive with lights, beckoning us down to life on earth again. We circled around the end of the Rock, over the lights of bobbing boats and as we dropped lower, we turned and banked, dipping one wing almost into the inky sea before straightening out to skim over the water and touch down on the tiny strip of runway which straddles the Rock. Now I felt an achingly long way from England, and much too far away from my other boys, but I was longing to see Simon and Jack again. As I walked through customs and out into the small arrivals area at the airport I saw them waiting by the rail. Big smiles and hugs all round, it was wonderful to be united again, but my head felt totally spaced out, as if I was continually in the wrong place, and I suddenly felt exhausted.

We awoke to a view of the Rock again and a wonderful sunny morning in La Linea. I still felt as if I were in some strange time warp and it took many days for me to get back into life on the road. We walked and talked on the beach and Jack collected yet more, small smooth pieces of coloured glass, for that mosaic that we would one day make. Then we packed up the motor home and headed back up the coast, with my eyes leaking periodically, each time I re-lived the recent roller coaster ride that I seemed to have been on. We called Peter daily now and continued to keep in close contact throughout the rest of the trip. We also decided that we would not try to go to Morocco. It seemed that we were fated not to get there and with time slipping by, we decided to head back up through Spain and on to Italy. That evening, we stopped on a quiet stretch of road next to the sea and after a barbecue we had a bonfire of driftwood, well into the night.

The next few days were hard for all of us. We had to settle back into a routine again and we were all feeling tired and emotionally spent. We were also still worried about Peter and what the final outcome of the accident would be, and although he assured us that he was ok, we knew that it was early days. We trundled along, through the usual beautiful countryside, but I found it hard to appreciate it and my mind was usually somewhere else, miles away. Simon was also feeling tired, having worried about Peter and me while I was away. So, with all of us in a bit of a state, it's not surprising that we have some fairly grim memories of Mojacar.

The town of Mojacar itself was fine, but us getting there was not so good. We had turned off the motorway just past Almeria, in order to head down to the coast to wild camp for the night. However, we had taken a very narrow road which followed a precarious route down to the sea and Simon had to concentrate hard to ensure that we stayed on the road and not in the ditch either side. I didn't make it any easier by twitching like a nervous wreck and repeatedly saying that we were 'awfully close to the edge' again. Then, when we were about to swing onto a very small, rather rickety looking wooden bridge, Jack chose that particular moment to try to get the camera out of the cupboard above his head. He reached the camera, but let the sprung cupboard door slam shut with a loud bang, at the very moment when Simon needed a steady hand at the wheel. The resulting jerk of Simon's head as he looked round to see what the hell the bang was, caused all of his neck muscles to leap into a spasm. Yep, it's funny how these little things can escalate into a disaster. Luckily, we hadn't hit anything, not that we could see anyway, but Simon's neck was now seized solid and he had to turn his whole body to look right or left, rather like a robot.

When we arrived in Mojacar you could have cut the air with a knife. We drove along the coastal road, looking for somewhere to stop and saw up ahead a large parking area. We were just about to swing into it, when once more I panicked about the rather high kerb and caused Simon to falter, seizing his neck muscles yet again! I felt absolutely miserable. As before, Jack did the sensible thing, got out his book and ignored us, while we had a fairly major row, well as best Simon could considering his inability to move his head anymore. Looking back on it now, we can laugh of course. But at the time... well you can imagine the rest. Needless to say, we stayed at Mojacar for a couple of days and it did us good to relax a little again. Jack and I cycled to the nearest pharmacy and managed to buy Simon several packets of Relaxabies, which were the recommended tablet for relaxing muscles and we just hoped that they didn't relax too

many of them. He spent two days with a hot water bottle against his neck, semi-co-
matose on Relaxabies and I tried not to be a complete pain in the arse anymore. Never
easy, I can tell you.

Well, we got our act together again. It didn't take long, just some good nights sleep,
and we were ready to head off. Up past Lorca, to Murcia, with its vast fertile plains of
neatly sown vegetable crops; mile after mile of orange, olive and almond groves; cherry
trees and grape vines as far as the eye could see, and all with a blush of bright spring
leaves. Up into Valencia's rolling hills, where we stopped in an empty motorway car
park for the night and had a fabulous view down a long valley to the coast and Valencia
itself.

Pressing on up the coast, we eventually stopped at a campsite at Villanova, about
forty kilometres south of the capitol of Catalonia. Yes, before we finally left Spain, we
were going to visit Barcelona.

They say that if you only visit one city in Spain, then it should be Barcelona and this
place certainly had it all as far as we were concerned. Spreading from the Costa Dorada
(the Golden Coast), back towards the lower foothills of the Pyrenees, this great Catalo-
nian city offers you tradition and modernism all in one breath and you will need a good
three days to enjoy just some of it.

Probably the most famous attraction in this exciting city is the modernist, art nouveau architecture of the late 19th and early 20th centuries. The mixture of Moorish,
Gothic and Art Nouveau is all eclipsed by the totally unique and uncompromising
work of Antoni Gaudi. His imprint on the city draws tourists from all over the world
and one thing is for sure, you may love them or you may hate them, but one thing you
cannot do, is ignore his buildings. We decided to just get our bearings on the first foray
in, so the next day, which was March 11th, we caught the public transport into the city
centre. A local bus ran every thirty minutes from the campsite gates to Villanova train
station, and the trains ran from there to Barcelona every fifteen minutes. We caught
the 9.30 bus in and then hopped onto the next train. The bus journey did become
rather tedious, as it took a meandering route through the town, but the trains were fast,
clean, electric and double-decker, with plenty of room. The whole journey took about
one hour but we thought that driving and parking would probably take as long and at
least we could relax and read while on the train.

We alighted at a fairly central underground station, (Passieg de Gracia) and walked
up the stairs to street level. Barcelona buzzed all around us and as we gazed in some
confusion at our surroundings, we saw directly opposite us our first Gaudi offering - the
Casa Batilo. This many storied building, with its weird and wonderfully shaped balconies and windows, has Gaudi's unmistakable signature of free flowing lines, rounded
edges and dripping stonework. Straight lines and sharp edges hardly exist in nature
and Gaudi's designs, based on natural forms, would not entertain them either. Like a
cake that has dripped its soft icing down the pillars and supports, over balconies and

doorways, this building looked good enough to eat. As always, it is a matter of taste, but I loved Gaudi's creations, if only because they always made me smile. Bizarre, crazy, unconventional; they were certainly different. We joined the masses and predictably photographed it from every angle.

Following our city map of Barcelona, with Jack leading the way as tour leader, we took a stroll down to the largest square in Spain, the Placa de Catalunya, with its fountains and statues and its wide-open space in the centre of the city. From there we headed down what must surely be, the most well known street in Barcelona – namely 'La Rambla'. You have got to walk down this famous boulevard as it has masses of entertainment value, even though, as a major tourist attraction, you may have to watch out for light fingered pick pockets. Wide and lined with shady trees, this pedestrian area takes you straight through the heart of the old quarter and then down to the towering column of Columbus and the newly developed harbour area. But you will not be able to hurry down La Rambla because at every step, you will want to stop and watch some elaborately dressed street artist, or hover at the edge of a crowd who are studying a gambling game, or admire some of the caged birds stacked five high and ten across at the pet stalls or simply sit on one of the available benches and people watch. We dawdled and wandered our way down, Simon usually in the lead trying to hustle Jack and me along a little faster than a snails pace. We couldn't resist studying the many, many street artists in their amazing costumes, who stood like statues and then, for a handful of small change, would perform a clockwork routine, ending perfectly statue-like again. Our favourite, who we just had to watch several times was the man dressed completely in yellow, with a whitened face, his hair and coat tails standing straight out behind him; he looked as if a strong wind was permanently blowing against him. He performed a slow motion run forward and then reversed back, ending like a statue again. A close second were the pair of silver angels, dressed in layers of long, flowing, silvery grey material, huge feathered wings on their backs, who acted out a slow motion dance, ending with a flourish as they handed you a little silver star as a keepsake. Che Guevara, President Lincoln, and moon-walking Michael Jackson, to name but a few, were all down this street.

Flower stalls competing for the best display of colourful blooms; stalls selling small yellow and blue song birds, singing heartily despite their confined surroundings; book stalls, pavement artists, beggars, and conmen with eastern European accents who worked in teams as they gathered in a crowd and took bets on which upturned cup had a ball beneath it. Older locals, plumped down onto plastic chairs at the side of the street with their shopping bags full of fresh market produce. They passed the time of day with acquaintances or just snoozed in the sun. It was fascinating. No wonder Simon had a problem keeping us moving. However, at last we found ourselves at the end of La Rambla and standing at the foot of the monument to Columbus.

Columbus was of course Italian by birth. He also lived in Portugal for some of his

are many great buildings in the world; from pyramids to mosques, castles to cathedrals, but this one has no comparison. It will surely be one of the Wonders of the World when it is finished. To date, only eight of the twelve, 100 meter tall, bell towers, dedicated to the Apostles, have been completed. The transept and the apse will be crowned by six domes, dedicated to the four Evangelists, the Virgin Mary and Jesus Christ. This last one will be 170 meters high and will be crowned with a cross. As Gaudi once said, "The Temple grows slowly, but this has always been the case with everything destined for a long life. Hundred year old oak trees take many years to grow; on the other hand, reeds grow quickly, but in autumn the wind blows them down and there is no more to be said". On that basis, I would say that the Sagrada Familia will be here to stay for centuries to come. Gaudi died in 1926, hit by a streetcar when crossing a road, and by that time he had dedicated 43 of his 74 years to this building.

We approached from the western side and entered through the 'Portals of Passion'. The roof of this façade, which represents the death of Christ, is supported by six sloping angular columns reminiscent of clean, stretched bones. Set into the walls above you, are groups of very angular, almost severe carved figures, with heads bowed in grief, epitomising agony, death and sorrow. These stark sculptures, by Joseph Ma. Subriachs, are quite unlike any others on the building. Joining the queue of multi-national visitors we shuffled our way forward, at last entering the nave and transept. The work here is only partially completed and we walked through a semi-building site of scaffolding and stone as we gazed ever upward through, what felt like, a forest canopy of stone columns and arches. Nothing is of regular shape here. Columns resemble trees, light recesses resemble flower heads, edges are curved and decoration is everywhere. Enormous stained glass windows tower upwards and before long we had neck ache again. Of course it was busy, and at some points we felt that we were on a conveyor belt of people, moving though the church, but it must be extremely difficult to balance the complex construction problems alongside the huge numbers of tourists who visit here daily, year round. As usual we had to get to the highest point possible, and soon joined the upwardly spiralling queue which was inching its way slowly to the top of one of the completed towers.

If you suffer from claustrophobia then spending a good half an hour, inching your way slowly up a tiny, spiral staircase inside a 100 meter tall stone tower is not for you. Occasionally we were able to glimpse Barcelona through thin slit windows, as it gradually diminished below us, but most of the time we enjoyed the view of a large Dutch bottom in front of us and a chasm like drop to the side. As time went by we all became quite chatty, which was just as well considering our proximity to each other. The casual conversation also prevented me from dwelling on the image of trying to extricate someone, from this completely blocked spiral staircase, in the event of a heart attack. Panic could easily have taken over, given the right set of circumstances, or maybe that was just my over active imagination getting bored. Anyway, eventually we reached the first of two balcony areas where we could step out and get a dizzying view of the awesome dimensions, both interior and exterior. Alongside us sculpted white doves decorated a swaying, leaf covered stone tower. Below us, were the pointed tops of other towers, with their bizarre and intricate carvings and below that, miniature people walked the streets. At this point we could explore several towers, like a maze at altitude, or a tree-top canopy. Crossing a stone arch, which linked one tower to the next, we started upward again to reach the very highest point. Here even Simon and Jack had vertigo. It was all quite staggering; the views of Barcelona and across to the sea, the sheer scale of the proposed buildings and the elaborate detail carved into every sinuous line and stylised flower. We came down through the one way system, eventually reaching terra firma again and worked our way round to the museum, where priceless original scale models and drawings beautifully illustrated what the completed building would look like.

We finally left by the Nativity portal, alongside a group of excited Japanese tourists who skittered back and forth taking it in turns to be photographed in front of this remarkable east facing façade. Dedicated to the birth and life of Christ, this entrance was supervised by Gaudi himself. His distinctive style is unmistakable here, as the stonework sweeps and flows over the building, every inch covered with elaborate carving. Angels, shepherds, birds, flowers and the story of Christ's early life materialise from the façade as you look more deeply into its depths. It is simply amazing and would be too much for some, but as always, it cannot be ignored.

That day we were going for broke, because after viewing the Sagrada Familia, we then got out our street map of Barcelona and put Jack in charge of guiding us to yet another Gaudi offering, wondering if this man ever slept in his incredibly creative life. Did I say that you would need a week to see Barcelona, I should have said a month, and Parc Guell should not be missed. This is where Gaudi turned his hand to landscape gardening and if you are expecting linear paths and regular flowerbeds, you will be in for yet another surprise. Today's landscape architects would be hard put to create a more bizarre and unusual park.

Commissioned by his wealthy friend, Count Eusebi Guell, Parc Guell was originally intended to be a housing development with a difference – but it was never completed and only two of the proposed sixty houses were ever built. One of them being the house that Gaudi lived in for the last twenty years of his life. It is almost the forerunner to Disneyland, such is its fairytale, gingerbread, organic style, with twisting walkways of warped imitation tree trunks, a lizard fountain of brightly coloured mosaic and snaking seating which wraps around a promenade giving panoramic views of Barcelona. Palm trees and exotic foliage decorate balconies and pagodas with all the supports and pillars designed along the lines of nature, although to me, the natural became the unnatural which almost became the natural again. It was almost too much, even for us. But whenever I saw Gaudi creations, they always made me smile and laugh; he broke all the rules and somehow got away with it. He pushed design and creation to its limits, demanding that you stop – and look, and think about your surroundings. There's nothing bland or safe about Gaudi creations, they shriek 'look at me, I'm different'.

Trekking around the Parc, liking some parts more than others, we eventually reached the very top plaza. Here we flopped down beside a line of tourists along the cliff-top edge of the large open square and dangled our aching legs over the drop. The grid like shape of Barcelona, stretched out before us beneath a sunny haze, as far as the eye could see, its famous landmarks clearly visible. Phew, one more Gaudi to go and then we would have seen the lot!

We slept almost all the way back to camp that evening, the train humming along with the usual commuters whose numbers gradually dwindled as the train got further and further away from the city. At Villanova the bus had just left, so we gratefully crawled into a taxi and took the quick route back to the campsite. The Beast, our home on wheels, was there waiting. We became so adept at living in our motor home that a routine had easily been established. I would start the food preparation while Si opened the wine. Jack would raid the fridge for a quick snack and then either watch TV or relax with his book. Habits of a life time are hard to break. That evening another big American RV rolled into our almost empty parking area, but we were too tired to socialise, so it was not until the next day that we met and got to know another set of new neighbours, namely Sean and Michelle.

This young couple had left England with the same plan as us, which was to spend a year in Europe, but they had had nothing but disasters since the moment they hit France. On the first night they'd awoken to find two men searching through the front section of their motor home. Luckily, Sean was a big man, so he had scared the intruders back out of the window that they'd broken in through. This had left them feeling very nervous about wild camping again. After that they'd been very unlucky with the campsites they'd selected and had spent a fortune driving a long way off their chosen route when trying to meet up with friends who never materialised. They were also towing a large trailer behind them, containing two Superbikes, a scooter and a complete mobile work shop, and we thought we were brave. Now, they were on their way down to southern Spain, but were being held up by an electrical problem on their RV which kept cutting out the wipers, indicators, electric steps and other essentials. They seemed doomed and we felt very sorry for them.

We were taking a day off to recover from touristing, but Simon soon had his tool box out and had joined with Sean in trying to discover where the problem lay. It was a tricky one, but after several hours on their backs under the chassis, they eventually found a well-hidden, partly severed cable, which was only connecting intermittently – problem solved. We spent the evening with them and next day they rolled on they're way again. They made it safely down to a campsite on the sunny Spanish coast and as far as we know are still there.

It was now mid March and the weather was good, with a warm sun and very little rain. The year was racing on. We had one more trip into Barcelona planned and then we too, would be heading off, but our next major stop would be in Italy. We were now quite used to catching buses and underground tube trains, to scoot from one area of Barcelona to another, so before long we were climbing the steps of the National Museum of Modern Art, another great building set majestically at the top of a wide avenue of steps and terraces, with flowing fountains cascading in tiers before it. Unfortunately, many of the exhibits were closed for alteration, so apart from Fortuny's famous and beautiful painting, 'Beach at Porcini,' we saw very little inside the gallery. On for a quick coffee and sandwich, and then back to the Guell Palace, for our booked tour of one of the first modern buildings to be declared part of the World Heritage by UNESCO in 1985.

Once again, the wealthy Eusebi Guell had commissioned Gaudi to design this city family-residence for himself, as an extension of the small palace he already had just around the corner, on la Rambla. (Both houses are connected by a devious passage through the city). This house has two main entities, which are almost in contrast with each other. One is the interior of the house, and the other is the rooftop. The main façade, built of local limestone, has magnificent wrought iron gates set in parabolic arches. Entwined serpents, twisted metal and the dark brooding shape of a phoenix rising from the ashes, greet the visitor as he walks through the entrance and into the double vestibule. Carriages would stop here, and the horses would be led down a spiralling brick ramp to the stables under the house. Even the stables were carefully designed in the modernistic style and the fungi-form capitols and columns, in exposed brick work, are some of best known of Gaudi's architectural perspectives. The rest of the house is almost brooding, with heavy iron, marble and dark wood, used in natural flowing shapes. The roof top on the other hand, is a complete contrast, as if Gaudi got bored with the gloom of the interior, and when reaching the roof, felt that he just had to introduce some colour somewhere. This is, of course, where you will find the famous gaudy, Gaudi chimneys, quite unique to him. Distorted shapes and fantastical decorations in fragmented tile or glass or pottery have transformed the twenty chimneys on this flat rooftop into something from Alice in Wonderland. No two chimneys are alike, and all are unlike any chimneys you will see anywhere else. He certainly knew how to make a statement. We must have photographed them all from every angle, before deciding that we really had walked one monument too many. We wandered back to the train station through the streets of Barcelona, taking one last look at this great city. As always, there were many wonderful sites that we still hadn't seen, but our time was up and we would now be leaving Spain. Italy was beckoning, our route was planned, and it was time to go.

Moving on, after a long stay somewhere, was never a problem because we had a good routine which ran like clockwork, with all three of us having a part to play. We did it so often that we could get it down to record time, which was sometimes essential. Outside lockers were all checked and secured, the roof lights were closed, hook up disconnected, TV aerial wound down and satellite dish secured. The legs were raised, awning wound in and picnic table pushed back into its slot. Inside, all lose items were quickly stowed to their right positions, cushions were stuffed into overhead cupboards to stop the contents from moving too much, the fridge contents were checked and secured, water pump turned off and drawers all put into locked position so that they didn't fly out as we went around corners. We gathered our books, drinks and camera into easily reached positions and off we went. Rather like living on a boat, every item had a specific place in the motor home and once we had got used to living this way, it was extremely easy. We could move our home daily and although our surroundings may change, our home remained exactly the same. Every night, Jack made his bed up and every morning he unmade it. This may sound tedious, but actually it took only minutes to do and was no problem. If we were leaving a campsite, it was Jack's job to fill the fresh water tank while Simon emptied the grey and black waste tanks. Most campsites had the facilities to do this and because of the large capacity of our tanks we could 'wild camp' and live independently for about three weeks at a time, when we wished to.

Back on the road again we left Spain and entered Southern France. How nice it was to be back amongst those great 'aires' which provided such good facilities to drivers. Following the motorway past Perpignan, we eventually pulled up just outside Narbonne, at a lake-side camp site in La Nautique. Something about seeing the name Narbonne on our map had made us decide to stop near there for the weekend to take a look around. We knew nothing about the area, but it had a pleasant feel, and warranted a visit. The campsite was run by a Dutch family who made us most welcome. Its quirky feature being that each pitch had its own toilet and shower house in the form of a small, wooden, chalet type building, to which you were given the key. Yet another variation on shower blocks around Europe.

The countryside around this area looked excellent for cycling, so we soon had our bikes off the back of the Beast for an exploratory run. Jack hadn't ridden his since he broke his arm in Tarifa, but after a long circuit of the lake he pronounced himself fit enough for the Tour de France. A little exaggeration maybe, but he felt great to be back in the saddle. Over that weekend we cycled the quiet lanes to Narbonne, a picturesque town of interesting buildings and bridges. Chaining our bikes to the ubiquitous lamppost, we wandered the Sunday morning market and food hall, tempted as always by the superbly fresh fish and vegetables. We bought duck breasts, salads, fruit and local wine, forgetting of course that we only had our ruck sacks and bikes to get it all home and Jack unerringly homed in on the only stall selling BB guns. How wonderfully focused kids can be, when it suits them.

Dividing the centre of this town is the Canal de la Robine , and complete with brightly painted, flower decked, canal boats, it was obviously well used. It joins a vast network of canals including the famous Canal du Midi and the extensive inland waterways would allow you to cross France and reach the Bay of Biscay if you wished. It would surely provide a wonderfully scenic route. Another long cycle ride took us through the countryside towards the coast. Again we followed quiet lanes alongside the picturesque canal. Over locks, past ruined houses that looked ripe for restoration and perfect mini chateaux that had already been rescued and redeemed. Lizards basked on stone walls in the warm sun and pretty views enticed us on. With the wind behind us, we went too far for too long, as always, and coming home, against the wind, took us twice the time and twice as much puff. We never reached the coast, which is only about 14 kilometres from Narbonne, but if we had we would have seen salt marshes, coastal lakes and sandy beaches. This whole area was very pleasant and unspoilt.

Our weekend break over, we motored on again, sleeping overnight along with the juggernaughts in the 'aires de service'. We stopped for lunch in a lay-by overlooking Cannes, and then sped on past the hectic resorts of Nice, Monaco, Monte-Carlo and Menton, before eventually crossing into Italy. With so much of Europe left to see, and with five months of our year already gone, we made a conscious decision not to stop in Southern France. Tempting and beautiful as that area was, we knew that we could easily go back there another day. We'd also left behind the warmer weather of southern Spain, and the cooler climate of the French Riviera in March was not nearly so appealing. It was time to tackle Italy, so armed with the maps, guide books and our Italian phrase book, we set our sites on Florence and with Maisy leading the way, we started down the long Italian coast in search of 'la dolce vita'.

had stopped early in the day, because by 5.45pm we were totally blocked in by lorries and coaches of all nationalities. Our neighbour, a French lorry driver, set about the ritual cooking of his evening meal 'a la primus stove' and shared it all with his Siamese cat, who sat contentedly on a cushioned platform area in the front window of his cab. A coach load of children pulled in on the other side of us; the children rapidly escaped and recklessly used the car park as a play area, whilst more lorries streamed in, until it was all nicely gridlocked.

No one was going to move on in a hurry, certainly not until Romanian, Spanish, French and Italian lorry drivers had stretched their legs and eaten some food. We put the kettle on and I started preparing our evening meal while Jack played a game on the lap top computer and Simon looked at the route for the next day. We could do all of this in the comfort of our home-on-wheels and still be mildly entertained by the argument which was building up to a crescendo in front of us, between a portly Spaniard, whose lorry had been well and truly blocked in and a verbose little Italian. Plenty of horn sounding, shouting and fist waving went on and once again, we could see that lorry drivers in Europe had serious problems when it came to parking for the night.

We slept reasonably well. Nose to tail and side-by-side, cosy you could say, with our multinational lorry drivers, and we were up and away by 7.0am the next morning. We stopped at 9.0am and in my diary I have written – "stopped at 9.0am for coffee and omelettes – feel like running straight back to France. Oh for those big aires and open spaces". It was obviously going to take us a while to settle into Italy. But eventually the landscape began to flatten out and we left the awesome Apennine Mountains behind us for a while. Turning inland, we entered Tuscany country and before long we were travelling through rolling hills, dotted with the famous statuesque cypress trees and ancient olive groves. Every view was a Renaissance painting, with squarely built red-roofed villas, chickens in the vineyards and picturesque woodland. Now all we had to do was find our next campsite.

The one we had chosen as our base was situated 15 kilometres south east of Florence at a small town called Troghi. We had telephoned ahead, concerned that they may not have space for us, but we need not have worried as the season in Italy had hardly begun and no self respecting Italian would be out camping until at least June. We turned off the main road and started to follow directions, but as the afternoon wore on and we delved deeper and deeper into the Tuscan countryside, a tremendous thunderstorm started brewing in the darkening skies above us. By 4.0 pm the heavens had opened with horizontal rain and a noisy and impressive lightening display. As the road began to flood and our visibility dropped to zero we pulled under some trees and gave up. Once more the kettle went on and we got out a pack of cards, ready to sit out the storm, wondering where on earth we were going to end up that night. Two hours later, the evening sun broke through and we headed off again. Five hundred yards later, only round the next few bends, the entrance to Camping Il Poggetto, presented itself.

Maisie got a good telling off for not doing her job a little better, and we rolled into yet another, almost empty campsite.

It had become very obvious, as we travelled around Europe in early spring that most motor-homers were not moving far from the warmth of southern Spain. We encountered fewer and fewer now and didn't really see any more English travellers until we reached Dubrovnik in Croatia, in June. Most of the tourists that we were encountering were obviously on package tours, just visiting the high spots. This campsite near Florence, was not officially opening for the season until the end of March, but they were happy for us and a few other travellers, to park up there and use the facilities.

The rain and storms returned that night and we awoke to a dismal, grey morning. A unanimous vote was soon taken to stay in bed for as long as possible and have a lazy day recovering from our hectic dash into Italy. We took it in turns to walk the three feet necessary to make a cup of tea, and thoroughly enjoyed snuggling under our duvets with good books. When the sun did finally appear again, Jack set up some targets and became 'Sniper Bob, on the job' with his new BB gun, while Simon walked to the village for fresh ciabatta bread and olives. The campsite owners pottered around us, tidying up the storm damage, and complaining about the un-seasonal weather, and as the clouds lifted, beautiful Tuscan views gradually emerged.

Next day, we were up with the Italian larks, (if there are any left in Italy, not in a paté or pie), to catch the bus into Florence. We were going to be able to buy our bus tickets from the campsite reception desk, so clutching our guide books and euros, a small excited group of us hovered there expectantly. However, the owners now pointed out that a spontaneous, nationwide transport strike had occurred, and no buses or trains were running. Oh these impulsive continentals, how they do like to upset things. There was no other way of getting into Florence that day, so that was that. Our little band of hopefuls stood despondent, realising that those carefully made sandwiches, which we were going to eat on the steps of the Uffizi, were now going to be consumed at camp. It just didn't have the same appeal, so we quickly made an alternative plan and persuaded the owners to lend us a detailed map of the area, so that we three could at least go walking.

Re-equipped, we set off again on a long circular ramble that took us up into the hills. It was a stunning day of spring sunshine, with soft blue skies and pillowy white clouds that raced high above us. We climbed the first hill, past fields of solid old olive trees, and lush pastures of yellow dandelions and purple anemones. Endless rows of knobbly, brown vines, lined up over the rolling landscape and thin spirals of smoke, betrayed small bonfires of prunings. There hardly seemed to be anybody else around in the world, except the habitual cockerels that called to each other across the valleys. The Tuscan countryside looked exactly as you see it on postcards; rolling hills dotted with shuttered stone farm houses, their red pan-tiled roofs smouldering in the sun; tall, dark, evergreens which stood together like exclamation marks on the landscape; olive groves, small woods and as a back drop to it all, the snow capped mountains of middle Italy. I absolutely fell in love with Tuscany on that day. It was warm and peaceful and the air smelt sweetly of spring, with just the occasional whiff of wood smoke. We followed the track up to a silent monastery, half hidden at the top of a wooded hill and stopped there on a low wall for a drink and a snack. The view was idyllic. A slender Italian girl, who could have come straight out of a TV advert for a stylish car, came strolling up the track from the other direction and we practised our "Buongiorno's", in unison, which instantly reduced us to hysterical giggles. Luckily for her, we didn't have a clue whether she was a signora or signorina, so we got no further with our conversational Italian. She politely replied and walked on by, probably wondering what three strange Brits were doing sitting on the wall by the monastery. The local cat, who had by this time found us, had no language barriers to bother him and he purred around us like an old friend as he nibbled his way through our biscuits. We continued on our stroll, over the top of the hill and down into the valley on the other side.

Following our map we wandered on, the path leading us through a scrubby wood where we stopped again for tuna rolls and a drink; then I lay down in the warm sun and dozed, while Jack and Simon had target practice with his BB Gun. Scenes from The Godfather drifted through my mind as Marlon Brando's voice was impersonated, and Al Pacino dashed from tree to tree. Boys will be boys, but I have to admit that I was not sad when Jack's cheap bit of plastic fell apart a few days later. We eventually returned to the campsite, having had a memorable and quite unexpected day. That evening we discussed our forthcoming tour of Florence.

"Don't let's try to do too much on the first day", we vowed. But of course, how could we resist!

Italy has so many famous cities, many of which are bursting with art and stuffed to the hilt with treasures, and it's difficult to know where to start. After a while you will become blasé as you walk past priceless statues and over floors of ancient Roman mosaics. We knew that we could never see it all, but as we travelled down the country, we hoped to visit Florence, Pisa, Rome, Pompeii, and Capri. We would then go to the Island of Sicily, and afterwards, we would travel back up Italy on the east coast, catching Venice before we moved on to Croatia. So, next day, with bus tickets in hand, we waited on the stone bridge outside the campsite for the 9.0am bus into Florence.

Italian men, especially those in their prime, have a certain reputation to uphold; be they high powered business men or high powered bus drivers – for there is no such thing as a lowly Italian man. I figured this out as we sat on the bus into Florence. Our driver was young, very well groomed and dressed in a crisp, white shirt and dark suit. (It surely couldn't have been his uniform). His black, immaculately cut hair, perfectly framed his olive skinned, angular face and I dare say that he had excellent eyes, but they were hidden for the whole journey behind sleek, designer sunglasses. And of course, he smelt divine. Yes, I am still describing the bus driver! For most of the ride he was talking animatedly on his mobile phone, which was sometimes wedged between his shoulder and chin and sometimes held in one hand, while he emphasised every point he made, with the other. Sometimes he had both hands waving in the air, as if his flamboyant, Italian gestures were visible to the person on the other end of the phone. We took a while to work out how he was steering our bus down the mountain roads, but finally realised that he was using his knees. A smooth operator. We were slightly worried, but mostly just impressed; in Italy, style is all.

We safely reached the central bus depot in Florence and with Jack holding the town map we headed straight to the main post office. This was not to see some great treasure, but to post letters and parcels to family back home. We regularly sent home a 'round robin' update with printed digital photos; and for our three little grandchildren, there was often a parcel of mementoes, from well-known places. You would think that posting parcels would not be that difficult, and we soon discovered that in some countries it was quite easy, while in others, you would almost have to take a DNA test to get the parcel accepted. At the post office in Florence, which was the most wonderful old building with a long colonnaded front, we had no problems. A few weeks later, when we were in Braccianno, Italian bureaucracy lived up to its reputation and it was a nightmare.

Our tour of the city was about to begin and from what we had read, we had plenty to see. Florence (Firenze), is the regional capitol of Tuscany and one of the most significant centres of the arts in Italy, perhaps even the world. Its long history would fill half of this book, so although I am doing it a great injustice, I will try to abbreviate its past. It is thought that the Etruscans founded Florentia (meaning 'flowering') as a small, fishing settlement on the banks of the river Arno. Around the middle of the first century BC, the Romans, with their canny eye for a good piece of real estate, realised the potential of this fertile river valley and encouraged agricultural and commercial development. The town grew rapidly, despite local wars, the plague and political and religious squabbles. By the 13th century it had become famous as a great trading centre, and for its wool and silk industries. Using secret techniques, they produced unique and highly coloured dyed cloths from Asian silk and un-corded wool, which had arrived from all over Europe through the nearby port of Pisa.

There was such a growth of wealth, that the city even produced its own Florin, made of 24 carat gold, which was accepted all over the known world. This commercial success led to the great building boom of the 13th and 14th centuries and to the creation of the highly important guilds of craftsmen. By the 15th century, wealthy families had risen to power, including the famous Medici family, and the great political and financial input of these families coincided with the revival of classical culture, or as we know it, The Renaissance. The re-birth of the arts.

A certain 'one-upmanship' between the powerful families also ensured that there was plenty of work for the artisans and artists, who were now drawn to the area. This

a living museum. The goldsmith's shops now look more like expensive tourist traps and it is hideously busy, but that probably isn't very different to the way it always was. Beggars, peddlers, con men and cafes vie for your money; it's only the goods that have changed. We peered at the overpriced gold bracelets, and fought off the salesmen who were convinced that we wanted to buy their tat, before deciding that we'd had enough and headed back to the bus station.

We had had quite a day and early the next morning I had some rebellion back at camp. A heated discussion arose about the virtues of art and Simon made it clear that he would rather be barbecuing fish on a beach than ogling oil on canvas amongst the crowds. It was expensive and pointless as far as he was concerned. I was hurt, to say the least, and fell into despondency. We had done everything together, and I wanted to share Florence with the others, even if they weren't that keen. Jack opted for the middle road, (he learned diplomacy if nothing else during that year), and said he was happy either way although he was missing his friends. Guilt, guilt and more guilt; just when I was thinking how good things were. We talked it through and I was beginning to admit defeat. "We needn't throw good money after bad. If I'm the only one that enjoys art, then we shouldn't go back to Florence", I said, which seemed to result in Simon and Jack then persuading me that we should go back and see the rest. I expect Freud would explain that one quite easily. Anyway, we quickly scrabbled our stuff together and ran up to reception to buy tickets for the early morning bus.

Waiting at reception were three American girls. They were on a three month back-packing tour of Europe, although one of them certainly had more than a back pack, judging by the enormous suitcase-on-wheels she was dragging around with her. They were friendly and fun and we chatted while we waited, wondering what had happened to the reception staff. The owner arrived at last, and proceeded to inform us that the clocks had changed the night before, it being that time of year, and we had missed the bus into town by one hour. It was also Sunday and the next bus was not until the after-noon. Why is this sort of thing so infuriating? Why don't camp owners put up huge notices or, as in our case, where there were only a few of us staying at this camp, didn't they let us know. How many times we gritted our teeth at the infuriating attitude of some campsites.

Well, we ranted and raved and so did the American girls who had ongoing train tickets booked and had to get to Florence, and eventually we arranged to share two taxis to get us to the nearest train station. From there we would get the next train into the city. The train station was about a twenty minute drive away at a town called Figline Valdarno. Totally in the wrong direction, away from Florence, but the train line from there would take us directly in. After a long wait and several phone calls, the taxis arrived. I suppose that the drivers were having a Sunday morning lay in and it probably hadn't helped that there was a full scale cycle race on the road between us and the train station, which was causing considerable delay. This was turning into one of those ugly days. The taxis whisked us to the station, in what must have been record time judging by the way they scattered the poor cycle race before them. It was now 10.30am, and we thought that we were back on schedule, until we heard that the next train was not due until 12.30pm. Yes, we all groaned, we know that it is Sunday. We could hardly fail to know because pretty much everything around the station was shut. A cup of good Italian coffee was desperately needed but we would have to walk up into town to get it, and get some more money as our cash was now running low.

We had two hours to kill, we wanted to be somewhere else, we were already tired and hungry and our money in Italy was going through our fingers like sand. Yes, we found Italy to be easily the most expensive country to be in. Food, drink and entrance into tourist attractions were all much, much higher priced than in Spain and drastically higher than Portugal or even France. We arranged to meet the American girls back at the station and walked up the road into town; and here we found, yet again, that you never know what is waiting for you round the next corner.

We walked through the quiet back streets until we came to the open, cobbled square; the essential meeting place of almost every Italian village and town that we visited. On this Sunday morning, in this sunny town square in Figline Valdarno, a large crowd had assembled. To begin with we couldn't see what they were all looking at, but as we got closer we realised that there were over a hundred little Fiat 500 cars, all lined up on display with their proud owners standing alongside. It was their annual rally. We made our way through the throng, and found a table at one of the street cafes. Strong Italian coffee and an expensive pastry each, was just what we needed. The rally was in its early stages, and at this point the devotees of this humble little car were more interested in seeing what extra variations had been added, than in driving them. All colours of the spectrum, but all the same size and shape; some had fancy wheels, some had extra holes in the bonnets and others were original in every way. Engines in the back, extremely small, like little beetles.

Eventually the owners squeezed themselves in, along with friends and relatives, who were going along for the ride. Engines revved and after much noise, the little cars all started heading off through the square. The lead car was not a Fiat, but was obviously owned by someone very special in the area. It was a tiny, miniature red Ferrari, driven by a young lad in red racing overalls and his dad. It must have cost a fortune. Then, cheered all the way, each Fiat sounding its unique horn, which ranged from Colonel Bogey to a siren sound and every variation in between, they gathered speed and whizzed off. One quick circuit of the narrow town streets, noise reverberating from every building, and they disappeared on a jolly into the countryside. Italians just love sounding their horns. While they were on the roads we suddenly felt quite glad that we would be travelling by train. Back at the station, the train arrived on time and we boarded, along with the three American girls with their baggage. It already felt like about 6 o'clock at night although it was actually only lunchtime.

We arrived in Florence and headed straight to the Galleria dell'Accademia, to see Michelangelo's famous sculpture of 'David'. Our spirits sank when we saw the length of the queues, but Simon had the bit between his teeth by now and went on a quick tour of the outside of the building, while we joined the line.

"Follow me", he muttered on his return.

We scuttled after him and were soon ushered through a smaller door further down the Academy; for an extra three euros each, given to a man at a side door, we were able to go straight in, and if those nine euros went straight towards his pizza for lunch we certainly didn't care— we were beginning to understand how Italy functioned.

For me, to see the statue of David in real life was a dream come true. Not just because of its immense beauty, every muscle and sinew, every line and expression conveying the perfection of an idealised hero, but also because Michelangelo himself had carved it. He was just 29 years old when it was completed; just one example of the prolific talent of this painter, architect, poet and sculptor whose genius and ability dominated the High Renaissance period. I could have looked at it all day, in fact if I ever return to Florence that's just what I might do, but there were other treasures to see at the Galleria.

Besides some beautiful paintings by Bottecelli and Lippi there were also the sculptures, again by Michelangelo, called 'The Slaves'. To us three, these four unfinished statues were almost more exciting than 'David'. The huge pieces of rough marble, which were selected for these sculptures, are halted forever in the process of changing, like a metamorphosis, into the shapes of people. It is as if the human shapes are trying to free themselves from the unshaped marble around them. They also emphasise the skill required to carve a figure as dramatic as 'David' from solid marble. The actual figure of 'David' stands 13 feet tall, without the base, and the 'Slaves' are of a similar height. All larger than life, yet not so much larger that they seem unreal. We left the Galleria with time to spare before our bus was due, and for once we didn't rush off and cram another sight-seeing tour in. Instead, we bought some huge cones of delicious Italian ice-cream, (the only thing that is cheap in Italy), and we joined lots of other people, who were laid on a spacious grass-covered area, close to the main bus station. From here we could watch the Florentines go by. This was something that we all loved to do.

In front of this small piece of city park, were two complicated interconnecting roundabouts. A type of organised chaos wove its way around them and we decided that this was a great place to study Italian driving skills. God must favour the brave, was all that we could think, as we watched cyclists, pedestrians and motorists hurl themselves along in the maelstrom. Also in front of us, was a hut where you could hire cycles. Bikes of varying size and condition were chained up alongside the hut and two young men lounged on folding chairs waiting for punters. We licked our ice creams and watched with interest as six older American tourists approached the stand and started to negotiate a deal with the lad in charge. They sorted out a variety of odd-looking bikes and eventually managed to mount them and launch themselves, one by one, out into the traffic. We held our breath in trepidation as they wobbled away into the paths of cars and buses, like six delicate butterflies fluttering along a river of snapping crocodiles. But with gay abandon, and shouting encouragement to each other, they cycled off to explore the back streets of Florence.

Although it was a Sunday afternoon, it was still incredibly busy. Dark haired Romany women, in long full skirts and baggy cardigans, hassled car drivers as they pulled up at the traffic lights; brazenly they washed the windscreens with mucky water from their buckets, before demanding payment, yelling to each other over the din of the traffic. The men folk of their group sprawled on the grass, like us, but they swigged beer and smoked cigarettes, while their brown skinned, raggedy children, swung over the railings and pestered passers by. Ambulances howled past with amazing frequency – could one of them be for the American cyclists we wondered, but then an ambulance screeched up alongside us and three young medics jumped out.

Everyone's gaze now shifted to this new form of entertainment, which centred around the steps leading down to the public toilets. The three medics disappeared down the steps, followed by the raggedy children and a few curious onlookers, and reappeared a little later supporting a staggering man between them. They sat him down on a bench, and we watched in amusement as they tried their best, to do something with him. He had a cut on his head, which they soon dealt with, and we decided, judging by the accompanying hand movements, that they were trying to convince him that if he didn't get into the ambulance with them then he would die and go to heaven. He was hard to convince though, and seemed more interested in kissing the hand of the pretty young female medic and inviting her to share some of the wine that he was still trying to swig from the bottle he had concealed in a paper bag. We gave the medics ten out of ten, for patience and staying power because it took a good half an hour of general group therapy before they finally got him into the ambulance. The crowd clapped as he was helped aboard and he took a drunken bow before being taken off to hospital or maybe even heaven. His rather shifty looking friend, who I had noticed hovering on the edge of the crowd all this while, furtively slipped the wine-bottle bag into his own carrier bag and disappeared down the toilet steps again. Ah well, it all makes work for the working man to do.

The six bells of the church of Saint Lorenzo started to peal out with such discord and ferocity that they even drowned out the traffic. Would anyone answer their call on this crazy Sunday afternoon we wondered? Our bus was due, so we would never know. We boarded, along with four new American backpackers, all men this time, and before too long we were back at the motor home. Mama Mia, Florence had more to offer than we had ever imagined.

We had booked tickets to visit the Uffizi, which was to be our last trip in. It was a Tuesday and definitely not as crowded as the weekend had been. With batteries re-charged, we were ready to visit Italy's most important art gallery, containing most of the world's well known Renaissance paintings. The Uffizi was designed by Vasari and built in the mid 16th century for Cosimo 1st of the Medici family. It was originally used as administrative and judicial offices, but was bequeathed in its entirety to the state of Tuscany in 1743, by Anna Maria Ludovica de'Medici, the last member of this prestigious family. By this time it had already become a gallery of some importance. Our visit started on the second floor of this most beautiful, U shaped building. Nothing really prepared us for the sheer number of priceless masterpieces that we stopped and admired, as we wandered through the rooms. I had made a short list of 'favourite artists to see', but it was hard not to deviate. Michelangelo and da Vinci were of course top of the list, with Canaletto, Botticelli, Titian, Rubens, Raphael, Bellini and Holbein as close seconds. And then of course there were the Caravaggio's and Goyas and not forgetting Bellini – oh but I've said him already. Well, you can see how hard it was to choose. I could have stayed there for ever, with so many wonderful works of art to gaze at. So, if I ever return to Florence I shall spend a day staring at the statue of David and a month staring at the breathtaking paintings in the Uffizi. Eventually, Simon dragged me away and we walked through the corridors towards the exit doors. Original Roman copies of original Greek busts, lined the walls of the corridors and ornately painted ceilings invited us to gaze ever upwards. There was always more to see in this gallery. Perhaps when I return I will spend two months at the Uffizi!

We had seen some wonderful art in Florence, but we had only scratched the surface and we could have spent much longer there. If you are thinking of visiting any of the highlights of Italy, I would give this advice. Entry to tourist attractions is not cheap and queues can be long, so it definitely pays to book tickets in advance and be there early. Early morning and evening viewing, is always better than mid day. Eating out is also not cheap, so if you can take food and drink with you it will help, although we did find it very difficult to find places to actually sit down and rest, while eating our packed lunches. The cafes are great, but expensive, and sometimes we would have an overpriced cup of coffee just so that we could sit down for half an hour. Public seating was not easily found and there were always hordes of tourists, like us, looking for somewhere to rest before trekking off to the next attraction. We didn't have time to see a fraction of the treasures that Florence has to offer – it is a truly amazing city with an important history – but with stamina and good planning you will find it well worth a visit. We, however, were heading on to our next delight; our music was playing and our wheels were turning – and Maisy was programmed for Pisa.

March

Pisa

Leaving Florence behind, we headed back to the coast for a few days at Pisa. Divided by the River Arno, which was once a great trade route, Pisa had its days of glory when it was a busy port, a commercial and artistic centre and the home to such benefactors as Hadrian, the Medici's and Galileo Galilei. So while it may not be of such strategic importance now, it has been left with a well laid out town, a university (the oldest in Italy) and some wonderful historical buildings, it's leaning tower of course, being the most easily recognisable tower in the world. Would Pisa be so famous if Bonanno Pisano had built the tower on more solid ground? Who knows, but even without the lean, it would be an interesting building.

Arriving on the outskirts of the town, we started to search for somewhere to park-up for a few days. There seemed to be plenty of car parks available, but we were having a problem working out exactly which part of the city would accommodate us best. Our solution was to pull into a lay by, get our bikes off the back and cycle in for a quick recce. (Our motor home was much too large to drive through the smaller streets). A thick city wall, much of which is still intact today, encloses the mediaeval section of the city, the gateways and arches providing good geographical reference points. Having sorted out where we were in relation to the Leaning Tower, we rode back and drove to a large car park that seemed ideal. "Fantastic", we enthused, "this car park even has electricity points, and a toilet block and water taps". Well done Italy, we said, but we had second thoughts about this a few days later.

Jack and I then cycled off to the local Carrefours, and returned with rucksacks laden. I seemed to find a million and one ways to cook a kilo of mince round Europe and home-made spaghetti bolognaise, with wonderfully fresh ingredients, was for supper that night. We all have different memories of the places we visited, but when I think of Pisa, I will always think of spaghetti bolognaise and Roy Orbison. For some unknown reason, we were now keen to sing along with Roy's classics. 'Only the lonely.... dum,dum,dum,dummy doo-ah,' being a favourite, along with 'Love Hurts' and those challenging high notes of 'It's Over.' So, if I want to remember Pisa, I simply put on his greatest hits CD and I'm back in that car park, cooking spaghetti and singing along with Simon, Jack and Roy.

Sunshine and blue skies were forecast and next day we once more rode into town like The Good, the Bad and the Ugly. We still hadn't determined who was going to be the Ugly though. Pisa was great fun to cycle around; the narrow cobbled streets of the old town criss-crossing with each other, leading us into squares, dead ends and twisting passages. The traffic was not too heavy, although it was still a law unto itself. We found our way to the Campo dei Miracoli (The Field of Miracles), which is without doubt the most beautiful setting for the three major buildings in Pisa. Enclosed on two sides by the city walls, a vast emerald- green lawn stretches across the Campo, bisected only by neat paths that lead you to the doors of the Cathedral, the Baptistery and the Bell Tower.

It was quiet and cool, with little sign of the crowds who would gather there later. We cycled through the stone entrance gate into the square, and saw before us the most perfect view. The light in Italy is sometimes quite ethereal and this was one of those mornings, when the sky was literally heavenly. The dazzling white marble of the buildings, the perfect green lawn and the translucent, blue sky .... I started taking yet more photographs while Simon and Jack went to buy tickets to enter the famous Leaning Tower. It's essential to buy a ticket for the tower, and as it gets busy quite quickly, we made that our first priority. Everyone wants to go up it, but only thirty people are allowed in at a time, with a guide, and the tour takes approximately 30 minutes. You are warned before hand not to lean out, not to stand under the bells and to be 'most prudent and orderly'! And with good reason, as the tower really does have a significant lean and offers plenty of opportunities to fall off, if you so wished. The inclination is about 5.5 degrees to the south, which means that the top-most section protrudes almost five meters over the bottom section. It has also subsided vertically by about 2.8 meters as a result of the unstable nature of the subsoil it was built on. It therefore seems to be coming out of a hole in the ground, rather like a trajectory missile being launched at the stars, but the building itself looks very delicate, a marble version of a tiered wedding cake, with slender arches encircling it all the way to the top. Walking up the 294 worn steps of spiralling staircase was apparently 'very weird' according to Jack, who said he would have preferred to crawl around the top viewing balcony on hands and knees, as it was so un-nerving to be stood at such an angle, on such a small circle of stone, at the top of a cylindrical column 60 meters high. I whimped out of this one and spent my time studying it from ground level. The two other buildings at this site are equally beautiful; the cathedral and the baptistery both exquisitely and delicately decorated, with similar slender arches in carved white marble. Their frescoed interiors with soaring columns and the dramatically carved pulpit by Giovano Pisano were well worth the queuing and entrance fee. There is nothing else to distract you here, except for a line of interesting market stalls which lean against one of the city walls. Apart from that you can sit on the grass, with your latest flavour in Italian ice-cream and enjoy these exquisite buildings.

We cycled on through the old town and found a small café in a sunny open piazza where we had the tastiest pasta lunch, while watching the Pisans go about their daily lives around us. The houses alongside the River Arno, unpretentious in their faded yellows and dusty reds, slightly crumbling and worn at the edges, epitomised the feeling of the town; busy and bustling, but not modern or ostentatious. Well-worn and totally original, and as always in Italian cities, full of life. We really liked Pisa, but of course, if we'd gone in the hot high season, we may have felt differently.

That night we stayed again at our big, empty car park just outside the city walls. Much of the evening was spent swatting the mosquitoes that obviously preferred us to the stagnant water down by the toilets. Their maddening hum made it impossible to sleep so we all got up and had a mass killing spree, notching them up on the handles of our fly swots. Jack had the most to deal with, as he was in the main part of the motor home, but he got well into it, leaping about in his boxer shorts swatting everything that moved until eventually, in the early hours, we reckoned to have got them all and fell into an itchy sleep. Distant thunder during the night hardly disturbed us, but rather odd noises started to drift into our semi-conscious heads at around dawn. A strange clanging sound infiltrated our dreams, followed by voices and car engines. "That sounds like tent poles", muttered Simon from under the mosquito resistant sheet that we had draped over our heads. Blearily we opened the blinds to see what was waking us up at six o'clock in the morning. Our empty car park now resembled a mini building site as a steady stream of white vans poured through the gates, found their preferred spaces and started throwing scaffolding poles onto the tarmac. (That would be the strange clanging sound then). Stalls were being assembled, tables erected and goods unpacked amidst much shouting and general banter. Now we understood why this 'wonderful' car park had electricity points and toilets. We were about to become part of the Saturday market. 'Operation Hasty Exit Two' swung into action as we flicked away dead mosquitoes and scrambled into last nights lazily discarded clothes. Loose items were thrown into cupboards and the bikes were slung on the back. We would never be able to get out of the car park once all the stalls were up, and we had plans to move on that day. Sleepy eyed, unwashed and unprepared, Simon revved her up and 'headed for the gate doin' ninety-eight – we let those truckers role, ten-four' - or in truth we lurched down the road and out of town, only to stop in the first possible lay by to start the day again with a cup of tea and breakfast. Ready or not we were leaving Pisa and heading for Rome.

Jack was a great travelling companion – most thirteen year olds, stuck with their whacky parents in a motor home for a year, would have rebelled – and with good reason – but he entered into the spirit of the whole adventure admirably. His main complaint was that he did miss his friends sometimes. We could quite understand his feelings and we felt bad about it. Another plan was hatched to give him a break from us and we invited one of his buddies to fly out and join us in Rome for the Easter holidays. Charles would be arriving at Leonardo da Vinci airport on April 5th, so we had two days to reach our next campsite.

We had chosen Camping Porticciolo, as our next base, a family-run, lakeside site, situated just below Bracciano about 30 kilometres outside Rome with a direct train line into the city. We thought that the boys could enjoy the activities at the lake in between our sight seeing trips into Rome. It didn't quite turn out that way but then, things never do. We drove down the coast from Pisa towards Rome, stopping at a huge supermarket to stock-up on essentials and then turned inland towards the town of Bracciano. We wild camped for one night in a lay-by, once again fighting off mosquitoes until well into the evening, and next morning we followed the campsite directions that guided our huge motor home around the old town and down to the lake. Without those directions we would have had serious problems, as one of the bridges to avoid was only 2.8 meters high.

We saw the entrance to the site and Simon groaned again, "another very tight turn, down a very steeply sloping, rough track", the poor Beast wasn't built for this kind of terrain. Wide, flat American highways, with huge turning circles, were what our motor home would have liked, but we could hardly blame Europe for our desire to drive a bungalow around. Simon drove brilliantly though, and we squeezed and bumped down the track and into a big open field of long grass. The owners looked at us in horrified amazement and walked slowly around the whole of our exterior, obviously not used to having a motor home the size of a luxury coach coming down their drive. They had mown a patch of grass for us to park on, which they quickly mowed again to ensure it was big enough, and we shunted into place and settled into life at Camping Porticiollo.

Alessandro and his wife were the charming owners of this pretty lakeside campsite and they could not have done more for us during our stay. Large pitches, shaded by well-tended trees, were situated on the lakeside shore next to a small private beach. Their own camp bus left at 9.0am every morning to ferry campers up the hill to the train station for the 9.15am train into Rome and the friendly bar and pizzeria opened every night. We were immediately provided with written information about the area, transport timetables and opening times of everything in the town of Bracciano. We imagined that it was the type of site which customers would return to regularly. It was rustic, friendly and peaceful.

Shortly after we had arrived and before we did anything else, Jack and I erected the small tent that we had brought along with us in case of visitors. Charles and Jack could easily have slept in the Beast but we thought that a bit of private space would be a novelty to us all. The boys could have the tent and Simon and I would have nights alone for the first time in six months. Jack and I collapsed in our usual heaps of laughter as we struggled to get the tent up, trying to remember what poles went where; but poor Simon had a worse job. He was doing running repairs to various parts of the motor home that had suffered general wear and tear as we had travelled. I had broken the leg of the folding dining table and the sink plug, to mention just the two jobs that I was admitting to and Jack owned up to a few more, so we left Si with the toolbox and, once we had got the tent to look as if it might actually remain standing and waterproof, Jack and I took a better look at our surroundings.

The camp was very quiet and had obviously only just opened for the season. Most of the grass was long and meadow like, dotted with wild flowers, and there were birds in abundance. Alessandro and his wife explained that they had not been able to cut the grass because of terrible recent storms, which had left plenty of clearing up to do. They both looked somewhat fraught as they set about their tasks, he stubble chinned, bookish and rather like a grumpy bear, and she petite and quiet, going quickly and purposefully about her jobs. It was about midday, but a thick mist blanketed the lake, shortening our view to just a few yards of eerie, silent, waters edge. Slowly, as the sun began to burn through the lifting haze, the whole of Lake Bracciano was revealed to us. It was far bigger than we had imagined, stretching further than the eye could see either way, with wooded hills and small towns visible on the far side. We folded our jumpers to make cushions on the damp stones and sat down to read our guidebook on the area.

Lake Bracciano is extremely deep, over 165 meters, lying in two craters of a volcano that has been extinct for thousands of years. It covers an area of 57 square kilometres and has a Neolithic village dating from 5500BC on its bed. No motorboats are allowed on the lake, just sail boats, canoes and windsurfers, along with local fishing boats that supply the excellent fish restaurants along the shores. It has provided drinking water to Rome, since early in the 17th century when an aqueduct was built, and much of the area is located within the Natural Park of the Bracciano Lake System. It was very peaceful and its beauty seemed totally unspoilt by any modern development. Looking down on the lake is the town of Bracciano, with the castle, Castello Odescalche, perched dramatically above the water, having a privileged view of the area. Jack and I watched as small green-backed lizards crept out to enjoy the growing heat of the day, and the lake waters turned to a brilliant blue, as the mist was replaced by a clear sky.

Early next morning our kind hosts gave us a lift to the station to catch the 8.15 into Rome. We joined the regular commuters and boarded the double-story, clean, fast train with its gentle piped music and comfortable seats. Our connection to Leonardo da Vinci airport was equally trouble free and before long we were waiting for Charles's plane to arrive. We scanned the faces of travellers as they came through 'arrivals' as if we wouldn't recognise him, but suddenly there he was, travelling light with just a rucksack on his back, looking exactly the same as six months ago when we had all said goodbye. It was great to see him again. He and Jack slipped straight back into a conversation about where they had got to with the latest computer game, as yet untroubled with the long preamble of politeness and formality which we adults go through when we insist on asking after the family and the weather. Kids have a wonderful 'here and now' attitude. So while Simon and I were looking around for the exit signs again, they were off together like greyhounds out of the stalls, heads down, chattering, and had already clocked exactly how to leave the airport building.

It was still early in the day and Charles seemed to have plenty of energy, so we decided that when in Rome, we should do what the Romans used to do, and visit the Colosseum. Rome's Metro system, The Metropolitana, has two lines, A and B, which cross at the central station called the Stazione Termine. These lines will take you very close to almost all the major highlights and are cheap and very easy to use. Tickets can be bought at machines or kiosks and as it is an integrated public transport system, you can use the same ticket for bus, train or metro – if used within 75 minutes, and don't forget to validate the ticket at the orange ticket boxes. We were soon zooming through subterranean Rome heading for Stazione Colosseo.

The Colosseum is a huge amphitheatre. It could seat up to 50,000 people in its gory hey-day, and considering the building was started in 72AD it is in very good condition. It stands on the site of an artificial lake, around which Nero's royal residence once existed, but Vespasion drained the lake when he ordered this new entertainment arcade to be built for the Roman people. Restoration has been underway since 1992, but restoring such an important and ancient structure is not a job to be rushed; there is still work to do. However, all of the main building is still there including the underground labyrinth of tunnels used to house the gladiators, slaves and animals. It is impressive in its complexity and structure and offers an excellent example of the life and skills of ancient Rome. Its present state, with roofs and floors absent, is almost a benefit because the complete skeleton of the building is revealed and you are able to see below the façade, to the workings and architectural bones.

Roman legionnaires continue to parade outside this amphitheatre, but they're not resting from the Punic wars, they are trying to persuade tourists to pose in full costume with them, exchanging a few pieces of silver for a gimmicky photo. Finding the actual entrance was somewhat difficult in the general melee; always a crowd-puller, the queues have remained the same as ever, and it is a bit of a bun fight to get in even if you have a reserved ticket. We didn't have tickets reserved, but Simon was now an old hand at doing things the Italian way and he soon zoomed in on an American tour operator who, for a few dollars more, whisked us in with his group. We followed in the footsteps of thousands before us as we climbed the stone steps to one of the higher levels. We would have been among the lucky ones. The less fortunate would only get above the subterranean level when they were being sent up on the elevators to die in the arena. The running of the Colosseum was an enormous operation, involving thousands of people and animals. Thousands died for the enjoyment of thousands more and looking at the ribs, arteries and heart of this unique example of Roman life, we got a good feel of what it must have been like when the crowds roared, louder than the lions.

We finally left Rome that evening and back in Bracciano, Jack and Charles once again took the lead, quickly finding the small country lane that led from the train station in the town, back down the hill, to the campsite by the lake. Simon and I staggered after them, munching bits of leftover pizza, with a cool bottle of Chianti in mind. The boys slept well in their tent and we had the luxury of a quiet night alone. There would be no more excursions for a day or two now, as we all needed a rest; the local market day would be soon enough for our next outing.

The market itself was not very interesting. Mostly tacky goods and the boys soon got bored and went back to camp. Simon accompanied me on one of my missions to the local post office to send home a parcel and some letters. It was three days to Easter weekend and I had found some Italian sweets and gifts for our three grandchildren. I have to admit that I never posted anything expensive or valuable, as I was fairly sceptical about the reliability of the overseas post. I had chosen very lightweight items and had parcelled them up in an old cardboard box.

When we reached the small, tired looking, post office, I took a numbered ticket and joined one of the many long queues for a cashier. Simon sensibly elected to wait outside in the shade. Slowly, very slowly, suffering the very hot, stuffy room and giving each other internationally-recognised long suffering looks, we all shuffled towards the counter. At last it was my turn, and in halting broken Italian, accompanied by bits of English, I explained the very obvious fact that I wanted to post a parcel to England. Reaching from behind towering piles of paperwork and an impressive array of rubber stamps, a stressed looking lady assistant took my parcel and gave me a grim, doubtful look. She tossed it around in her hands and flicked it over and over, tutting continuously. Then off she went to her friend further down the counter and they tutted together, as they tossed it around some more while giving me disgusted looks. Eventually she returned and threw it back to me. "No", she said, followed by the Italian equivalent to, "Signora, itsa notta possible to posta this worthless parcel because itsa notta wrapped correctly. You musta cover alla ova the boxa so that only the addressa is showing!!!!" All conversations in Italy end with either a question mark or an exclamation mark, and raised hands. Just to emphasise the drama of life.

I remonstrated slightly, purely to keep face, but with little heart as I knew that I would never win and took my parcel back outside to my now very bored and irritable husband, who did not view this kind of problem as the same kind of challenge as I did. He would have thrown it in the bin at this point but I had spotted what looked like a gift and paper shop just up the road, so there I headed. Mutton headed to the end. A quick search revealed rolls of brown sticky tape, so together we managed to completely cover the box in brown tape, apart from the address. A chainsaw would now be useful to open it. Back to the post office we went, for another ticket, another long queue with more long suffering, sighing people and an even more irritable husband shuffling along beside me. At last I reached the counter again… "Bellisimo!", she smiled, reaching through the towers of paperwork to take the parcel and weigh it. "19 euros!", she pronounced. "19 euros?" I gasped. "The contents only cost me ten!" She shrugged and started to fill in the required triplication of forms, rubber-stamping everything like a line dancer in wellies, before taking my money and eventually sending me on my way. Was it ever worth it I wondered? Some time later I spoke to my daughter-in-law on the phone, and asked her if she had received the parcel. "What parcel?" she asked.

Ah well, what's a few euros anyway.

April

Ripped off in Rome

Unsettled weather dogged our stay in Bracciano. Good followed bad, followed good –often chilly and damp although when the sun did come out, it was hot. The next day looked good and according to the campsite weather forecast, pinned to the notice board, it would remain fair. The white camp bus, an ancient relic in itself that travelled under a cloak of belching black smoke, delivered us to the station for the train to Rome. It was going to be a marathon day of touristing with Charles. One hour later we disembarked Line A metro at Ottoviano St. Pietro and walked the short distance to St Peters Square and the Vatican City.

Designed by Bernini, this vast Holy Square stands on a site that was once home to Nero's gardens and stadium, where crowds once gathered to watch gladiatorial combats and chariot races. The tall, simple obelisk which stands in the centre of the square was brought to Rome by the infamous emperor Caligula, and has remained close to St Peters Basilica ever since. There was a great feeling of space and sky as we stood in the square; an enormous ellipse measuring 240 meters at its widest diameter. On either side of us, 140 statues of the saints, all twice life size, stared down from the tops of imposing semi-circular colonnades. Each long, curving colonnade, made up of four rows of marching Doric columns, offering us cool shade from the sun-beaten Piazza. Before us stood St Peters, the most important church in the Christian world. Designed to impress and inspire the masses that gathered in the square before it, this is no humble church. To me it looked the epitome of power and authority and man's ability to amaze and impress himself by his own skills and it is steeped in history. It is the corner stone of millions of people's lives, its pale fabric, holding the desires and ambitions of many – emperors, kings, popes, and artists such as Michelangelo and Raphael, to name but a few. I am not a 'believer' as such, so I could only marvel at the architecture. The queues to the Sistine Chapel were hideously long, so we turned back to face the city and moved on to the Piazza Navona. I would have to return another day to see the 'Pieta', Michelangelo's famous sculpture, completed when he was only 24 years old and of course his beautiful frescoes.

Most tourist attractions that we visited in Rome were already standing on land of historical significance; such is the depth and layered history of this city. The Piazza Navona is a large and beautiful square lined with baroque palaces. It has three fountains, the most famous of which is Bernini's 'The Four Rivers', which we wanted to see. This plaza was laid out on the site of Emperor Domitian's stadium where chariot races

running repairs), and we all went cycling around the shore of the lake. The road was good and not too busy and we soon reached Anguillara, a small picturesque town that reaches down to the water from a tiny peninsular. All along the shore, we were amazed to see swans and ducks competing with South American coypus for scraps of our bread. At first we thought that these furry, guinea-pig like creatures were over grown water rats, but when we asked a young local about them he said that they had escaped from a nearby breeding farm and were now a normal inhabitant of the area.

We locked our bikes together and explored the tiny steep streets of this very un-touristy old town. Tottering houses with pretty flowered balconies, miniature court-yards and twisting alleyways, led us up to the large white church from where we could look down over the higgledy-piggledy rooftops and out over the deep blue lake. Far across the lake on distant green hillsides, white-faced houses and flashing car windows caught the sun. The boys soon got bored and raced off on their bikes, finding an 'alter-native' route home that involved muddy tracks along the shore, leaving Simon and I to enjoy this very beautiful area in peace.

That evening, which was Easter Saturday, we were planning to eat at the campsite pizzeria, but our kind camp hostess came pedalling round on her bike to tell us that, that night, a pageant was taking place in Bracianno town. The camp bus would take all those interested up to the town at eight o'clock and return at eleven o'clock. She even recommended a good restaurant in town, so we decided to eat there. By 8.30pm, we were enjoying excellent pasta in a friendly, family restaurant with a warm log fire and good local wine. Outside, as night fell, we could hear the town livening up and when we tottered out, at about ten o'clock, we joined the throng of people heading up to the castle. Streets lights had been replaced with flaming torches and music was coming from the floodlit castle on the hill. In the torch lit, cobbled square, below the castle walls, crowds had gathered under the canopy of a dark, starlit sky. The weather was going to be kind to us that night. Jack and Charles soon took advantage of the situation to roam off around the crowded square, while we waited patiently for the 'Pageant of the Crucifixion' to begin.

The festive music eventually stopped and a new composition started. This was much more dramatic, serious music, and from down the dark torch lit street, a proces-sion of six soldiers came slowly riding up, on strong, stamping horses. The soldiers were dressed as Roman legionnaires, carrying swords and spears; their decorated hors-es clattering over the shiny cobbles. Behind them were two lines of foot soldiers, carry-ing flaming torches and cracking whips into the air, and between them, being whipped as they walked along, were Jesus, and the two thieves who were crucified alongside him. They were bare footed and had full size, heavy wooden crosses, which were weighting down their shoulders as they dragged them up the street. They passed through the crowd and continued up to the gate in the castle wall. The music filled the black night, and we waited for the next part of the pageant.

Along the top of the ramparts more torches were lit as soldiers took their places at regular spaces. We were stood in the square just below the wall, and now the entire crowd that we were amongst, moved forward to look upwards to the castle. The music changed again and became even more dramatic as, against a backdrop of the night sky, Jesus and the two thieves were hoisted up, strapped to their crosses. Lightening flashed repeatedly onto the walls and the music reached a thundering crescendo. The soldiers stood illuminated by the glow of torches, as two women went to the foot of Jesus' cross. The crowd murmured its appreciation and as the music reached its finale, the central cross wasped slowly lowered and a lasered image of Jesus was seen slowly rising through the sky. Fireworks and jubilant music exploded into the air and the crowd then burst into wild applause for what had been a very dramatic and ambitious portrayal of the crucifixion. For a small country town, we thought that this had been an excellent dramatisation and we were most impressed. It was now well past 11.30pm, so we quickly rounded up the boys and ran back to the town centre, to catch our lift back to camp. The town was still heaving as men, women and children headed home. There were no drunks, no yobs, and no threatening behaviour, just families out at night, having fun. (So many times in Europe, we admired this quality of life). The big camp bus belched and burped its way back down the hill, full of cheerful San Marino campers and us four Brits…. We staggered into bed yet again!

Easter Sunday started slowly with us all having another lay-in. Simon connected an extension lead to the laptop computer and the boys scoffed huge Easter eggs while they lay in their little tent and played a game. Paradise in Italy for them. The San Marino motor homers were up and about, and the couple in the motor home next to us were soon knocking on our door, with a gift of four, decorated hard-boiled eggs. It was a tradition, and most kind of them, so we had a simple breakfast and decided to have a lazy day. We soon realised that prising the boys out of their tent would be like picking winkles from their shells without a pin, so we left them to it and went for a long walk along the lakeshore on our own. We had been totally mistaken in thinking that there would be plenty to do on this lake. We had expected to see Pedalos, canoes, or sailing at least, but it was obviously far too early in the season for the Italians to hit the water, and all of the hire shops were still closed. Very few of the restaurants were open, but there was one doing a good trade, so Simon and I decided to leave the boys in peace while we enjoyed a tasty fish lunch, alongside local Italian families. Grannies and grandchildren, all dressed in their Sunday best along with whole extended families, gathered around tables which were pushed together to accommodate everyone; babies slept in pushchairs and grandfathers dozed in corners as the long lazy meal was consumed. No one was rushing the food; the meal was excellent and a very social occasion.

When we returned to the motorhome, the boys' empty stomachs had got the better of them and they were in full production cooking pancakes. Charles neatly dressed in my apron and in charge of the frying pan and Jack mixing the batter, with eggs, flour, milk, jam, lemons and sugar working its way across all available surfaces. They became obsessed with pancake making over the next few days and, whenever we turned our backs, they were glued to the cooker making another fresh batch. They experimented with stomach churning fillings and emptied my larder, but at least we know that they won't starve when they leave home. The holidaymakers from San Marino were also enjoying a good lunch. They had set up long tables outside their motor homes and had gathered together in large groups for the meal. Plenty of wine bottles, plenty of food and then organised games around the campsite. The games becoming noisier and crazier as the wine bottles emptied, until eventually the rain returned and they called it a night. They certainly know how to party in Royal San Marino.

The weather was miserable for the next few days, with rain showers spoiling the few hours of sun. We explored locally and enjoyed the area as best we could. The San Marino motor homers all left on the Easter Monday and like a flock of departing, white sea birds, they flew off in a flurry of tooting horns and flying mud, leaving the camp site silent and slightly dazed. We thought that we would be on our own again then but as they left, two new families arrived, and to our utter amazement they were both English. We had not seen any other English travellers for many weeks.

The first to arrive was a small yellow dormer van. The owners of 'Jimmy the Van' were Nigel and Nicky and little Charlotte. Once again, who said that this is a lonely planet; now back in England they are still our friends. Nigel, taller than the average Englishman, seemed to fold himself double to squeeze into 'Jimmy', while Nicky, who usually worked in a bank, organised their small living area with great skill, and lovely Charlotte, a bright little five year old, rode her small pink bicycle around the camp endearing herself to everyone. They were taking six months off work, to travel, and were managing incredibly well.

The other English family to arrive were also to become good friends. They were John and Gill with their three children, Sarah, Hannah and Daniel. With just a car and caravan, these intrepid travellers had, like us, sold their home, given away or sold most of their worldly belongings and were taking two years off to see the world. They were taking a similar route as us around Europe but were then going on to Malaysia and the East before finishing in Australia. Their children were keeping up with their education as they went, and again, we have very fond memories of them and we still keep in touch. When we last heard from them, they had helped to rebuild a village in Thailand, which had been wrecked by the Tsunami, and had eventually reached Australia. Daniel was twelve, Hannah was fourteen and Sarah was sixteen and a dedicated Goth. How she managed to emerge from the small caravan every morning, dressed from head to foot in elaborate, black cult clothing, was a credit to her determination, and Gill and John's patience. We had a long chat with them that day, and swapped a box of eleven books, so we all had some new reading. We met up with them all again later in the trip; wonderful people whom we had good times with – so read on and you will learn more about them. They had all just arrived at Bracciano, but we were shortly to be moving on, because Charles's holiday was now over and he was due on a plane back to England.

So, next morning, we swapped mobile phone numbers with them all, and said goodbye to our new friends. Alessandro and his lovely wife gave us wine, postcards and mementos to leave with and even promised to send off some letters for us. They were exceptionally kind hosts and I would recommend anyone to visit their camp site. We packed up, putting the motor home back into driving order after ten days at Bracianno, and swung out of the campsite. That night, we parked and slept in the coach car park of Leonardo-da-Vinci airport, in Rome. Very early the next morning, as the sun was creeping over the horizon, we caught the shuttle bus to terminal C, departures, and waved goodbye to Charles. It was just the three of us again, a long way from home, and still only half way through our trip. And where were we heading for next? Well, it had to be the wondrous or not so wondrous delights, of Pompeii.

were left and Fiorelli poured liquid plaster into these cavities or moulds and hence had exact replicas. A fascinating, if gruesome epitaph to the last moments of the inhabitants of Pompeii.

The next day we caught the local train to Ercolano, the nearby city that was also devastated by the eruption. Ercolano (or Herculaneum, supposedly founded by Hercules), was not covered by ash, but by a mudslide, thirty meters high. Here the ruins are better preserved with better examples of frescoes, mosaics and furniture and we found it smaller and, in some ways, easier to understand than Pompeii. In both cases we were amazed at the lack of information available as you walked around. Dirt and muck covered many of the mosaic floors and general chaos seemed to surround it all. Maybe when a country has so many unique examples of its past it becomes blasé about it or maybe we are just spoiled by the way our English heritage is protected and displayed. Anyway, we found it all fascinating, although it was hard to believe that the peaceful mountain in the far distance could have caused so much havoc. When we climbed Vesuvius a few days later, and looked down on the towns, we could see that the distance was not so great for such a powerful force of nature.

Back at camp the next day, heavy rain and flash floods caused havoc outside. Rotten lemons floated in deep, black puddles which swamped the small, congested road and toppled over rubbish bins. The huge tourist coaches squeezed themselves in and out, disgorging bewildered, plastic-macked sightseers, and horns sounded almost permanently. We bought some fresh fish for tea, posted some letters back home and then spent the afternoon in the Beast discussing Pompeii, while we cut up cereal boxes into small squares and made our own mosaics – which proved much more complicated than we had imagined.

That night it rained heavily again, pounding the roof of the motor home, and we all slept badly, but, next day the sky had cleared, the sun was out and we caught the train to Naples to visit the Archaeological Museum – or at least that's what we were hoping to do!

The journey to Naples, from the station just outside our campsite, only took forty minutes and cost just four euros each, return, but it was so busy that it was standing room only all the way. A quick metro ride after that, followed by a short stroll and we were standing outside the rather grim looking Museum. Around us was a city bursting at the seams in every direction, with traffic so clogged that you wondered how it functioned at all. People, fumes, noise, dust, car horns, battered buildings, fraught looking traffic police, and in one corner by the station, a group of thirty, elderly men, quietly playing cards around picnic tables. Naples looked like a city that you could either love or hate.

The Museum holds, amongst many other riches, the art treasures rescued from Pompeii and Ercolano, which we had come to see – if we could only find a way in. Eventually, after circling it several times, we discovered that, contrary to all information that we had, the museum was shut on Tuesdays, and today was Tuesday. It was supposed to be closed on Mondays; our long journey had been in vain and at that point I felt like adding an extra brick, through the window, to the huge, filthy, old building. But maybe that was a little excessive. Deflated, we were reluctant to make the arduous journey back to camp having achieved nothing, and, being true Brits with some pioneering spirit, we decided to get the train to Ercolano and climb Vesuvius instead.

By mid-day, we were walking to the bus stop for transport to the lower slope of the mountain. But, in true Italian style, the predatory taxi drivers who lurked there, soon pounced on us with tales of long, unreliable bus rides and crowded return journeys. "We must take a taxi, we would surely regret it if we didn't", they said. We ummed and ahhed and tried to bargain and in the end we teamed up with a friendly young Dutch couple who were having the same problem and we all shared a taxi up. At the drop-off point we started the one and a half kilometre walk up a wide, well-marked path of cinder-like stone, and just before we reached the last section up to the summit, we were pounced upon by the next group of salesmen. They pronounced an 'obligatory' fee of seven euros each to be accompanied by the 'compulsory' guide. Everyone had to pay the fee, - but the guides were nowhere to be seen, (unless that was them, sitting in the hut drinking coffee).

The volcano was, of course, very impressive. Almost as impressive as the determination of some Italians to pry the last euro out of you, as you visit this unusual landscape. At the summit we turned our backs on the tacky souvenir/ food shop and looked out over the beautiful Bay of Naples and the Island of Capri in the distance. Well, it looked beautiful from where we stood. The sprawling city lay far below us and we realised how terrifying the eruption must have seemed. Once again, the only information about the formation of the volcano was a small display board, all in Italian, although most visitors were foreign tourists. We turned and peered over the rim and down into the massive crater of the sleeping volcano. Hot air and steam jets rose up the sides and we huddled behind a rock and ate our homemade sandwiches. Somehow, it wasn't quite what we had expected. Vesuvius is impressive, the views are great and you get a good idea of the power of a volcano when you see the old lava flows, far down the mountainsides. So why did we feel ripped off in Italy, yet again?

Back at the pick up point the taxi was waiting to take us, and the Dutch couple, back down to Ercolano. "Go, have a coffee first", the drivers tried to insist, but we all declined, fearing the price might be extortionate and they may charge us extra for the cup to put it in. Back at the station we all clambered out. "You had a good ride? I give good service? You tip me!" muscled the burly driver as he tried to block our exit. Then the boss came hefting over to collect his fifty euros, "You had good driver? You tip him!" he ordered.

Bloody mafia, we think, all of them looking like fat Al Pacino's with their sunglasses and slick hair. We found four euros between us and pushed our way through them.

Vesuvius dix point – but Italy nil point. This was one place that we wouldn't recommend visiting – but maybe someone else will have a better time there, or maybe its time that Vesuvius erupted again and got rid of the robbers who lurk on her slopes.

T'was on the Isle of Capri

When you're travelling, you can predict nothing. The day can be good, bad or indifferent, and as we had discovered, the trip to Vesuvius had definitely been indifferent. We were to going have much better times ahead and the next day was one of the best on the whole trip. The sun shone again, in a clear blue sky, so we were up and away early, on a day-trip to the Isle of Capri. Simon had done his research well and our route by train and boat was all planned. We caught the train at our local station. This would take us quite quickly down the coast to Sorrento, and from there we would catch one of the regular ferries over to Capri. We boarded the train and settled down.

A short while later the train halted at another station and more passengers boarded, and although we were more interested in the scenery than who was getting on and off, Simon was sure that he now recognised the backs of three heads. I tapped one of them on the shoulder, and yes, it was Nigel, with Nicky and little Charlotte, our friends from Bracianno campsite. They were staying at a campsite just past Pompeii and they had planned the same kind of day as us, so without any hesitation, we agreed to join forces and do Capri together.

We reached Sorrento, which looked beautiful, a town of ornate buildings that sits on the edge of a stunning peninsular and the breathtaking Amalfi Coast, although we only glimpsed its sophisticated streets as we marched through, anxious to book tickets on the next ferry going to Capri. The port was crowded, but our boat wouldn't leave for forty minutes so we had time to sit down by the seashore, with a cup of cappuccino and catch up on their news while we waited for the boat.

The ferry that day was packed with an outing of noisy Italian school children that got great pleasure from the heavy swell of the rolling sea and I take my hat off to teachers the world over. The mesmerising water shimmered in the heat; a deep, rich, Mediterranean blue, with two lines of white foaming suds trailing our stern. We stood along the sides of the deck, hanging on to the rails and let the wind blow our sun-covered faces; Charlotte holding on tight in Nigel's arms. Capri appeared before us, a green emerald on a blue cloth, its jagged coastline only broken to allow boats to dock at the Marina Grande. This enchanting island, of just 13 square kilometres, has a rocky shoreline indented with grottos, like the famously deep Grota Azurra, (The Blue Cave). We were all keen to see this and to take a trip around the whole island by sea, so we bought more tickets at one of the busy, tourist-attraction huts and clambered down into a much smaller, faster boat, driven by yet another Greek god in sunglasses.

If the scenery ever got boring you could always sit and admire him. His technique for driving this boat was similar to driving a racing car, full acceleration all the way with thrills and spills every minute, so we had a breathtaking trip, stopping briefly to drift into the famous Blue Grotto to stare into indigo depths, and The Green Grotto and even the White Grotto….. all of these cavernous holes casting the waters into strange shades. Through the 'Lucky Arch' which linked a trio of rocky islets, the sea chopping and charging at us as we circled and swung around and then on round the full circumference of Capri until we were back at the Grand Marina.

Back on land again, we said goodbye to our Adonis and went looking for the correct bus to take us up to Anacapri, the smaller town situated uphill of Capri itself. The queue for this little bus was long, but we all squashed aboard, standing room only, and held on tight as we wriggled along a tiny road carved into the cliff wall, with the scariest of sheer drops down to a transparent blue ocean below us. Our bus driver had confidence enough for us all, as he coolly swerved past traffic and squeezed between houses. He obviously knew this route like the back of his hand and before long we were skidding to a halt at Anacapri.

Anacapri is the sister town to Capri, and at one time there was some dispute between the two communes as to who should have jurisdiction on the island. It is built on the lower slopes of Mount Solaro, although the entire island has steeply rising cliffs and a precipitous interior. Early discoveries date back to the Neolithic and Bronze ages and, as usual, it has a varied history of domination by raiding pirates, squabbling nations and the ubiquitous plague, but once again it's most prominent history dates to a Roman Emperor, Caesar Augustus who re-discovered Capri on his way back from the Eastern campaigns. He was so enamoured with its tranquil, undisturbed beauty, that he traded Ischia for it with the city of Naples. When he died, his successor Emperor Tiberius made Capri his golden exile and lived there for the last ten years of his life; between them, these two emperors developed the island and built twelve villas, some still standing today.

The Capri that we know now was re-discovered in the 1950's, when writers, poets and artists fell under its spell. And it is easy to see why they did. A Mediterranean jewel, that manages to retain its magic, despite the latest raiding tourists. Stunning scenery, set under a huge clear sky, in a sea of blue. The westerly winds fan it with fresh cooling air, fragrant flowers adorn it and once again, rather like Tuscany, I absolutely fell in love with Capri. I could happily wake up there every morning, to the dazzling panoramic views across to the Bay of Naples. Ah well, one day………

We rambled through the streets of Anacapri, admiring the petite white washed houses, flowered balconies and shady courtyards, and ignored the restaurant owners who were trying to wave us into their cafes. Take-away pizza from a busy street seller was fine for us, before making our way to the chair lift that would take us to the very top of Mount Solaro. This lift, of single chairs with a safety bar across, rather like a child's high chair, whisked you to the top-most point in about ten minutes. We stood in line to be popped into a moving chair by two assistants, little Charlotte on Nigel's lap again, and all rucksacks held in front of us. These chairs were quite small and it was quite a squeeze to get in. Then we were flying up over hillsides of meadow grass and spring flowers, pine treetops and patchwork houses, our legs swinging in the breeze. Below us we looked down on tiny terraced gardens, manicured rows of potatoes and peas and green leafed fruit trees. Donkeys and goats munched on their small patches of grass, and vines shaded haphazard patios. Across to our right, the most amazing panorama stretched across to the Bay of Naples and the Island of Ischia.

At the top, we were scooped off our chairs by two well practised attendants, and then headed for the open terrazzo to indulge in a cup of sweet, strong Italian coffee. From there we gazed at the most beautiful view you could ever wish to see. Capri basked under a golden sun and floated in the bluest of waters, with mainland Italy across in the distance. We looked over the cliff top, down through a clear sea and could almost see fish swimming way below us. I was hooked and I wanted to stay there forever – it was so utterly romantic – but there was more. We all decided to walk back down Mount Solaro, back to Anacapri, on a track through the natural, unspoilt pinewoods. This easy, well-worn path, called the Via Crucis, zig-zagged down through flower covered hillsides and sweet smelling, shady, dells and was regularly dotted with numbered, intricately engraved shrines. We skipped and jumped our way down, Charlotte swinging along on the ends of Nicky's fingers or riding high on Nigel's shoulders. We had a long way to walk back and we wanted to eat at one of the quay-side restaurants before the ferry left again. At Anacapri, we again opted to continue walking rather than take the little bus, but this time we went down 'The Steps'. We were still very high up and the drop down to Capri was almost vertical; running like six, manic, mountain goats, we flew down the 850 stone steps that steeply wound their way, back and forth, through tunnels under roads and past houses. After about 200 steps I managed to develop a sort of goat-hop, with arms flailing, to bounce myself down, getting hotter and hotter as we careered. Running down that many steps is surprisingly hard work and all the way down Nigel kept us breathless, as he taught us the complete version of that old sweet song, "T'was on the Isle of Capri that I found her", which he swore he'd learnt on his mother's knee.

We fell off the last steps and had about one hour before the ferry left. A quick run through the streets got us back down to the port, where we found a cheap restaurant and ordered much needed beers. The owner took us in hand, and fed us rich, stuffed Cannelloni and yet more pizzas, before we were galloping off again, laughing and burping, to catch the last ferry home. Red faced and wind blown we squeezed on. It looked like everyone waited for the last ferry before they left, and we waved goodbye to lovely Capri. Charlotte fell asleep on Nicky's lap and only woke when we boarded the train at Sorrento, for the ride back to camp. When Nicky, Nigel and Charlotte got off at their station, we swapped addresses, mobile numbers and kissed goodbye. They would be heading for Brindisi and Greece and we would be heading for Sicily next. Would we ever see them again……luckily yes, we all met up back in England. We staggered home to the waiting Beast, -"T'was goodbye to the Isle of Capri".

The following day we rested; our faces feeling like sun-baked tomatoes and our leg muscles twinging every time we faced even the smallest step up or down. Our maps were spread out on the dining table of the motor home and Simon and Jack programmed Maisy to take us on to Sicily. The road down the Amalfi Coast, which we would have liked to have seen, had been blocked by a landslide, so we would initially use the motorway and then join the A road which ran parallel with the sea all the way down the western coast to the toe of Italy. We gave the motor home a quick clean up and then, before we moved on, Simon got under the kitchen sink to change the filter that provided filtered water to our separate drinking-water tap. We rarely bought bottled water. Ever since leaving England we had been religious about using the filtered water for drinking, as we were keen to avoid stomach upsets. However, when he dismantled it to remove the old filter, he discovered that there was no filter in it anyway. We'd assumed that the motor home dealer had put a new one in as part of its ready-to-roll service. We had obviously been drinking various countries' waters, with absolutely no problem. Which says a lot for the water around Europe.

Early morning and as we left Camping Zeus, Pompeii was in its usual turmoil of hooting, tooting traffic. A quick swing into the supermarket car park for a mammoth stock up of food and we were off, bumping our way down the fairly rough motorway past Solerno. Rich, green countryside melted into spring mountain slopes, as we drove alongside almost continuous high ranges and small villages perched or nestled wherever they could get a good grip, or a good view between the steep V shaped valleys. We turned off just before Lagonegro to join the coastal A road over viaducts and through tunnels, until turning off again onto a smaller road. We finally ground to a halt at a sandy beach, and wild camped for the night. This whole coastline was quite different to our experience further north. Quieter, with much less tourism; almost deserted and wild in comparison. That night I cooked sausages with a medley of fresh vegetables and we ate our supper round a campfire on the beach. How good it was to be back in the wilds, after the madness of Pompeii.

We felt so relaxed at this little spot that we decided to spend the next day there as well; the gentle waves were such a relief. The few beach bars and shops were not yet open for the season and everything looked rather shabby, but we enjoyed pottering as usual, gathering driftwood along the long stretch of sand. Between the beach and the main road was a rough meadow area, quite large, sprinkled with miniature red poppies and wild plants. Small birds busied themselves amongst this rough land and all day we could hear the trill of a Whimbrel; eventually we spotted him through our binoculars and Jack and I did our familiar 'creeping up' technique, as we followed him through the grasses. A little further inland, hills spread back into mountains and in the distance, we could see snow-topped, far-away peaks. It was a good resting place.

That evening we had another beach fire of collected driftwood. Jack loved this kind of evening, when he was in charge of keeping the fire alive; creating tiny sparks that rose up into the night sky, or running off bare- foot down the dark beach, to gather more wood. I cooked another easy meal and we completed it with a sampling of some delicious Italian cheeses. I became completely hooked on Ricotto al Forno and spent the rest of our time in Italy and Sicily, ensuring that we always had some in the fridge. It was a smooth cheese, soft and creamy, with a dark, burnt edge, rather like the burnt skin on a rice pudding. That and the yummy Mozzarella became my passion.

We travelled on the following day, working our way slowly down the coast. It was a Sunday and the roads were quiet, apart from a swarm of Sunday motor- bikers and a long cycle race that passed us by on the other side of the road. At the town of Diamante, the rather grey looking sand changed to yellow and urbanisation increased, but it was still quite rural with olive groves, sheep pastures, and small holdings of cultivation. We joined the motorway again at Rosarno, filling up with diesel and sleeping in the motorway car park for the night, along with the lorries again. We were now close to the toe of Italy, where we could cross to Sicily, and the next day would take us to the ferry terminal at Villa Giovanni.

My diary for 26th April reads, "Scariest bit of road yet. Motorway reduced to one lane each way, extremely high on flyovers, over sea and deep gorges. Can't look, absolutely terrifying!" We were very close to the edge, yet again. The landscape in this corner of Southern Italy was stunning to say the least. Very green and lush at this time of the year, with fast flowing rivers, dense woodland, and a dramatic, precipitous coastline that kept us gripped all the way..... mostly to the edges of our seats. The ferry port at Villa Giovanni was small, but very easy to find, and when we rolled into the parking area there were only two or three other vehicles waiting to cross to Sicily. The ferry charge, at that time of the year, was very reasonable, only 35 euros for a sixty day return ticket, and it would only take about half an hour to cross. We hadn't known what to expect at this ferry port, so it was a great relief to find an easy roll on, roll off service. We rolled on and were soon rolling off at the busy port of Messina.

I had never thought that I would ever be able to visit Sicily, an island that had always captured my imagination. Wild, warm, and romantic was how I had always thought of it, and actually yes, we did love it there. It is the largest island in the Mediterranean Sea and yet is still small enough to allow you to see most of its treasures and terrain over a few weeks. Three seas surround it: the Ionian, the Tyrrhenian and the Med, and the volcanic Aeolian (or Lipari) Islands, including the active volcanic island of Stromboli, lie just off its northern coast. Sicily is mountainous, with Mount Etna being the highest volcano in Europe, on its east coast. But it also has two very fertile inland plains and as we travelled we saw olive and orange groves, heavily laden lemon

charming man then insisted that I try these fruits, freshly picked from his garden and we sat and ate our way through them; eating them whole, pith, pips and all, sweet and sharp and delicious. I eventually left, boarded my bike and was starting to ride back to camp, when round the corner came Simon and Jack. Their jaws dropped as they did a double take of this glamorous new hairstyle and for a few minutes they were speechless. Mama Mia, I felt quite light-headed. A new me and all for fifteen euros.....definitely a Sicilian bargain.

The delightful smell of orange blossom filled the air at this campsite. Jack tracked geckoes and lizards as they moved around the olive trees following the sun, and captured huge, yellow and black striped, flying insects under glass to examine them. Next to the site was a Nature Park and lagoon where we took evening walks, the sea on one side and cliffs on the other and here we saw our first Squacco Heron: a small brown-backed, bittern-like heron that bursts into a dazzling white when it takes flight and shows its wings. But the weather had now become changeable, either very hot or very squally, which was making it difficult for us to book our boat trip to Stromboli. The boats just didn't run if the weather looked stormy, but we booked it for the coming Sunday and hoped for the best. That was of course, if Aeolus was willing.

May

The Aeolian Islands

The Aeolian Islands (also known as the Lipari Islands) are named after Aeolus, the Greek god of wind, who supposedly confined the winds in a cave. Seven Islands make up this archipelago off the north east coast of Sicily and two of the islands still have active volcanoes. Stromboli is easily reached and eruptions can be seen regularly, especially at night, when glowing lumps of lava are hurled above the crater rim to illuminate the dark sky. It is one of the most active volcanoes on earth, being in nearly continuous eruption for the last 2000 years or more, and although it hasn't caused major damage, it has caused some fatalities. In 1919 four people were killed and twelve homes destroyed by gigantic rocks hurled over the rim. In 1930, three people were killed by pyroclastic flows and a fourth person was scalded to death in the sea where the flows entered the water; in 1986 a biologist was killed by flying rock and in 2002 the collapse of an unstable slope caused a small tsunami which damaged the village below and for the first time ever, caused a complete, temporary, evacuation of the island. So, although most eruptions are relatively harmless, it is still an unknown quantity, capable of killing. The cone-like shape of the crater usually contains the lava flow and protects the island from further damage. It's possible to hire a guide and walk to the top of the volcano but as the explosions in recent years have become fiercer, a review of tourism is under-way.

We boarded the ferry at mid-day, along with about sixty other tourists, and found spaces above deck on the canopied seating area. The first stop on our 'Stromboli By Night' tour was at Panarea, a small but incongruously jet-set like island. As we approached the quay, loud thumping music blared across the stage of an outdoor, aerobics area. We felt as if we had landed on a miniature Ibiza. The male DJ, (I think he was male), bizarrely clothed in a leopard skin dress, sunglasses and wide, plumed hat, strutted amongst the young and not so young exercisers, as they stamped and stretched and wiggled their bottoms to disco-baby songs, while other young-and-beautiful types paraded around them. Now we felt as if we had landed on Mars. Yachts and speed boats in the bay, decked out in bikini-gorgeous girls and brown hunky men in shades, basked in the world of Panarea – but we scuttled off as fast as possible from this nightmare area and headed up into the hills. We only had a few hours at this island, which we spent walking one of the narrow coastal paths, past scattered white washed houses baking in the sun with stunning views of the sea. Our picnic lunch we ate on a pebbly, shadeless beach, downwind of the yellowy, sulphurous fumaroles, the exit holes for the rotten-egg smelling gas, which seeps out from the volcanic base of the island. Then we made our way back to the busy little quay to board the boat again. Shops and restaurants were still doing a good trade and the music was still blaring away.

Stromboli, was a completely different experience. As we approached, over a shimmering, sapphire sea, the huge classic volcano shape of the island appeared on the horizon ahead of us. This whole island is the volcano; steep sloping sides flow into the water and a cone shaped top, puffs continuous white gas clouds up into the blue sky. The sleepy, one street town of Stromboli speckles the waters edge, diminutive in comparison. We circled the island, viewing the steaming lava flows on their slow journey into the sea, before disembarking at the small jetty where little children played and dogs rolled in the sun. I had the feeling that life would never get too hectic on this island unless the volcano felt like causing a stir. This place had a very definite, laid back character of its own.

With no-where much to go, we walked up what appeared to be the one and only main street and had a beer at a small bar, where a young DJ was playing great acid-jazz music. Occasionally, small, three wheeled cars went by, or the odd scooter appeared, but on this road, children and dogs definitely had right of way. Our trip was called 'Stromboli By Night' and as the sun set, we boarded the boat again for a supper of pasta and fish with local red wine and soft bread, before motoring round to the side of the island where we moored up to watch the volcano. Wrapped up against the chill night, we sat on the open deck and enjoyed a display of belching smoke and intermittent eruptions of fire and brimstone, glowing red against the black sky. Every flare and flash brought ooohs and aaahs from our bobbing boat and it was with some reluctance that we finally left such a great sight and motored back over the inky-black sea to mainland Sicily.

Next day, later than we'd planned, we packed up and drove on towards our next destination. A strong, warm Sahara wind was whipping up the sea again, so we felt lucky that we had managed to take the boat trip the day before. We wanted to travel further east in Sicily now, and then head across the island to the south-western coast. All through that day we followed the quiet, unspoilt coastline, alongside the crystal clear sea. Fat yellow lemons hung on the trees, and again bright red poppy fields flanked us, but the wind now gusted so strongly that we were continuously buffeted across the motorway. I think that Aeolus must have released one of those captured winds. At last, Simon gave up trying to manhandle the motor home against the Gods and with aching arms he pulled into a sheltered service station car park where we slept the night. It had been empty when we had arrived, but in the morning lorries once more surrounded us: alongside, behind, in front, up close and personal again, but we hadn't heard any of them arrive in the night.

The wind disappeared as quickly as it had arrived, and next day promised to be scorchio. With the air conditioning on, we crossed rugged green Sicily on the raised A19 road that flew us over hills, vales and plains. Without a doubt the Italians are master road builders and excel when it comes to flyovers. We joined the road to Agrigento, but took a wrong turn and detoured over a mountain, through sumptuous green countryside and the busy old town of Caltanisseta, a fascinating place that we vowed to go back to one day in a Fiat 500, not an American RV. Then down to the coast and the Valley of the Temples. This route across the centre of Sicily was exceptionally pretty at this time of the year; almost continuous swathes of small red poppies in Monet-like green fields, sprinkled with flora of yellow, purple and blue, steadily rolled by us. Acres of vines in young green leaf disappeared over rounded hills and ancient olive groves and almond trees stood on floors of fresh spring grass. Small herds of goats, with soft floppy ears and ding-dong bells, pottered down roughened tracks and we hardly saw a person all day.

Agrigento, the most ancient town in Sicily, sits strategically on a small plain between two hills, close to the sea. The Valley of the Temples, containing five important Greek Doric temples, is near by. We decided to visit these, as we were going to pass by so close, and followed Maisie's directions as she led us up towards them. Only two of the temples are still standing, in relatively good condition, the rest having been destroyed by earthquakes and early Christian vandalism. As we approached we could clearly see the Temple of Concordia, positioned majestically on the top of a small hill; a large building of golden weathered stone, its once impressive roof supported by around eighty, tall, Doric columns in long rows, its graceful lines and imposing proportions dominating the landscape. This wide valley was once central to religious life and is littered with the remains of ancient buildings constructed in the 5th century BC. We had hoped to find a good parking area, so that we could take a day to explore it all, but as we approached the main entrance, we realised that this was not going to happen. As we often found in Italy, the organisation and accommodation required for the armies of tourists who are drawn to these spots was completely inadequate. The entrance to the site was situated on the small but main highway into Agrigento, so cars, lorries, buses, motor homes and all else who would normally use this two way road, had to contend with parties of bemused tourists who ground traffic to a halt as they unloaded from coaches. Touting salesmen hindered cars which tried to squirm between it all and we made yet another hasty twelve point turn at the first opportunity and got the hell out of there. Back down the road, some way from the entrance, we found a large lay-by where we stopped and had lunch. Luckily, we could easily admire the impressive Temple from there, and read about its history while we had a civilised salad with a glass of chilled wine. That was as good as it was going to get for us and it suited us just fine.

Our next stop, a quick detour down to a beach, put us in the path of another touting salesman, who appeared alongside us as we stood admiring the crashing surf. This time it was an older man, slightly bent and weathered brown, but driving a smart little car. He had no doubt in his mind that we should buy some of his homemade olive oil, which we had to admit looked good, but we really didn't want five litres of it. His insistence started to put our backs up, after all we hadn't asked him to stop and sell us olive oil and how did he think we would store five litres, did he think we were running the engine on it. Eventually he admitted that he had smaller quantities in his boot and we bought two, half litre bottles. But, the smile had disappeared and he drove off without even a thank you. Well, it takes all sorts, and we certainly met most of them on our travels.

The next sort we met was a real character, and I smile to this day when I think of him. We drove on down the coast and stopped to wild camp for the night in a large, bumpy parking area, right by the beach, next to a gently rolling sea. It was a peaceful spot and far from town, in fact we were the only ones there. Jack jumped out to stretch his legs on the sand and Simon wound up the satellite dish to check the news and weather report. He soon discovered that there would be a full eclipse of the moon that night and we were in one of the best areas in Europe to see it – and clear skies were forecast. Our evening entertainment sounded all set so I cooked chicken stir-fry, Jack gathered some driftwood for a fire and we relaxed. A gentle stray puppy had befriended us when we arrived, firstly by rolling on the sand with our own young puppy and then by sticking doggedly to Simon who fed her the last tin of dog food that we still had from our stay in Ronda. The sun began to set over the sea and we all settled down on the beach to await the rising moon, with a glass of wine by the fire. At that moment, up rolled a battered red car and out jumped a small, even more battered, dark-skinned Sicilian man clutching a grubby plastic cup and a bottle of red wine.

"Buonasera, Buonasera", he greeted us, with a great toothless smile.

"Buonasera" we happily replied, while he filled his glass, topped-up ours and introduced himself as a local. (We never did catch his name).

He and Simon immediately got into long and jovial conversation, as best they could, as neither spoke the others language and much was translated by drawing in the sand with sticks. After a while Jack and I retreated to the motor home, slightly unsure of this rather strange, new visitor. As the night wore on the moon rose and the wine went down (quickly) and before long our new friend was beckoning me out again. This time, he first shook Simon's hand and then sidled very close to me with murmurings of "Bella Signora, Bella Signora".

Then with a sudden and rather manic desperation he grasped my hand securely in both of his and his eyes took on a rather doleful, blood hound look as we shook hands, and he pressed closer. But the handshake that I got was either some secret Mafia signal or, (and this is what I've always believed), it's a suggestive handshake where his middle finger tickled my palm! I was so surprised that I jumped a mile but the leery look in his eyes left me in no doubt about what he was thinking. I didn't know whether to laugh or run. He was definitely no Adonis, but that obviously didn't stop the hot Italian blood from coursing through his veins and for the rest of the evening, he gave me long, meaningful looks over his white plastic cup, which had me and Jack in stitches. As I write this now, I'm still laughing and feel like squirming when I think of his grubby handshake. You've got to give it to these Italians, they don't waste much time.

Well, we all stood and watched as the earth blotted out a wonderful, huge, bright moon that seemed to hang in the air over the murky sea and surf; the fire died down leaving a cold empty beach and our friend gave up the chase, skidding cheerfully away into the black night. He promised to return the next morning, and needless to say we were up and away early. Our biggest regret was saying goodbye to the dear little dog, who had been such a good companion. We left her with food and fresh water, but we always wished we had taken her with us....... And if ever we go back, we hope that she at least, will still be there.

Our rather loose plan now was to go to Siracuse, but we decided that we would follow the coast around the end of Sicily, and if we saw a pleasant place to stop, then we would take a few days to explore the area on the way. The land became flatter as we travelled south and west, and before long we were passing through poly-tunnel, vegetable growing land again. We homed in on Punta Bracetto, a small fishing village in the province of Ragussa, where we knew there to be a good campsite. We sometimes gathered information about campsites as we went along, but we had also bought a great CD disc, which we could run on our laptop, and which itemised camp-sites in most countries in Europe. Scarabeo Camping was one of those lucky finds that we feel like keeping to ourselves, but I guess I should share it with you.

We arrived to find the campsite only just open for the season, but with a friendly smile and much encouragement they got us through their entrance gates and we found a place to park up. Once again, we were a little on the big side. One look at this beautifully positioned, un-assuming site and we thought that we had found heaven. Opened in 1968 by Professor Giuseppe Nobile, it had regularly won the Award for Quality and Courtesy. In 2001 it was taken over by his nephew and niece and they have continued to keep up his high standards. This is not a site for those who like a noisy and hectic holiday; it is quite small and very peaceful. The building materials are mainly traditional and are as natural as possible, just local stone, terracotta, bamboo and wood. Its simple lay-out accommodates tents, caravans and motor homes but its biggest attraction by far is its idyllic location. Warm, wooden steps, edged with palm trees, lead you straight from the campsite to a beautiful sheltered bay of fine, silver sand. The peaceful beach with a shallow, blue sea is just the place to go if you are ready to relax with a good book for a week or two. Even in May it was hot enough to swim and the free sunshades provided, were a must. The only other occupants on the beach were the abundant and industrious little Scarab beetles, after whom the site is named. They scuttled through the soft sand on endless missions, leaving tiny footprints for us to follow. Jack had his surfboard out and was in the sea before we could put the kettle on and that was the start of a most enjoyable stay at this site.

Next morning we cycled down to the local bakery, and bought our ciabatta bread. The small, dark haired owner, with her ready smile, was soon giving us fresh home-grown lemons and selling us a huge bottle of home made wine, "multo forte" and " good for the stomach" but which I have to admit was too strong even for us, and eventually went down a drain in Croatia. Our cycle rides took us along flat roads, to the nearby towns of Scalambri and Marina di Ragusa. Although quite small and quiet, they had elaborate baroque buildings and spacious, well used squares. Walks along the coast took us past banks of bright pink, star shaped succulents sheltering curious green backed lizards. Jack caught endless insects – from flying grasshoppers, to weird and wonderful caterpillars and an enormous horned beetle. We thoroughly enjoyed this quiet corner of Sicily, and spent many days on the beach, snorkelling in the bay when the water was clear. Six days later we thought we had better get on to Syracuse, so we said goodbye to Concietta and the rest of the campsite crew, gave the lady at the bakery a big hug, and we headed off. That's the joy of independent travel; when you find a special spot, you can stay there for as long as you want. One day we must go back to Camping Scarabeo.

Sicily in late spring was a delight, and as we drove we once again admired her co-lours and clear seas. With too many enticing wild camps, rushing was out of the ques-tion but we had to keep moving or we would never get to Syracuse. The only campsite we had seen advertised was situated about four kilometres outside the city. We planned to park up there and ride our bikes in, although you could catch a local bus. We arrived at the campsite at about nine o'clock in the morning and waited for the owner to unlock the gate. It was basically an overgrown olive grove with minimal facilities, the owner was not the happiest of souls and it was expensive. It was also swarming with mozzies, and they zoomed in on Simon while he worked outside, hooking up to the electrical supply. Even with fly screens on all windows and doors they cunningly invaded us, making our stay miserable, but within the hour we were all set up and keen to see Syracuse, so we made a dash for our bikes and cycled in single file along the main route into town. I would say that this road was not one for the faint hearted. Very busy, and used by huge lorries and coaches, I probably lost several kilos in weight from the sheer fear factor alone as we pedalled single file, trying to avoid slip-streaming under the wheels of juggernaughts. We arrived unscathed but not un-scared and locked our bikes together around a support on the wide Ponte Umberto Bridge.

This elaborate bridge links the slightly younger Syracuse with the small island of Ortygia, which was the original centre of the city. The history of Syracuse takes some unravelling. Its ancient ties to Greece, its Carthaginian settlements and its fear of Rome caused it to waver dangerously between one stool and the next, eventually falling to a Roman conquest. In 264 BC, Syracuse was a Greek city, but when Rome set her eyes on Carthage in the First Punic War, King Hiero II, King of Syracuse, found him-self caught between two mighty empires. He initially supported Carthage, as Syracuse had many Carthaginian settlements, but was coerced to pay tribute and supply grain to Rome. In the second Punic Wars, 218 BC, Hannibal of Carthage led his army to victory against the Romans when he crossed the Alps into Italy and many Siracusans wanted to ally themselves with him again. But King Hiero continued to honour his treaty with Rome: when he died, his fifteen year old grandson, who had started to re-negotiate with Hannibal, succeeded him. The city became divided between Roman and Carthaginian supporters and a civil war followed the assassination of the young King. The Carthaginian supporters won a brief victory and Rome was forced to send an army to deal with the situation and promptly lay siege to the city. However, for many years, the great Archimedes had been military advisor to old King Hiero, and he had made good preparations for such an attack. After three years, Marcus Marcellus did breach the inland walls and Syracuse was sacked with around 2000 Cartheginians brutally slain including Archimedes. Marcus Marcellus had intended that he should be spared, as his wisdom and inventions were already much admired.

Like much of Italy, history is soaked into layer upon layer of this city. Greek, Roman, and every dominating nation thereafter, have left their mark. We walked the maze of medieval streets and alleyways in Ortygia, marvelling at the fancy 17th century baroque architecture which curls around every doorway, balcony and window. Wide, shaded paths edged with restaurants led us around the city sea walls and past the Greek temple dedicated to Apollo. At lunchtime we bought rich anchovy pizzas and yummy pistachio ice cream, and then walked down to the picturesque waterfront on the Via Pichareli, and to the famous Fountain of Arethusa. We couldn't believe how much history was woven into this ancient city and wondered how much more could we take in one day?

Well, it was easy really, because old Ortygia was a very pleasant place to be. However, we did have a cycle ride ahead, so we risked our lives again in the slightly chaotic traffic and pedalled furiously back to camp. We rushed straight into the Beast and slammed the door shut – there wouldn't be any fraternising with fellow campers on this site, because any glimpse of flesh was immediately attacked by the hoards of mozzies. Armed with our individual fly swots, we searched every nook and cranny before going to bed, but we still spent the first hour or two before sleep, jumping up shouting, "there's another one", and leaping off to kill it. By morning, the pale roof-lining of the motor home was dotted with dead bodies and our blood, each mark showing where we had zapped the satiated little devils.

Even after our restless night, we managed to get into town by about ten o'clock next day. The ride in had been another hell raiser – our single file, weaving along, Simon in front, Jack in the middle and me at the rear signalling furiously when required. This time we scooted through the main town to find a back route to the honeycomb-shaped Archaeological Museum. Our devious route took us through a very pretty park that had a most unusually shaped modern building. Simon was on a mission to reach the museum, but Jack and I skidded to a halt, intrigued by what we soon discovered to be, The Sanctuary of Our Lady of Tears.

In 1953, a modest plaster image of the Madonna, belonging to a poor family, miraculously shed tears. It was a sensational event, causing amazement in Italy and Europe, and as word spread, crowds of pilgrims and worshippers, the sick and the dedicated, went to pray at the small shrine. Many cures were attested to the tears of the image and in 1954 Pope Pius XII provided a final blessing when he gave a radio speech supporting the virtues of the icon. By 1968 the present sanctuary or church, had been built and the plaster image of Our Lady of Tears was carried there, before a crowd of tens of thousands of people. We studied the exterior of this ultra-modern building, which dominates the skyline of the city and is designed in the shape of a huge teardrop. A massive circular base, with regularly spaced entrances, converges to a single central point 102 meters high. We parked our bikes and went inside to discover a round, cavernous, cone shaped church, with slanting light stabbing through from above. Built on a cantilevered design, this is a very contemporary building, but inside, it manages to retain a feeling of complete peacefulness and unity. The image of the Madonna rests in a silver framed hollow, above white marble steps. When we were there, the Church was being attended by many people of all ages and appeared to be as popular today as it had ever been. If you are in Syracuse and are interested in architecture, it is well worth a visit.

We cycled on, and eventually reached the Archaeological Museum, Paolo Orsi, which houses an amazing 18,000 or more ancient artefacts, dating back a staggering 6000 years – tools, decorated pots, jewellery etc from 4000 BC. It is a modern building where the displays are clearly laid out in chronological order, depicting life throughout the past six millennia. The wealth of information soon had Jack and I staggering boggle eyed; for us it was almost overload, but Simon, who kept saying, "you must look at this one", had the stamina to work his way through the whole museum. Jack and I soon disappeared outside and found a shady spot in the gardens to recover and discuss the merits of different ice cream flavours. We had a nasty feeling that we were definitely going to overdo it that day and would need all the strength we could get.

The mid-afternoon sun was now beating down mercilessly, and we had to cycle along a ludicrously long, dusty road to reach the last item on our agenda - the large archaeological park on top of a dusty hill overlooking Syracuse. The largest feature here is a 5th century BC Greek semi-circular theatre, which had been literally carved out of the rocky hill side. We flopped for a while on the warm stone seating that circled the stage and imagined the entertainment on offer to those living in the area at that time. Behind us was the necropolis, containing the tombs of the dead, from the same period. Jack was keen to do a little exploration here, just to see if there were any bones lying about, so before we got arrested, we dragged him off to an interesting cave named Dionysius's Ear. According to legend, Dionysius used this cave as a prison, because the acoustics were so outstanding that he could hear the prisoners' whispered conversations. Its cool, dark, towering interior reminded me of the inside of a snail shell, the rock walls curving round to a large open area at the centre. We tried whispering in there, but our whispers were drowned out by a body of tourists who broke into a noisy, many times repeated rendition, of their national anthem. We backed out, much too politely, and went off muttering about national characteristics again. Perhaps it was time we headed home.

The Park also contained a very well preserved Roman amphitheatre but by this time we were feeling shattered. There is only so much that you can take in, in one day, and as usual we had overdone it. We wobbled like reckless, sun-crazed insects, expecting to be squashed at any moment, back along the busy main road to camp, dashed into the motor home and sat with our feet in bowls of cold water. A last muster of energy for another mass mozzie kill and we were in bed with our books by 8.45pm. Wild elephants could have thundered through the Beast that night, but dead to the world, we slept like logs and woke early next morning keen to move on and leave the mozzies behind.

Our route now took us up the east coast of Sicily, past Mount Etna and on to Taormina, a spectacularly situated tourist spot. We had seen a campsite advertised along this piece of coast and hoped to stop there, but as so often before, this was not quite the way it turned out. At first our road was quiet and wide, but before long it had changed to a small A road and the hot- bloodied, impulsive, racing Italians were around us again. We sped on as fast as we dared, but with reckless determination, cars overtook us, four at a time, whizzing in and out of gaps, with no room to spare. Bunches of wilting flowers lined the roadside, commemorating those who hadn't quite judged it right.

The day was scorching hot, but the summit of Mount Etna was shrouded in low cloud, and we had become so blasé about mountains that we gave it a miss. Vesuvius and Stromboli had satisfied our appetites for volcanoes and by now we were keen to reach Paradise Camping, our next beachfront campsite. We followed Maisie's directions, and the turning approached. Great, we thought, that wasn't too bad – however, it wasn't going to be that simple. We were ready to leave the busy main road and all looked good, including the inviting coastline below us. We should have known it was too good to be true and we should have spotted the railway line that ran alongside the coast.

The campsite was well signed and we turned hard right into it, through a narrow arch followed by a very hard 90 degree left, going steeply downhill. At the bottom, another hard 90 degree right, again with a serious drop, took us onto a long very narrow lane. This entrance was just about manageable for long vehicles but we were now well and truly committed to going in this direction. You have probably guessed what was then ahead of us – yes, the usual extremely low bridge, in this instance with a height clearance of 3.4 meters. We were 3.7 meters and short of taking the air-condition-ing, satellite dish, aerial and skylights off the roof, there is no way we would go under it. The lane was too narrow to turn around, and our only option was to reverse back up this very steep twisting lane of sharp bends, and back-out onto the hellishly busy main road. What is it with some campsite owners? Why don't they have the sense to put a sign at the entrance warning of low bridges? We surely weren't the first vehicle to have this problem. We practically stamped up and down in the lane, such was our frustration. To add to our growing anger, the owner now wandered up the lane to us and with complete indifference shrugged her shoulders, turned around and walked off again. We had deliberately phoned ahead to this site, giving our dimensions, to ensure that they would have room for us, so why didn't they mention the bridge! Just a helpful word of commiseration would now have gone such a long way, although we might have given her a few words of advice about where to put a sign. We resigned ourselves to a difficult reverse back up the obstacle course. At the main road, I sprinted down to a bend and flagged down the speeding traffic so that Simon could back out, then I raced back to the motor home and clumsily jumped aboard as we moved off again. About two hours later, after a three-point turn on a busy sea front and a fair bit of cursing and swearing, we found a super little campsite, swung in and pulled on the hand brake. A cup of tea was totally inadequate, but several cold beers helped us calm down and once again we took in our new surroundings. Jack got the bikes off the back, set up the bar-becue and pulled out the awning and we ate our supper under a shady tree, overlooking a calming sea. Just another day on the road!

Once again, we had found a friendly family run site, this time at Sant'Allessio Si-culo, a small seaside resort just twelve kilometres north of Taormina. Flowers bloomed profusely, the sun shone brightly, Goldfinches enchanted us daily, and the builder's yard next door gave us some brief entertainment. Monday morning started with a huge argument, coming clearly from the yard. At 8.0'clock the boss had arrived in his over-large 4X4 car and weighty leather jacket. At top volume he yelled at his line of men who stood or slouched before him, banging his hands on his car bonnet and waving his arms in the air to add emphasis. With some reluctance they were bullied into shouting back and before long a full-scale row was brewing. We wondered what the problem could be; could it be Italy's choice of entry into the Eurovision song contest, or the poor results of their local football team, or just the price of bread. Whatever, it got them all very heated and at one point he jumped in his car, skidded round the yard, then got back out again and carried on the argument. He was one mad Italian. He obviously didn't believe in taking his group of employees into the office for a quiet word in their shell-like – aahh, if only we understood the language, or perhaps it was better not to know. Anyway, he eventually left; only to return just minutes later to vent the last of his spleen, before roaring off again for good. The unimpressed men shrugged their shoulders and ambled off to have a fag before starting work. Maybe it was the Italian equivalent to a Monday morning pep talk, who knows?

That day we caught the local bus to Taormina. This intriguing town perches high on a coastal hilltop, with an almost perpendicular slope down to the sea on one side and a dramatic view of Etna on the other. The main motorway runs through a tunnel, bored straight through the rock beneath this settlement, which leaves it in splendid isolation. However, it has long been a favourite haunt of European jet setters and is now firmly on the tourist trail. The local bus wound its way up the snaking road, dropping us off with still some way to walk up to the town. Expensive shops, elaborate buildings of baroque architecture and the gothic Duomo kept our camera busy, not to mention the staggering views down and along the whole mountainous coastline and out to sea. We took our time strolling through the fascinating streets, but ground to a halt when we discovered one of the best music shops that we had encountered on our trip. The Funivia (cable car) took us back down the quick way, almost vertically, offering us a fabulous panoramic view over the sun-covered land and stunningly beautiful sea shore. From there, we walked around the corner to paradise - Isola Bella Beach, which curves out into the transparent sea, forming a shallow sheltered inlet, punctuated by a fairy-tale island. Deep cerise bougainvillea with young green leaves, swayed against a clear blue sky and here we flopped and swam and lay in the sun until it was time to get our bus back to camp.

Next day I awoke slowly to the gentle mantra of woodpigeons, the long, descending trill of the brightly decked goldfinches and the rhythmic pace of the early train to Messina. The warmth of the sun was already heating up the air and we decided to take a picnic back to Isola Bella again. With snorkels, flippers and food, all packed into our backpacks, we caught the bus and spoilt ourselves for another day. Within twenty-four hours we would be leaving Sicily and be heading across the Southern coast of Italy. We had really loved our stay on this island and could easily have spent more time there. The people were generally friendly, the food delicious, the scenery spectacular and there was so much more that we could have seen and done. One day..... one day..... we would love to return, but now we had an appointment to keep in Monza – and before that of course, would be Venice.

Venice and Formula-One-Fun

By 11.20 the next morning we were rolling off the ferry, back onto mainland Italy. We'd arranged to meet Stella, Simon's sister, at the formula one race track in Monza in two weeks time and we wanted to visit Venice first, so we were heading straight up the east coast of Italy, from toe to top, and would wild camp every night on the way. The weather was really warming up now, but the air conditioning unit in the motor home was working well and it was a comfortable ride. The only slightly worrying aspect was that the parking brake light was remaining on while we were driving. Maybe it was just faulty wiring: it didn't seem to be affecting progress, and so we carried on. The scenery in southern Italy was dramatically beautiful with wild sandy beaches, verdant green hills and more swathes of red poppies. May was a wonderful time to visit; we guessed that a few months later, the land would be sucked dry by the relentless heat.

Our first wild camp was in a large lay-by, pleasantly shaded by tall eucalyptus trees, just off the motorway. Lorries pulled in during the evening and we watched them coming and going as we sat and played cards at the dining table. A small car had also arrived, initially rushing around the car park, before individually circling round the stationary lorries. The driver appeared to be using the little car to almost flirt with the trucks, twisting and turning, driving slowly alongside and then flouncing off to the other end of the car park. Another lorry rolled in and the little car rushed over, doing a few provocative turns in front of it, after which the driver of the lorry and the driver of the car both left their vehicles and went into the trees together. That was a new one on us, and we hastily shut the blinds. He was definitely selling something and we could make a few good guesses what it was.

Even with the night time entertainment going on we slept well, but next morning posed a problem. All ready to roll, with everything packed away and seat belts on, Simon started the engine. But when he went to move off, the motor home wouldn't budge. The auto-park brake would not dis-engage which meant that we were going no-where fast. We all exchanged silent glances, and a few silent prayers. I put the kettle back on, for that always helpful cup of tea, and Simon got out and got under to find the cause. The auto-brake transmission oil reservoir had leaked and was empty, and he thought he couldn't fix it without parts from the UK. This was a huge problem. We were stuck in a motorway lay-by, a long way between service stations, with no way of driving. If we'd been in a car it would have seemed better, but with all our worldly goods, our life, and our home contained in this giant vehicle that we had no way of moving, I couldn't imagine what we'd do and wondered if we'd spend the rest of our year in an Italian lay-by. So, while I stared dejectedly out of the window, watching our gay motoring friend as he now minced suggestively round the car park on foot, Simon trawled through the manuals and worked out that he couldn't fix the leak but he could disconnect the auto-park brake if we could get hold of a litre of transmission oil. This didn't make any sense at all to me, but Simon explained that we needed the oil in order to temporarily activate the auto-brake, so that he could disconnect it. Then we would just use the manual hand brake when parking. (It was still a little beyond me).

Basically, we needed transmission oil, but I thought that manna from heaven might have been easier to get at that point. Then he remembered that we had RAC euro- breakdown cover. Have you ever tried getting breakdown assistance while you're abroad? It isn't that hard so long as you have infinite patience and don't panic, so I would be useless at it. Simon however was brilliant. He called the RAC in England and explained our situation. They contacted their Italian counterparts and explained the problem to them. The Italians then called us and we emphasised repeatedly that we were huge, could not be towed anywhere but just needed one litre of transmission oil to fix our problem. They eventually arrived with a large tow truck and no transmission oil. At this point I wanted to put my head in a bucket of sand, (an ostriches life looked better than mine) and Jack said he was going to pray or cry but couldn't decide which would help most. This had all taken several hours, many phone calls and plenty of coffee, but at least we now had two big, burly, Italian car mechanics with us. They scratched their heads as Simon tried to explain the problem, and eventually one went off to get the oil while the other admired the motor home. When the oil finally arrived Simon disconnected the brake and we were ready to roll again. He also phoned a supplier back in England, asking them to send the spare parts to our next planned campsite. Eventually, thank god, we left our gay car park. I took two Relaxaby tablets and fell asleep in the back, while Simon drove us on, praying that we wouldn't have any more problems.

That evening we stopped for the night at a small service station and after supper we took a stroll down a grassy lane to a picturesque wood. I collected wild poppies and some wonderful grasses, and then from the pinewood we heard the distinct and unmistakable, fluted song of the Golden Oriole. We never did see him, but his song was good enough to cheer us up. Yep, just another day on the road, never a dull moment.

Jack notched up twenty-seven mozzie kills that night. He was leaping around until gone midnight, but in the morning we were all covered in red bites, so some had managed to escape him. We pressed on up the coast of Italy, through the flat agricultural plains of Puglia and up to the more touristy areas around Pescara and Ancona. An uneventful overnight stop and then over the River Po and we were approaching Venice. We were heading for a large campsite at the tip of the Punta Sabbioni peninsular. From there we knew that we could catch the regular ferryboat across the Lido to Venice. The long, thin Sabbioni peninsular was crammed with campsites and its singular road had become very congested. Even at low season it was busy, but once we were settled on our pitch, we knew that we could leave the Beast on site and it was an easy bike ride down to the ferry.

We took a cycle ride down to the quayside that evening and rode along the track that led out to the lighthouse. I tried to imagine what it must have felt like all those centuries ago when refugees from the nearby Veneto region had fled to these small islands in the lagoon to escape the pursuing Huns. There they had stayed, on those dank, misty, scraps of land, building their homes on wooden piles driven into the marshy ground. Gradually Venice had grown, eventually becoming a prosperous, independent trading nation, boasting of explorers like Marco Polo, who left from there on his voyage to China.

It continued to flourish until 1797, when it was overthrown by Napoleon, and did not become part of the kingdom of Italy again until 1866.

The sea has been pivotal to its history, helping with early defence and providing a gateway to trade routes with the world. But water may also be its eventual destruction, as it slowly erodes the foundations of the present buildings. Venice looks much the same now as it did in the 13th century, although then, we would have seen the white sails of cargo boats in the harbours and canals instead of the motorboats of today. The huge Venetian lagoon, the largest area of wetland in Italy, is the result of sea currents and tides moving in one direction and water channels laden with sediment moving in the other. Human intervention adds the last dimension. The resulting montage of islands resembles the flat bones of an ancient dinosaur revealed in the water, with Venice at the heart.

Approaching by ferry is the best way to first see Venice, and as we followed the deep-water channels through the blue-green lagoon, pale coloured stone buildings with rusty-red roofs, and the famous pointed tower, all became apparent in the distance, although the cities' flat outline hardly made any difference to the line of the horizon. Our first destination had to be St Marks Square, with its two airy piazzas originally laid out in the 9th century AD. The marvellous architecture of the buildings, which surround these most beautiful squares, is well worth dawdling over and I could have dawdled forever. Delicate, intricately carved and decorated buildings with long, shady loggias, edged the squares while the Campanile (Bell Tower) offers views across the lagoon and the city, to the far off Alps. From this tower Galileo tried out his telescope – I wonder what he saw in those days?

The decorated blue and gold Clock Tower, whose mechanism is a work of art, not only strikes the hour but also indicates the passing of the seasons, the phases of the moon and the movement of the sun from one zodiac sign to another. And rather like Trafalgar Square, St Marks would not be St Marks without the pigeons, which swamped us for our handfuls of corn. But how can you be there and not have a pigeon on your head? They must be the best fed birds in Italy. Dominating it all is the Basilica, the final burial place of St Mark. It would be quite impossible for me to describe this lavish, beautifully proportioned building and its breath- taking interior, or the arched Palace of the Doges which stands alongside it and is the first building you see when you arrive by boat. All I can say is that if you haven't seen Venice, then you must.

I could have spent the rest of the day in the square, gawping at the buildings or just window-shopping for exquisite, unnecessary objects, ridiculously expensive adorable clothes or superb, delicate glass baubles that I wouldn't know what to do with. Oh, if only there had been another female to enjoy all that with me. But I was out-numbered two to one and had no chance, eventually being dragged away by the hand. We moved on to catch the Number 1 vaporetto and ogled the eclectic mix of construction, from gothic to rococo, on palaces, churches and houses that lined the Grand Canal. We had bought the ten-euro tickets that allowed you 'all day' use of the vaporetti (ferry) and traghetto (water buses), which meant that we could travel cheaply and as much as we liked. So, hopping off at the Rialto Bridge, famous for the row of narrow shops that line it, we decided to see more of the city by foot on a route through the back streets of Venice. This is the best way to get a feel for life in this amazing city, although even with a map, it's easy to get lost. If you can imagine that every street and alleyway is flooded with water, with houses whose doors step straight out into that water, then you begin to understand how unusual this city is. Tiny, hunched bridges arch steeply from one island to the next and archetypal gondoliers weave their slim-line, pencil thin boats through slender passages and watery streets.

We passed the Bridge of Sighs, named for the sighing of prisoners as they crossed it on their way to the dungeons, and then detoured to take in an exhibition of scale models that explained some of Leonardo de Vinci's inventions, before eventually returning to catch the ferry back. The next day we did some of it all over again, just for the fun of it. Venice is another absolutely unique city. A constant pleasure to the eye but as usual, even in May, it was busy. In mid summer it would be very hot and very, very busy, and I for one would not want to be there then. Not for all the pigeons in St Marks Square!

We had been on the road now for eight months and we were well settled into life in the motor home. We still missed our family, the other boys and our friends, but we were looking forward to seeing Croatia and Slovenia before starting the home run. We had no idea what we would do when we returned to England, or if indeed we would still return. We phoned home regularly to catch up with everyone's news and nothing seemed to have changed there. Stella would be able to give us a better up-date when we met her in Monza. We were also in touch with John and Gill and their family who we had first met at Easter in Braccianno, Italy. They had got to Dubrovnic and were heading up Croatia, so we agreed to try to meet them half way down that coastline at a later date. Mobile phones make communication so easy when you're travelling. We texted people like Gill and John frequently and Jack was always communicating with his friends back home. It was reasonably cheap and easy to use, but for longer calls we bought the local phone card and used kiosks.

So, leaving Venice, we took a detour inland to Monza, which sits just north of Milan, part of the huge fertile plain bordered by the long stretch of the Alps to the north and west. The National Autodrome of Monza hosts Italy's top automobile racing events, the Formula 1 and Superbikes, but is also used as a test circuit and for walking races. The track was completed in 1928, in record time with a huge workforce, through the initiative of the Automobile Club of Milan; its situation is surprising because it snakes through the woods of Monza Park, an area covering 800 hectares. The park was originally part of the estate belonging to the nearby 'Villa Reale', a stately neo-classical pile, built in the late 1700's by the archduke Ferdinand of Austria, who like many before him, appreciated Monza's countryside and closeness to Milan, the capitol of Lombardy. Today, the park contains not only the impressive Villa Reale (now the civic art gallery and museum), but also the Mirabello horse racing track, two golf courses, a polo field, a public open air swimming pool, a camp site and of course the National Autodrome. It is the cycling, walking and leisure place for the fortunate people of Monza. We were joining up with Simon's sister, as she was one of the co-ordinators of the Historic Grand Prix Car Association races (HGPCA). Cars from the 1920s to 1960s, many with great racing provenance are lovingly pushed to their limits by dedicated enthusiasts at events all over Europe, and we would be lucky enough to attend this one.

We rolled into Monza Autodrome, following directions to the paddock and once again there was Stella, waving us in to park-up alongside the likes of Maserati and Ferrari owners. For months it had been 'just the three of us,' but now suddenly we were literally in the midst of English speaking, fellow Brits, involved in a busy, social weekend. Slightly antiquated racing cars were being tuned-up with ear-splitting results, but after practice time we managed to squeeze in a cycle ride, around the whole race track. Our bikes were once again invaluable at Monza. We could easily ride through the wooded parkland, so cool and tranquil, to reach any of the spectators stands, where we sat in the hot sun and watched the deafening cars come roaring by. If we cycled outside the autodrome area, into the rest of the park, we joined other cyclists, joggers and walkers enjoying a natural environment in this busy city and it was fun to be so sociable again. We squeezed eight people into the motor home for dinner that evening, Simon conjuring up a massive paella. The wine flowed and Stella promised that the next day, she would drive us into Milan in her car and show us the sights.

Milan is huge, the fashion and financial centre of Italy, but luckily, the major sights are all fairly central, and can be reached quite easily by taking the underground trains or walking. We parked on the outskirts, and caught a tube train to see the Duomo. When we got there, it was completely covered with protective material as it was undergoing restoration works, so unfortunately we wouldn't see one of the largest churches in the world, said to be a surprising display of bizarre, gothic design. However, another building, namely the Central Train Station, had already greatly impressed us. Thousands of people travel to and from this station every day and many homeless sleep in it at night. It is a practical building for the people and yet it is heroic in proportion and style. No modest station this, but colossal and heavily faced with strong art nouveau lines in grey stone, elaborated with gargoyle-like faces and huge winged horses, it must be one of the largest and most impressive railway stations in Europe. Outside, set in one wall, a fountain of water gushes from the gaping mouth of a grim, angular face. Inside, vaulted ceilings of glass, towering walls of marble and marvellous carved panels, dwarf the commuters. It was designed in 1912 but not completed until 1931, the time when Mussolini was at the height of his power and it is well worth a look if you are in Milan.

We wandered around the back streets, dodging the cities' orange trams, and after a leisurely pasta lunch at a street cafe, retraced our steps to the Piazza del Duomo and the glorious Galleria Vittorio Emanuel 2nd – a shopping arcade like no other; the absolute opposite to the austere Central Station. If you have the money, then you can spend plenty in the sumptuous shops that line this extraordinary arcade. Golden light floods through the arched, glass and iron roof 96 feet above you, and mosaics in richly coloured marbles lay beneath your feet. The two inter-crossing streets adorned and decorated with statues and sweeping baroque garlands, meet under a stunning central dome of coloured glass. Linking the Piazza Duomo and the La Scala Opera Theatre, this was where the rich paraded at the end of the 19th century. Guiseppi Mengoni designed it, but he tragically fell from the roof of this very beautiful arcade, and died just days before it was due to open.

That evening we dug out some of our vaguely respectable clothes and joined the HGPCA dinner at the luxurious Hotel de la Ville. There we drank champagne and dined like Maseratti owners – very nice if you can get it – and the next day we joined the throngs for Race Day at the track. The noise was deafening, (and that was just the Italian commentator), and the buzz of excitement and enthusiasm rubbed off on us. Strolling amongst the powerful cars, we felt that we were definitely part of the jet set. Another dinner out that evening and then they were all heading home again, so all too soon we were waving goodbye to dear Stella, Martin and the Historic Grand Prix Car Association. They disappeared through the gates, a convoy of trucks, motor homes and friends, leaving just a big empty space and us feeling rather flat and lonely.

So, there we were, just the three of us again, parked up in an empty field in beautiful Monza Park – but the weather was good and the Formula 1 racing car trials were about to begin, so 'here and now' we decided to stay over and watch them. At 9.45 the next morning we were sitting in the almost empty stands opposite the pits while McClaren, Honda, Ferrari, BMW and most of the other famous names, tweaked their cars to perfection before screaming round the track. Each team had their own pit area, well separated from the others by screens and barriers so that no trade secrets could be stolen. The mechanics, in uniform, fifteen to twenty of them at a time, fussed over cars and drivers like mothers over their babies. When the car was rolled out of the pits, the driver was shaded by a large umbrella and supplied with drink through a straw. Heat covers were ready to warm the tyres and final smears of speed reducing dust were removed. Then the stomach churning roar as they revved up and left the pits, reaching a squealing crescendo as they pulled out onto the track and thundered away. Gradually quiet returned, with just a far- away scream of engines as they raced around the park, through the chicanes and down the straights, and an ear-slitting neeeeooooooowwww as they came screaming by again at top speed. Small, powerful and very fast; the earplugs helped, but not a great deal. But then, half the fun is in the excitement of the noise so Jack simply wore his newly acquired Ducatti cap and sunglasses and stayed cool, dismissing the earplugs as things that only boring old farts used. Well, that put me in my rightful place anyway!

side rock or chair that they can find there. We wondered if it was meant to be a sign of great wealth, rather like the Tudor days when a big belly was to be proud of. Their female counterparts were in hot competition with large bosoms, bellies and bottoms to match and we just thanked god that they didn't tend to go naked. After all, much of this coast is designated for naturism. As it was, there were plenty of bikini clad, grossly overweight, overcooked ladies, beached on the rocks. They dominated all sea-front positions with their caravans and tents, boats and trailers and I have to admit that they were the rudest people we had come across on the trip. Maybe it was just a certain nationality and type that you got there. The Croatians were slim, mild mannered and always polite in contrast. Needless to say, we found a quiet pitch, back from the busy beachfront and, as we had arrived on Simon's birthday, we celebrated with a local meal of fresh fish in the excellent camp restaurant.

We planned to spend about a week here, going as far as we could on our bikes and also hiring a small car to explore some of the 360 square miles of the peninsular. Next day we rode along the flat, well-used cycle path that follows the beautiful shore line through the Punta Corrente Forest all the way to Rovinj. Just off shore, serene green islands dotted the clear, clean blue sea and white sailed yachts drifted in and out of bays. Rovinj itself is a charm, set in the jewelled bracelet of the Adriatic; on a high peninsular, next to the sea, it is the prettiest town in Istria. We locked our bikes to yet another lamppost (a useful common denominator in all countries) and walked the stone cobbled streets that were so warm and smooth that I preferred to take my sandals off and go barefoot. There's no doubt that this famous town deliberately attracts tourists but it is a genuinely busy fishing port too; working boats small and large plied back and forth to the harbour and tangled black nets were spread along the wide, waters edge, to be mended in the sun by old, seated, sea-farers. Tourists strolled amongst the restaurants and craft shops and artists captured it all on their carefully composed canvases. Pastel coloured houses, their stonework crumbling and dog-eared, were shuttered against the hot sun and the glare from the deep blue sea. This place, with its relaxed atmosphere, was somewhere that we could have lived quite happily. Above the town, dominating the sky line was the lofty tower of the baroque Saint Euphemia Cathedral; its wide, smooth steps providing a shady resting place for us after the long walk up. Steep, narrow streets of pale Istrian cobbles and dark open doorways, accommodated playing children, and lines of gaily-coloured washing decorated the houses. We wandered back to our bikes and cycled home for a cat-nap before taking an evening ride along the coast the other way. A very pleasant start, to our stay in Croatia.

Simon collected the hire car on the Sunday morning and with sandwiches, coffee flask and a million other things we 'might need,' we spent a day inland. The central Istrian peninsular is a mixture of rolling green highlands and valleys, mainly farmland and woodland, which changes to a fertile plain in the southwest. Northern Istria consists of mountain massifs, which were historically difficult to cross. Most towns and villages were built in circular form on hilltops, for natural defence, and the town of Motovun, perched 270 meters above sea level, is a classic example of this. This fortress town has a magnificent view of the fertile wooded valley of the River Mirna. A chunky stone wall surrounds it and steep cobbled streets, so shiny that they appeared wet, led us through solid stone arches and up to a wonderful open sided, forum. The view from there, across the silent valleys, was utterly peaceful, so we sat on the silky stone benches that ran around the inside of the building, took our sandals off so that we could feel the smooth, warm floor and ate our picnic. The air had that wonderful heat, that when you sucked it deeply into your lungs, seemed to warm right into your bones and relax all your muscles. Lying on the bench with a full stomach, like a well fed puppy, Jack fell asleep, and we almost did the same. Croatia seemed to have the same timeless pace that we had found in Portugal, with none of the franticness of northern Italy.

Arriving back at camp that evening, we unloaded the car and had just grabbed a beer when we heard our names being called out by five people walking towards us. It was the Doherty's; Gill and John with Hannah, Daniel and Sarah, who we had first met at Braccianno in Italy. It was good to see them again and we all immediately took up where we had last left off and exchanged stories and information about our travels. They pitched their caravan and awning next to us and we spent many evenings together before we all moved on again. As I write this, we are still in touch by email. They are in their second year of travelling and have reached Australia, all well and happy. They were the only other English people that we saw on this campsite apart from one man we met, who had a Slovenian wife. We saw no other English motor homes on the roads until we reached Dubrovnic, although there were plenty of French, Italian and German.

The next day we should have used the hire car but we were so tired from a late night, us talking and the kids disappearing on an owl hunt until one in the morning, that we spent the day snorkelling in the clear sea and laying on the rocks. Croatia has very few long sandy beaches, most of the coastline is made up of flat, smooth, sloping rocks that are good to sit and lay on, and a few small sandy coves. Shoals of fish were easy to see when snorkelling and in June the water was warm. Many beaches were designated for naturalists, as was half of our campsite. We got fairly used to suddenly meeting naked people, although Jack would usually do a rapid 'U' turn when he saw them coming – his age, I guess. There was also a fjord close to Rovinj; the 'Limski Zalijev', and Simon, Jack and I had allowed ourselves to be persuaded by Nicky, the camp activity organiser, to join a boat excursion there the next day. This was a first for us – normally we orchestrated our own expeditions, and we soon regretted our rather rash decision.

I feel that all nations have predominant characteristics but I certainly wouldn't denigrate a whole nation just because of the actions of a few. Our boat trip up the fjord could have turned us against one certain nation for life but how foolish would we be to let that happen! We boarded our 'pleasure' boat at 9.30 in the morning, a jolly

Croatian captain and the cook welcoming us on board. They were mild mannered, enduring people. The boat was filled to capacity, and we all sat on benches and around central tables on the open, canopied deck. At 9.45 am we were heading for the fjords and the first of the Schnapps was brought around. We gave that a miss, just a little early in the day for us, but most of the jolly Germans on board, who made up about 90% of the passengers, threw it back with gusto and enthusiasm. Loud, tinny, yo-ho-ho music blared from the overhead tannoys and we realised that this was not quite the informative trip that we were expecting. Apart from us three lone Brits, there were a quiet young Slovenian couple with their small daughter, a few older Italians, and a very large, long haired dog who took up most of the floor space, (and the large German contingent, who now appeared to be all together, or soon were after the Schnapps had gone down.) By 10.30am, plates of ham and bread appeared along with the first of a non-stop supply of rough local wine. Brought out in small crates, one crate per table, with plastic cups to swig it down, it looked like we were in for one long booze cruise with no escape. We groaned, silently of course because we are English, and the German party started up a singsong in competition to the tannoy.

We motored around Rovinj bay and then up the entrance of the fjord where we moored up at a regular tourist spot. Here we all got out to inspect a 'pirates' cave. Well, pirates were certainly running it now, even if they weren't before we got there, because we were fleeced to enter a dingy hole and expected to buy postcards to get out again. Black Beard would have been proud of them. Back on board, wine still appearing from the hold, the singing continued while the cook barbecued fresh sardines on a grill which hung over the stern of the boat, and people took it in turns to don a pirates hat, pipe and eye patch and have their photo taken sitting behind the ships' wheel in the captains chair. We gave up at this point and had some of the wine, hoping to anaesthetise ourselves. Jack declared that he might actually throw himself overboard rather than suffer on the boat, but decided to wait until after the sardines. Half way up the fjord we stopped for lunch. Some people got off and swam from the rocks in the deliciously cool water but others stayed at their tables, unable to move far by now and continued drinking. To be honest, there was very little to see in the geography of the fjord and as no educational information was being provided, you could have had a similar time in the local bar.

The food served was excellent though, and the Croatian hosts were unbelievably polite. Now we turned and headed back, which seemed to be the 'go ahead', for the party to move up a notch. The main contingent, all in about their thirties, now red faced, still drinking and swaying ominously, really got underway and we wouldn't have been surprised if they hadn't started dancing on the tables and slapping their thighs. The small group of older Italians tried to compete with a few nostalgic melodies, but for sheer volume, lasting power and boring repetition, the Germans had it. Of course, being British, we kept quiet. We couldn't think of anything to sing except Robbie

Williams and that didn't seem quite the thing anyway, and we're not sure of the words unless he's singing along with us, so we suffered in silence and Jack said that if he threw himself into the sea, we shouldn't try to rescue him because he might still be alive. The large dog continued to spread himself out on the floor, despite yelping loudly every time he was trodden on. Eventually, at about six o'clock, worn out by the sun, wind and noise we staggered off the boat. The German party, bottles in hand, looking as if they'd spent a week at a beer fest, staggered away too, thank god in the opposite direction. Of course, I wouldn't denigrate a whole nation just because of the actions of a few, but it would be oh, so tempting!

Next day, Jack did the sensible thing and had a day at camp with Gill and John's kids; swimming, playing on lilo's and watching 'Bend it Like Beckham' on the lap top in the comfy air-conditioned peace of the Beast. Why didn't we think of that instead of going off in the hire car again to explore more of Istria. Still, that's adults for you. We worked our way across the peninsular, over Mount Ucka to elegant Rijeka and then returned along the coastal road taking in Opatija en route. This 'old' sea-side resort, the place to be seen before the First World War, still boasts grand, ornate residences which once housed kings, tsars, celebrities and the wealthy. Now turned into elegant hotels these lavish mansions attract wealthy, Italian tourists in the summer and well-heeled elderly Europeans who enjoy quiet warm winters. It had always been the Dalmatian Riviera.

The sparsely populated inland areas, with woods, mountains and flat plains offer wonderful diverse scenery, but the coast is always stunning and the best way to see it would be by boat. That evening we stuffed ourselves at one of the many roadside restaurants which tempted you in by cooking whole suckling pigs, on turning spits over hot coals, at the roadside. The smell was delicious and the price was very reasonable. Agritourism has really taken off in Croatia and everywhere we went we saw signs for rooms to let in family homes and farms. It is their equivalent to B and B and using this accommodation would be an excellent way to travel through the country.

We had the car for two more days and wanted to make the most of it. Early next morning we drove down to the southernmost tip of Istria to the Kamenjak Nature Park. This long narrow peninsular is famous for its untouched, extremely indented coastline, its warm clear seas and the abundance of wild flowers, including several species of orchid. It is also quite rightly called the Terrae Magicae. Clouds of dust followed us as we drove over the dirt roads that led down to the beaches. We chose Kolombarica Beach, with its flat slab rocks which gave easy access to the sea, and there we snorkelled and swam for the day, following shoals of gleaming fish. Swimming round the shore to another area, we found the well-known sea cave whose punctured ceiling allows shafts of sunlight to slant through the clear water. We snorkelled for hours, until we were cold and then went in search of the only watering hole on this quiet peninsular.

Wooden signs pointed the way to a café that remains one of our favourites to this

hunks of soft brown bread and sizzling sausages had never tasted so good.

About half of the National Park is covered with forest; holm oak, holly, and fig, but mostly it is beech and pine. Everything needed, has to be brought up the gorge on pack animals, not just for the café but also for the few remaining residents who are allowed to continue living in their old stone houses higher up on the alpine meadows. We continued upwards, the spectacular Velebit Mountains gradually getting closer and closer and seemingly even higher. Their huge, stone, rock faces shifted colours and shadows, as the sun traversed the clear, blue sky. Eventually, by mid afternoon, we reached the alpine level, a strange contrast of gentle slopes covered with wild sage, thyme and low pretty flowers. The air was fresh here, scented with herbs, and again birds and butterflies were everywhere. Here also was a long, well equipped, mountain hut where you could arrange to spend the night and continue the next day to the peak of Vaganski Vrh at 1757 meters. We would love to do it one day, but at that moment we were simply grateful to stretch out on the benches and fall asleep for half an hour under some shady trees. Beyond the hut, the meadow became hilly again, and almost hidden amongst the trees were scattered a few small, stone farmhouses, some of them built into the rock faces. It was absolutely peaceful up there, completely untouched by modernisation. We saw only one person, a tiny old lady, dressed in black, sitting outside her tumble-down, stone house feeding lean looking chickens, a silent dog by her side, although there was a strange feeling that others might be watching us.

By now we were all suffering. My knees were aching, Jack's feet were killing him and Simon's calve muscles were seizing up, and we still had the long hike back down. The return walk gave us superb views of the gorge and, as the sun was dropping low in the sky, the towering cliffs were a kaleidoscope of colours. Half way down we stripped off and swam in a deep, cool pool of icy water, which was constantly filled by a crystal clear waterfall. Back at our bikes, we just about managed to freewheel down to the campsite where, too tired to cook, we ate in a restaurant – we were so weary that we wondered if they could carry us home to our beds. Paklenica Gorge was well worth it though and would be just as stunning in winter. We can't wait to go back one day and walk it again.

Next day we struggled to do anything, other than sitting on the beach watching a large, spotted toad as he scuffed out a cool hole under the low beach wall. It was a scorchio day and he was having none of it. Eating ants in the shade was his idea of heaven, so we lay on our towels and idly watched him work while we thought about our next destination, namely Krka National Park.

Dubrovnik and Croatia's Gems

Krka National Park (pronounced Kurka), is situated in Sibenik and Knin county about half way down the coast towards Dubrovnik. We arrived a few kilometres from it on the following evening, after a steady drive and a huge risotto lunch at a quiet beach side café. We ate out more in Croatia than anywhere else, mainly because the food was so good and so cheap. There were few opportunities to wild camp, so that night we pulled into a local families' camping field (agri-tourism in action), and paid about £3 each for a nights stay with use of shower and toilets if required. Tourism is undeniably important, as the wife explained to us that evening. They owned a small herd of cows and some chickens, which they raised on the old family farm. The barn buildings were solid but basic and the family were obviously not affluent. They had two children and her mother lived with them too; she was busy hoeing the large, well-tended vegetable patch in their modest garden. The wife explained that her husband had recently been made redundant from the local fabrication factory and now they had to make a go of the camping field. To supplement their earnings she got up at 4.am every morning to deliver her eggs, milk and cheese to the market in Sibenik. It didn't look an easy life and they didn't have the usual trappings of European wealth, but Croatia is still emerging from a difficult recent history. It has come a long way, and so far has retained an unaffected, natural charm and pride. It was a blessed relief to visit three of its most important National Parks, and some of its major attractions and never, ever, be hassled or harassed by money- grabbing, touting taxi drivers, guides or salesmen, as we had been in some other countries. Yet tourism is their main source of income.

Early next morning we said goodbye to the friendly campsite owners and drove on down a descending road until we reached a large car park by the wide river at Skradin. There are two ways of entering Krka Park; either by road at the top or by boat at the bottom. The boat trip up the river was a great way to approach it.

The Krka National Park was proclaimed the seventh national park of Croatia in 1985 and encompasses an area of 109 square miles along the River Krka. From its source at the base of the Dinaric Mountains the river drops 242 meters to the sea, and it includes areas of unusual, preserved ecosystems. It is exceptionally rich in varied flora and fauna, with eight hundred and sixty species and sub-species of plants recorded growing in the park and eighteen kinds of fish, including ten endemic species, living in the river. The reed beds and water meadows are alive with amphibians and water birds, and reptiles abound in the shrubby, dry, stony areas. The majority of visitors, including us, only see the spectacular travertine cascades, but there would be much more to see if you wished.

These famous cascades and small waterfalls have evolved over thousands of years by a series of rather complicated and unique physiochemical factors. The river passes through terrain that consists mostly of limestone. As the limestone is dissolved it leaves calcium carbonate in the water, which under certain circumstances, remains as undissolved particles. As these particles have passed along the river, aquatic mosses have retained them, and that has caused a gradual build up of rocky, travertine layers. What you see now are a series of seven travertine waterfalls, created by limestone sediments, covered with mosses and water plants.

The first ferry left the small dock at Skradin at nine o'clock in the morning and we were aboard with our food, drinks, swimming costumes and towels. (Take swimming costumes and jelly shoes with you if you can, because you will have the opportunity to swim at the falls.) The wide river spread like a mill pond ahead of us and reflected perfectly the sloping, wooded hills either side of the valley and one small white cloud in the clear sky. The morning sun had not yet risen above the hilltops and was just a pale hint of the day to come. We motored up the river, which gradually narrowed, past quiet fishermen who silently watched us as we chugged by. Huge, darting dragonflies skimmed the water's surface and the dark silhouettes of fish disappeared before our eyes down into the greeny-blue depths. At length we reached a wooden jetty close to a small wood. Here we disembarked and walked up through shady trees suddenly emerging into the sunlight, with the cascading falls ahead of us. White, frothing water sprayed over the bright green, moss-covered travertine rocks, layer upon layer, as far back as we could see, and a thin mist rose up from the torrent, the sun now making it all glisten and sparkle. The path ahead led to a low, wooden boardwalk, which guided us meandering for hours over waterfalls and clear pools, through shady areas and open vistas. The water was consistently perfectly clear, often with shoals of basking fish only inches away from our fingertips. Long, thin, water snakes slid amongst the reeds; frogs, large and small, gathered everywhere and fat green lizards sat by their holes in the sun. Small blue damselflies flitted from one plant to the next and we spent the whole day simply wandering through this amazing and unique river habitat. We weren't alone; crocodiles of brightly capped little children and other wandering families were there too, but it wasn't too busy. There were no hawkers or traders and, like all the national parks we visited in Croatia, the facilities for tourists were kept as natural and simple as possible.

At the end of the walk was Skradinski Buk, a massive, clear, natural pool with quite high waterfalls at one end and cascades at the other. Here, most people had donned their costumes and were thoroughly enjoying a cooling swim. Kids were playing in and out of the waterfalls, which we could all stand behind, and one daredevil young man was diving off the top of some high rocks. A lifeguard paddled around in a rubber boat, just to keep an eye on things and we got our costumes on and joined in. Jack absolutely loved swimming in this natural environment and messing about in the falls. I just couldn't see this happening in England, even if we had the weather. Coffee, beer, ice-creams and barbecue meals were all available from the open air café, but believe it or not there were no gimmicky tourist shops selling ghastly, plastic replicas of squeaking frogs or rubber fish or waterfalls. It was as natural as it could be whilst still allowing visitors to enjoy it.

We caught the 5.30 pm ferry back to Skradin and walked the few steps to the car park and motor home. Jack flopped there, guarding the van while Simon and I explored Skradin itself. A quiet town with a central square, where chatty groups of little girls played at pushing their dolls around in prams, imitating the strolling young mothers and babies. In a shaded open bar, football was showing on a large screen watched by the laid-back husbands, each with a beer in front of them, and little boys, brown skinned and dark haired, in clean bright T-shirts and shorts, kicked their football around practicing for the Croatian football team. On the corner of the square, three workmen in blue overalls worked on into the evening to erect a large, ornate street lamp. The smart new marina held expensive, white yachts and gleaming motorboats which had come up from the coast. Behind the waterfront, just one street back, the brightness faded, the streets looked poorer, the houses marked with old bullet holes sprayed into the plaster; new paint and even new plaster being an unaffordable luxury. The affluence of the front marina hadn't quite reached beyond the harbour. In one doorway, two little boys had hand painted shells for sale on a small rickety table, while a grandmother sat knitting close by. I couldn't resist of course, and my dull green, splodgily painted little shell will always remind me instantly of Skradin and the fits of giggles that the boys disintegrated into as they tried to negotiate a sale. I can see them to this day.

Early next morning I took a short walk over to a church across the road. The ornate iron gates to the cemetery were open and I walked in, curious about the history of this area. A few people had died in the most recent war and some graves were sprayed with gunfire, as was the church. Some nameplates had been removed and small, basic wooden crosses had been put in place. It was a vivid reminder that we were close to the Bosnian border. For the next two days we drove on down the coast of Croatia, wild camping wherever we could at night, heading for Dubrovnik.

The weather was hot now, 25 – 27 degrees, so we were up and on the road early every morning, and as the road still hugged the sea shore, we stopped on both days in deserted coves, to swim and snorkel at lunch time, and then take a short siesta before we headed on again. We passed the big islands of Brac, Hvar and Korcula, baking under the sun, and stopped to buy fresh vegetables and fruit from roadside stalls. The coast was sparsely populated, with small, low level towns and villages; clusters of fishermen's cottages nestled in niches, each with its own jetty. The exception to this was busy Split, whose tower blocks and sprawling development reached right back into the foothills of the mountains. As we neared Dubrovnik it gradually began to look more affluent, and the red roofed houses were replaced by restored white villas. I can only hope that as Croatia becomes more popular it does not lose its new found peace and natural beauty.

Dubrovnik is heralded by a rather wonderful, modern bridge, which spans the wide, deep fjord that you must cross or go around to reach the city. We got caught up in a small convoy of French motor-caravans as we trundled over this bridge and eventually all ended up in the same lay-by like Barnum's travelling circus. We had a camp-site in mind, as there would be nowhere to wild camp, and without too much trouble we found it and pulled into the entrance area. Simon jumped out and was about to walk to the campsite office when he spotted that one of our back tyres was rapidly deflating. Luckily the back wheels were doubles, so we were able to limp onto a pitch before making another of those calls to euro-assistance. Changing our own tyres was impracticable on the Beast as they were the size of lorry tyres and we could never have jacked it up anyway. However after some problems getting a jack man-enough for the job, (we needed a ten ton jack, not a four ton jack), a good natured garage owner took the old tyre to his garage, repaired it and brought it back good as new. Simon and he worked hard under the baking hot sun to re-fit the tyre and eventually all was ok. We took a look around the campsite, which was not awe-inspiring for such a major town, but adequate, and I hit the laundrette with four loads of washing, which dried in an instant on our washing line between the trees. This was a large site, not very busy, but there were a few other GB plates here and we briefly met a few other English and American travellers. It looked like everyone had ended up down in this small corner of Croatia. The camp had great beach access though and the wonderful views across the sea to a small island meant that the sunsets from here were picture-postcard perfect.

We made a rule not to overdo it on the first day in Dubrovnik, so next morning we caught the number six bus and got off at Pile Gate which is the main entrance to the old town. This arched gate, with its heavy wooden drawbridge, is set in an immense city wall that is completely intact and encircles the entire old city in over two kilometres of solid stone, up to twenty-five meters high. Built into the wall are also two enormous round towers, fourteen square towers, a large fortress and two smaller corner fortresses. It is said to be the best example of a walled city in the world and it certainly is very, very impressive.

Invaders approaching from the sea must have been quite daunted by the thought of attacking such a solid defence, but even so, Ragusa (as it was called until 1918) has been invaded many times in ancient and recent history. Its geographical position made it extremely desirable, especially once it had grown into the most powerful trading centre in the Southern Mediterranean, with a large fleet of merchant and war ships equalled only by Venice. As a result of earthquakes and various wars the city has been partially destroyed and rebuilt several times. It has been over-run and occupied, including during the Second World War, first by the Italian army and then by the Germans. Its troubles didn't end there though, because in1991 during the collapse of Yugoslav Federation, it was attacked by the Serb-Montenegrin army and was under siege for seven long months. In May 1992 the Croatian army liberated it, although it was not free of all conflict for another three years. Subsequently, yet another re-building programme had to be organised as almost two thirds of the city had been severely damaged by shelling.

The city is being re-built in a massive restoration project, adhering strictly to re-placing like with like, rather than designing a new Dubrovnik. The replacement of old materials is a daunting challenge, particularly when it comes to finding enough of the uniquely honey-coloured roof tiles which are a dominant feature of the skyline. The need to reconstruct has enabled the architects to build-in some provision for future earthquakes and hopefully the city is stronger now than it has ever been before. Tourism was badly hit after the war ended, but now this truly handsome, restored city attracts many visitors and it is definitely back on the tourist trail.

So, now we had come through the Pile Gate and were standing just inside the city walls. The massive Onofrio Fountain (1438) was just before us and beyond that stretched the long, wide promenade with its smooth-as-silk, polished marble pavement. In perfect symmetry down either side, light coloured stone buildings, four stories high with arched doorways and shuttered windows offered a little welcome shade and res-taurants with brightly striped awnings tempted strollers to stop for a coffee. No traffic is allowed within the city walls so it is a pedestrian's heaven. We three strolled down to the end of the Placa and viewed the elaborate baroque-style St Blaises' Church. After that we just wandered, eating ice cream as we went, stopping to take an ice cold drink at a carved marble fountain and enjoy lunch at a street café. This small city has a great feeling of spaciousness, even with tourists around, because the main thor-oughfares and squares are very generous and all stonework has a wonderful luminosity. Smaller, steeper, cobbled streets radiate off the main area and lead up into the labyrinth of old houses and flats rented by locals. Washing lines hang high above narrow alleys and children play in the shade, giving it a quiet but very 'lived in' feel. Unfortunately property prices have risen astronomically in recent years and investors own most of Dubrovnik now, making it the most expensive real estate in Croatia. We caught the bus back to camp in the stifling heat of mid-afternoon and went down to the beach for a swim in the bay. The next day we would walk the walls.

Up with the larks, we were soon back at Pile gate to start exploring while it was still cool. We entered the peaceful city once more, and climbed the narrow, stone steps which led almost vertically up to the top of the city wall. At the small payment kiosk we hired headsets from a chatty, young American student – (it's a small world and students seem to hop through countries with the greatest of ease). The path around the top of the walls can be as much as six meters wide; although in most places it was around two meters, with constant changes in height and direction, as it wove its way around the uneven perimeter. The famous honey coloured roof tiles spread out below us, with slight variations in colour showing clearly where damage had been repaired. Views down into thin dark alleyways, small courtyards and spacious squares were revealed within, while without were the harbour and the blue, open sea. The temperature up on that exposed walkway was rapidly rising, and after a while we were crouching for a rest in any shade that we could find. Jack had a cotton handkerchief draped from the back of his cap, giving him a very foreign legion look, and we pitied the poor soldiers who had once spent long hours on this battlement, watching the horizon for tell tale white sails. We walked the whole circumference and it took us the best part of two hours. As city walls go it must be one of the most beautiful; its light, smooth, stone, curved towers and stunning views giving it grace and elegance.

That evening, when it had cooled down, we went up to the campsite bar and joined Richard and Louise, a young couple from England. The UEFA Cup football match was on again, England versus Portugal, and a small crowd had gathered to sit under the stars and watch the sport. It went to a nail biting penalty kick-off and Portugal eventually won a well-played and most enjoyable game. Richard was surprised but not upset; he was a fervent Arsenal fan, never missing a game he said, but he obviously enjoyed all football. The following evening we watched Greece beat the favourites, France. Richard and Louise had moved on, but we guessed that they would have found a bar somewhere, to stop and watch the match.

Lovely as it was, we were ready to leave Dubrovnik. The temperature had suddenly soared up to the mid thirties, and by nine o'clock in the morning it was almost too hot to move. Jack, with his ginger hair and fair skin, had got rather sunburned when he'd been swimming without a T-shirt on and we needed to find some cooler weather. We had gone as far south as we were going, we would now start heading north, eventually crossing back to England. We were going to drive up through inland Croatia and then into Slovenia. We would wild camp en route, and reckoned that the next stop would be Plitvicka, the third and last national park on our list.

Our wild camp, on the way up to the Park, was in a lay-by beside a long, thin lake, Pervcko Jezero. We were on an inland road that ran between the coast and the border of Bosnia Herzegovina. This countryside was all on a huge scale; huge mountains, huge plains and huge empty spaces; the scrub covered land occasionally dotted with red-roofed angular houses, either in small clusters or standing alone. Throughout this area the results of war were still to be seen in the bullet strafed, burnt out shells of deserted homes. Sometimes they were isolated houses, sometimes in small groups and sometimes just one house damaged amongst many undamaged, occupied ones. We rolled on down the almost deserted road, watching the scenery unfold as we ate up the miles. Occasionally we would see old ladies, dressed from head to foot in black, carrying big bunches of greenery. They walked resolutely, with heads down, though not a house could be seen for miles and we always wondered where they had come from and where they were going. It looked as if time had slowed to a halt in this dramatic scenery. We journeyed passed farmers in their fields using pronged wooden hay-forks to gather hay into loosely stacked cones, drying it in the sun in pointed stacks. Occasionally we'd pass an isolated road side stall where a patient lady sat under the shade of a large umbrella, hoping to sell a round of cheese or some homemade honey. With few tourists around, they weren't doing a roaring trade.

By early afternoon we'd reached Plitvicka National Park and had pulled into the spacious coach parking area, where we made ourselves a quick lunch before walking round to the entrance. In my diary I have written that this is yet another of Croatia's little wonders - but I should say big wonders. Declared a National Park in 1949, it was entered into the UNESCO World Heritage List in 1979. Sixteen lakes of crystal clear, blue-green water are connected to each other by cascades and spectacular waterfalls, which were all naturally created by the same process of lime deposition on mosses, as we had previously seen at Krka National Park. This is all situated amongst 266 square kilometres of verdant vegetation, wooded hillsides and craggy gorges of pale rock. Eighteen kilometres of low, wide, wooden walkways and footpaths carry you only inches from tumbling, churning water and the damp cooling mists of lofty waterfalls. There are very few barriers or handrails, so you feel very much part of this river valley.

There were various routes to explore, but as it was already late afternoon we bought our tickets and chose to catch a ferry boat across one of the lower lakes. The path then led us alongside the water to reach a point where we could catch a Park bus back to the entrance and a fantastic view down onto the turquoise coloured waters in the gorge. At the top of the lake you could hire a rowing boat and drift alongside some of the tumbling streams which cascade through thick, green vegetation. So, late as it was, we had to hire one, and Jack rowed us out onto the lake, a perfect reflection of the surrounding hillsides – and then attempted to sink us by trying to get my end of the boat under a waterfall. Well, that's what boys do I guess. It would be much too boring to just row a boat, and Jack was anything but boring. He had been travelling with us for ten months now and knew how to make the most of every day. Before much longer he would be back behind a desk pushing a pen, not rowing a boat across a lake in one of Croatia's beautiful national parks. We caught the almost empty bus down to the entrance again and then drove the motor home a short distance to Autocamp Korano, where we stayed for that night – and another two after that.

The best time to see the lakes was early in the morning, when there were few other people around and it was cool and quiet. We were now at the end of June and, even inland, it was getting very, very warm. We were up by seven o'clock next morning, and had driven back to the National Park by eight thirty. We left the Beast in the coach parking area again and caught the first available bus up to the second lake area. At the upper lake we took one of the small electric and very sedate ferry boats across the water and then walked the Upper Lakes and Falls. I feel almost embarrassed to tell you that we spent ten hours on this walk, probably the record breaker for overdoing it. Definitely 'here and now'. At first we followed the board-walks over waterfalls and clear lakes where fish swarmed in shoals at the surface of water clear enough to drink from. We passed endless frogs, camouflaged in croaking choruses, and damsel flies and dragonflies imitating mini Harrier jump jets; then we turned away from the lakes and took the path through dappled beech woods from where we glimpsed the occasional view down into the water-filled gorge. The usual green and brown lizards basked in dust, almost too lazy to move as we walked by, and shield bugs and beetles we saw by the score. No wolves or bears – but then, the park is so big that they would be mad to come anywhere near the tourists. We did see a horned viper though, being heckled by a fierce little robin, until he eventually glided away into the undergrowth.

Our route-march eventually took us back to the ferry and then down to the lower lakes again. I was almost asleep on the boat, I now felt so tired. The towering water falls, with great view-points alongside them, had to be explored though, until we had eventually 'done it all'. We would love to visit the superb parks of Croatia again; they shine in summer, would be a glorious show of colours in autumn and stunning in winter with the edge of frost and deep snow. They are well signed and well priced, (a one day ticket is valid for three days as long as you stay in the area), but we by now, were well exhausted! Back at camp we just about managed to rustle up some tinned sardines and salad before we all fell into bed, waking in the night to a fantastic display of thunder, lightening and torrential rain. At least that would cool the air down a little which would be good, although we were now going to move on, heading inland towards Zagreb and then to another place which had definitely caught our eye – a little-known town called Varazdin.

Varazdin and into Slovenia

Turning away from the coast, heading inland, we wouldn't see the sea again until we reached Northern France and Brittany in early autumn. As we approached Zagreb the mountains and gorges slid behind us and we entered a very English looking landscape of rolling hills and green plains. It became more populated, although you could hardly say over-developed; more cars were on the roads and there were often queues of elderly locals waiting at bus stops along the route. Being the same size and shape, we were often mistaken for the local bus and people would put out their hands to try and stop us; we even got the impression that if we slowed down too much we would have them all climbing on board pressing kuna into our palms and asking to be dropped off at the market – so we drove on by rapidly and waved apologetically, leaving them looking a bit puzzled. The houses, with red pan-tiled roofs as always, were now chalet style and the whole area had a more alpine appearance. Everywhere was neat and tidy; wooden bal-conies edged with red geraniums, immaculate gardens with trim lawns and full flower beds. I was always prodding Jack to look out of the window, but he spent a large part of this particular journey making moving objects out of wine corks, wooden kebab sticks and rubber bands. His allotted cupboard space had filled up months ago with books, tapes, models, drawings and weird and wonderful pebbles, sticks and fossils. Luckily we had masses of storage space on the Beast, both inside and out. My storage area was filling with odd mementoes and masses of literature. Simon's had our travelling library of reading books and maps. The huge space under our bed held our pantry of staple foodstuffs and all of our un-seasonable clothes, most of which hadn't been worn. We had skis, boots and ski suits, flippers, snorkels, surfboards, kites, badminton and ten-nis racquets, balls – in other words the toy department, in outside lockers, along with repair tools, motor spares, wine, cartons of fruit juice – well just about everything you would keep in a house. Our three bikes were strapped on the back of course. It's always surprising how quickly we humans can gather 'stuff' to fill all available spaces.

Anyway, we motored on, boycotting Zagreb as we didn't feel up to another major city, and reached Varazdin late in the afternoon. Circling the town on the main road, we eventual spotted what looked like the overflow car park of a useful supermarket. Simon managed to squeeze down some small backstreets to find the entrance, and there we parked, tucked behind a huge billboard advertising Rovinj, which almost hid us completely. It wasn't the most salubrious of wild camps, beside a busy road and a housing estate, but it would do for us. Yet again, as everywhere we travelled, we were left in peace, even though we didn't exactly blend in with our surroundings. We all had a shower, one of the luxuries of the motor home, and then went for an evening walk around Varazdin.

I'll never forget this town, and if there was ever somewhere that I would like us to spend one complete year in, enjoying every season, then this would be the place. It seemed to hold something for everyone. Once a strategic crossing point of Roman roads, it went on to become an important administrative and cultural centre and a favourite haunt of political high flyers. It prospered and grew, providing work for artisans and masons who left their mark on the baroque style, stucco decorated buildings, pleasant open squares, ornamental gardens, mansions, town hall, tower and castle. It's also famous for its music school and music festivals and is home to the Croatian National Theatre. It has a vibrant, youthful feel, like a small university town, with cafes spilling onto streets and cyclists of all ages, from children to grandparents, criss-crossing the squares on bikes of all sizes and design, in fact this is a town of cyclists – with around 22,000 bicycles in a town of 43,000 inhabitants. I would love to get to know this town a little better. I could imagine the stone buildings and pretty squares covered in snow on a winter's eve with warm lively pubs, open fires and festivities in the streets; or flowers in spring and fresh green leaves on the trees surrounding the castle; or autumn days, when smoke from wood fires would settle over the town. I guess I'm just an old romantic at heart, but one day – one day, I would love us to live for one year in Varazdin.

For now though, we had just a couple of days to see the sights and find the acclaimed entomology museum that we had seen advertised. That summer evening we joined with everyone else, and strolled the elegant old streets of small shops, many of which were open due to the custom of taking a long lunch and opening again late afternoon. The central square was busy with local families, meeting at the pavement cafes, and, like the Italians, an amazing number of men, women and children were eating ice-cream. There was a wide range of flavours and a huge scoop of this rich and creamy specialty only cost twenty pence. We consulted our local map and guide book and eventually found 'The Golden Goose' where we ate a slap-up, three course meal each, including wine for about thirty-five pounds. A real treat for us.

That night was swelteringly hot again and we didn't sleep very well. Even so, we had found the local market by 8.30 next morning and were soon buying fresh produce. The market holders appeared to be all locals, mostly ladies dressed in wrap-around overalls and sensible shoes, who stood behind long trestle-like tables in a covered arcade, with their freshly picked vegetables, fruit and flowers laid out before them; broad beans, new potatoes, big hearty lettuces, gypsophila, lilies, dahlias and a whole heap of camomile flower heads. Meat, fresh bread, and home made wines; the sight and smell was a joy to the senses and I doubt if any of it had travelled more than ten miles and a few hours from production to sales. One whole building was devoted to cheeses and eggs, and all heads turned our way as we entered, being the only obvious tourists around, in fact the only customers in the building at that time. With some embarrassment we walked up and down the silent aisles, admiring one display after another but feeling incredibly self-conscious as we tried to decide what to buy from whom..... we were surely going to upset quite a few people in there. Eventually one forthright lady collared us as we approached her wares, and before I knew it she had my arm in hers, and was dollopping a splodge of soured cream onto the back of my hand from a ladle. She mimed for me to lick it off, to taste its good flavour, which I willingly did, while my bag of tomatoes cascaded to the floor. Jack started for the exit, guessing that this was going to go from bad to worse and Simon soon followed him, (rats up a drain pipe came to mind), while I struggled to gather the escaping tomatoes, juggle with a kilo of cherries and buy a huge lump of feta cheese from the lady. The other stall holders looked on probably wondering what the hell I was going to do with it all.

Following our town map, Jack led us to the unpretentious, well worn exterior of the Entomology Museum. There were no opening hours displayed and the door was locked, so we rang the bell and waited. A cleaning lady opened the door and explained that she was still busy with mop and bucket on the stone floors and could we return in half an hour. In some places this would have seemed annoying but somehow, in Croatia, where the pace of life is much more laid back, we didn't mind in the least. We went off in search of a cup of coffee and an internet café to collect and send our emails and found both in an open fronted bar, somewhat 'gay' in its orientation. Unfortunately, the internet connection was so flaky that we merely picked up our messages and then sat for a while nursing cups of coffee in the square while we watched the world cycle by. Simon read aloud from the information we had about the intriguing legacy of Franjo Koscec; teacher, scientific researcher, entomologist, inventor, draughtsman and famous citizen of Varazdin, because the entomology museum is based around his lifetimes work.

Koscec settled in Varazdin, teaching biology, chemistry and physics at the local grammar school. He was also a committed scientific researcher and had collected and catalogued thousands of insect specimens over several decades, eventually totalling as many as 70,000. He collected mostly in the greater Varazdin area, in the meadows and forests around the Drava River and in the nearby mountains. For many years he documented the fauna of the area, and the copious notes and diagrams provide a fascinating insight into the effects of social development, food production, transport, industry, tourism and insecticides upon the insect world. This quiet unassuming man was involved in the funding of the town museum in 1925 and, along with friends, developed a framework of societies to educate the people of the town. The small, beautifully laid out museum, explains the biology of insects, their irreplaceable necessity for the future of man and presents a historical overview of his work as founder of the entomology section.

We finished our coffee in the square, returned to the old baroque Herzer Palace where the museum is situated and walked into the shaded, arched entrance. We rang the bell, were soon admitted and led up a flight of stone steps to the upper floor. There the English speaking curator sold us a family ticket for about £5 and encouraged us to –"wander, explore and discover – you are the only visitors today". A polished, intricately designed parquet floor complimented the floor to ceiling, pale wood display drawers and glass fronted cases. The beauty of this museum was not just the interesting exhibits, but also the exquisite presentation, personally and lovingly designed by Koscec. Every perfect drawer, that smoothly slid open, revealed immaculately displayed families of insects, ranging from death's-head moth and blow fly to ladybird, aphid and locusts. Every developmental stage was explained with exhibits, along with habitat and life cycle. Glass sided cases had enlarged cross-section models of the detailed insect world to explain the most significant phenomena of their lives. We wandered for several hours through these fascinating rooms, before emerging again onto the streets and heading off to find the next item on our agenda, namely the moated castle in the 'Stari Grad' or 'Old Town' area.

A high, grassy embankment surrounds this white washed, lovingly preserved example of a mediaeval fortress, which once defended the region from invading Ottoman Turks. But, with its softly rounded towers, gracious courtyards and wide, three storey corridors it resembles a story book castle rather than a fortress. Once again, out of season, we had the place to ourselves and after paying a modest entrance fee a quiet young assistant led us on a guided tour explaining everything in excellent English. The castle is a living museum, furnished as a home with paintings, furniture, household items, decorative objects and weapons from Varazdin's past. By the end of the tour I felt that we had struck up a good enough relationship with our guide for me to ask him a question which had often been on our minds as we had travelled through Croatia. I wanted to know how he felt about the fairly recent war and how he saw the future of his country. We had a short awkward silence when I asked this, and I wondered if I had overstepped the mark. He chose his words of explanation carefully, and said that he was proud of his beautiful country but that many Croatians were embarrassed and sad that such a vicious war had happened; they no longer talk about it and look forward to a brighter future. The subject was closed and we said our thanks and walked out into the bright warm sunshine. We felt that he had conveyed more in the words left unsaid than in any long diatribe that he could have given us – it was in the past, it was time to move on.

Outside in the castle grounds, under the shade of leafy trees, we flopped onto park benches and indulged yet again in cones of ridiculously cheap, creamy ice-cream. I finished mine and lay down on the bench with my eyes shut, listening to the local sounds. Church bells rang out the hour, ducks quacked on the nearby pond, and the gravel paths softly crunched with the feet of occasional passers-by and the rhythmic tick of bicycles. The warm air filled our lungs and seeped into our bones. Maybe it was Varazdin that had seeped into mine.

Eventually, we headed back to the motor home. Varazdin would have had much more to offer, with festivals, theatre, music and sport just for starters, but July was just around the corner and once again we had to move on. So, after a quick shower each, we pulled out from behind our big, protective bill-board and started off in search of somewhere closer to the Slovenian border to wild camp for the night. Several hours and failed attempts later, we realized that a wild camp area was going to be hard to find. A small garage, on a long country road, looked like a possibility so we pulled in and asked the owner if he knew of anywhere. He explained, as best he could, that we couldn't park at his garage but, after a quick discussion with his mate, he jumped into his car and signalled for us to follow him down the road. We trundled behind and were soon guided down a side street in the next village and into an empty parking area, which I'm sure we wouldn't have spotted without his help. The wide river Mura, which denotes the Slovenian border, flowed along next to the car park and the border crossing was just down the road. This was a great find and it even included some evening enter-tainment for Jack, because within ten minutes of our arrival, a group of teenagers had drifted, one by one, into the car park. Each carried or scooted on a skate board; well used ramps and jumps were pulled out of hiding places and like teenagers the world over they spent the evening practising their skateboarding techniques and 'hanging out'. That night it rained heavily, which after the heat of the previous days was a pleasure to hear. We woke at around mid-night with the rain drumming on the roof and saw that this car park on the Slovenian border, like many others in Europe, was a meeting place for amorous young car owners. All very quiet though and no hint of trouble.

Next morning, with English-style drizzle still coming down, we checked our maps and crossed into Slovenia. We didn't have GPS discs (Global Positioning System) for Slovenia, so Maisy would be taking a rest for a while. On slightly bumpy, rather narrow roads we headed for the most northern corner of the Pannonian plain to a town called Murska Sobota. It was a bit like driving through the English countryside of the 1950's, before tourism took over, except that the neat, flowered-decked houses had roll-down shutters at the windows, cycle paths were frequent and storks nested on the top of most telegraph posts. Grey haired ladies in floral, ever-fashionable, wrap-around aprons, cycled slowly to the corner shops on sturdy black bikes, while holding umbrellas over their heads, and all was quiet.

Slovenia is a small country, sitting in central Europe, with Italy and Austria on the west and north, and Croatia and Hungary on the south and east. Its only coastline giving access to the Adriatic Sea is just 46 kilometres long. Slovenia has always been a gateway to the Balkans and has a widely diverse landscape - from the mountainous Alps and Dinaric ranges to the Pannonian plains and because of its geographical diver-sity the climate covers three prevailing types: Alpine, Continental and Mediterranean, with temperatures ranging from -26C to 38C. Forests cover half of Slovene territory and there are many natural parks where wild life, including lynx and brown bear, is protected. Perhaps the most famous is the Triglav National Park situated in the central region of the Julian Alps, with Mount Triglav as the highest mountain at 2,864 meters. In this small country it only takes a matter of hours to travel from towering snow covered mountains to vine covered plains or the blue sea of the Adriatic, and the Slovenes make the most of it all by being great weekenders.

We reached our destination, which was a large Spa campsite at Moravske Toplice in the Mura Region. There are fifteen Spa's in this country, most situated in the Pannonian area, where natural thermal and mineral waters flow up to the surface. The mineral waters have been drunk for centuries and the thermal bathing waters, which vary from 32 to above 73 degrees, have long been popular with locals and tourists. The Spa's have developed big leisure complexes with hotels, golf courses, restaurants and swimming pools and the site that we had chosen had all of these. We had decided to make it our base camp while we hired a car and explored this corner of Slovenia.

Parking-up was easy, with plenty of room on a flat, grassy area. It was still raining hard but we didn't feel like sitting in the motor home for the afternoon so we grabbed our swimming costumes, got out the umbrella and walked across the camp site to explore the swimming pool complex. The water which feeds this resort springs from a depth of around 1300 meters at a minimum of 72 degrees centigrade, containing sodium chloride and hydrogen carbonate. When you visit this Spa, the brochure assures you that, quote "a world of aquatic pleasure and joy awaits you, and in the 'comfly' and warm cradle of life a thought dawns on you spontaneously... into the blue I will be rocked!" Which all sounded pretty good to us! On looking through the brochure we saw that if we went golfing we should expect this experience, "While the 'storch' makes a loud smack with its long beak, you will feel like singing these words... into the green I am going to wrap myself!" We weren't too sure about that one. So much is gained in translation, hey!

The pool complex was great, with twenty-two interconnecting, indoor and outdoor pools. These varied from small Jacuzzi to Olympic size and from warm to very, very hot; from quite clear water, to water which resembled hot, salty, oily mud. Four water slides, including one that was a vertical 'free-fall' and another that sent you down 170 meters of twirling tube from a great height, kept Jack amused for hours and even in the rain we enjoyed it. Swimming from the indoor pools through small passageways, we reached the outside pools of very hot water, water falls and swirling whirlpools. From there we got out and walked across to the round 'mud' pool, which apparently eased muscular and rheumatic ailments. Entering this was rather like stepping into a shoulder-deep, muddy, smelly, slightly gritty, water-hole. All around the edge of this pool men and women, mostly the senior variety, were lined up with their backs to the wall looking very serious, if not downright depressed. This was obviously not meant to be a happy or enjoyable experience. Maybe they'd all just got the bill for staying at the hotel, or they all had horrible diseases or they were all a 'certain nationality'. Anyway, we didn't stay long in that pool, in case we caught a case of the miseries ourselves.

The rain had cleared by next morning and sunny blue skies had returned. I cycled into town for fresh bread and a look at the tourist office. We would hire a car for Monday morning, which gave us the weekend to relax beforehand. Green lawns surrounded the pool complex and sun beds were provided free, so we took our books and sun cream and actually relaxed for two days while Jack made friends with two Slovenian boys and spent six hours a day in the pools enjoying himself. An Austrian family, in a caravan near to us, became weekend friends and we joined the many Germans, Austrians and Slovenians, young and old, taking a break at the Spa. It made a good start to our stay in this country.

Over the next three days we drove our hire car around the wooded hills and flat, open, cultivated valleys of the Mura region. We had a great feeling of space in this immaculate, well-organised corner of the country. Close to Hungary and Austria, the stone houses, with neatly stacked log piles and huge tidy bundles of kindling wood, had a very rural feel. The roads were quiet, but it certainly didn't feel 'poor'. German was definitely the second language and we saw no other English travellers. Slovenia's recent history is one of domination and communist control within the old Yugoslav Federation, but in 1992 it was recognised by the EC and UN as an independent country; for a land about the size of Wales, and against great odds, it has successfully achieved a passive emergence into modern Europe.

We were now keen to see more of Slovenia and were soon travelling in the motor home again on our way to the capital city. A simple network of motorways and principle highways takes you very easily through this country. We took the main road to Maribor and then joined the motorway to Ljubljana. Skiing is a major sport in Slovenia and there are ample opportunities to do it. Rising just southwest of the city of Maribor, is the Pohorje Massif, the largest skiing centre in the country and one which regularly hosts world cup races. Kranjska Gora, in the Julian Alps, is another mecca for skiing enthusiasts as the World Cup slalom and giant slalom events are held there, and these are but two of many ski resorts available at substantially less cost than the nearby Italian and Austrian runs. While we were driving from Maribor to Ljubljana I had my diary open and as usual was scribbling furiously as I tried to describe the changing landscape. The houses took on a more Austrian appearance, with wide wooden balconies, carved balustrades and shuttered windows. Every garden, large or small, seemed to have its own vineyard, and the distinctive Slovene hay drying racks, dotted the nearby fields. We had long since left behind the countries where small white villages perched themselves on top of precipitous hills and we were now in wide open spaces. A cloth of green covers the hills and vales of Slovenia in July, with woods of beech, oak and fir sprinkled on the top. Snow topped mountains are never far away, their scenic valleys and gorges cutting down into the centre of the country. They would provide fabulous walking holidays; something else that we would have to do another day.

Before long we were rolling into Ljubljana and then through the gates of Jezica Autocamp, a pleasant, well-placed camp site just outside the centre. From there we could catch the local bus, which ran every five minutes into the centre of town. As usual, Simon had steered us safely from one place to the next, as he did brilliantly all through our travels. It was hard that he was the only driver but it would have been too nerve wracking for everyone if I had to get behind the wheel of the Beast. In fact I doubt if we would have ever got out of England – let alone reached Ljubljana in Slovenia.

July

Ljubljana and the Julian Alps

Just as Gaudi left his unmistakable mark on Barcelona, so Plecnik, a modest, contemporary architect of the nineteenth century, has left his signature on the delightful city of Ljubljana. As capital cities go, this isn't a large one, but what it lacks in size it more than makes up for in warmth and vitality. With a large university and three art academies it has a youthful feel, without any of the hustle and bustle of bigger metropolises. In its past it has experienced a history similar to many other towns that were initially founded by the Romans. Sieges, occupation and earthquakes were repeated over the years and with every change came another layer of history, architecture and society. Today, tucked into the shelter of three formidable mountain ranges, it is sufficiently guarded from the rest of Europe to have thankfully missed out on chain store shops, skyscrapers and fast food outlets. It spreads either side of the winding Ljubljanica river; a pleasant mix of Austrian and Slav with a good helping of baroque, renaissance, art nouveau and contemporary thrown in.

We caught the spotlessly clean number six bus (it always seemed to be the number six), into the centre and started our tour in the 'old' town. Here there were no noisy motorbikes and hooting car horns, just wide cobbled streets and elegant pale coloured buildings. Residents and tourists strolled and street cafes did good business. We made our way to the first of the three famous bridges which cross the Ljubljanica River, namely the Cobblers Bridge. Designed by Plecnik, it is of a simple yet unusual construction; a wide span with plain, white stone columns, which links the old town to the new. Following the river, we came to the second bridge – the Triple Bridge which was originally one single bridge built in 1842, but to which Plecnik added two arched side bridges. Then passing through the long colonnade of the gently curving covered market, we finally reached the Dragon Bridge, which was definitely our favourite. Built in 1901 of iron and concrete, this bridge was the one which we wouldn't forget and which Jack has pictures of in his album. A pair of vast winged dragons stand at either end of this angular structure, with evil staring eyes, clawed feet and mouths wide open. Their scaly tails curl around the back of the bridge and smaller entwined dragons with forked tongues decorate the balustrades. This is the dragon that was slain by Jason of the Argonauts when he and his men were fleeing from the Black Sea to the Adriatic with the Golden Fleece. Trapped, when they reached the source of the Ljubljanica River, they dismantled their boat, and were carrying it in pieces across land to the Adriatic when they came to a massive marshy lake. The dragon rose from

the lake and Jason fought long and hard before he killed it. So, what better reason do you need to have a most superb bridge decorated with glowering dragons.......
..........No better reason at all.

Before we stopped for lunch, we walked up to the old castle which sits, surveying all, high above the town. The small tourist train then took us back down for a massive family-sized pizza, after which we decided to split up and do a little personal shopping, which was something of a novelty because after ten months of doing mostly boysy stuff I had almost given up all idea of looking in shop windows at girly things. Simon had noticed an excellent book shop and Jack elected to stay with me to ensure that I didn't get lost. We wandered the streets, window shopping at last. Jack was searching for a new airfix model and I was hoping for anything with feminine appeal. We found both, and after selecting a good model, he patiently waited for me on the steps of the Three Rivers Fountain, (a copy of the one in Rome) while I spent about twenty minutes trying to decide what to buy from a shop selling 'all natural' soaps and perfumes. Eventually, I bought a bar of organic foot balm, which shows just how out of touch I had become with female shopping. I thought that this momentous purchase of mine smelt really nice, but over the next few days, as it warmed up in the hot interior of the Beast, there were loud cries of " what is that disgusting smell" every time I got it out to rub it on my aching feet. It was also melting rather rapidly and turning into one revolting gooey mess, so I was soon forced to ditch it. However, strangely enough, the all-pervading smell of airfix glue, and half-made model bits labelled 'don't touch', was not frowned upon at all, and I sometimes did wonder if our large American motor home was really big enough for the three of us.

Back at camp that afternoon Jack made a bee-line for an interesting adventure course that was being run by two young Slovenian rock climbers. It was aptly named 'Adrenalinski Park'. A stand of very tall trees grew at one side of the camp site and strung between these were rope ladders, beams, bridges and high wires, forming an aerial assault course about forty feet up. Kitted out with helmet and safety harness, Jack fearlessly clambered amongst the leafy canopy, finishing with a great zip-wire ride down to the ground. He spent two hours enjoying this fun 'tree-experience' under the guidance of the English speaking climbers and decided that some form of altitude climbing might be added to his growing list of 'things to do when I'm older'. A list which seemed to consist of activities with a certain degree of danger, like hang gliding, white water rafting, scuba diving and extreme snow boarding. What's wrong with art or theatre I frequently countered to deaf ears.

That evening, as we sat outside the motor home planning the next days itinerary, a friendly Dutch couple came over and introduced themselves to us asking if we would like to join them for a drink. Just like us, Rick and Pia had sold their house and were travelling for a year. They had only been on the road for eleven weeks and were already in a dilemma as to where to go next. She didn't like the heat but he did, so they were torn between going north or south – as simple as that. They had a car and caravan, but as the temperature was now around 28 degrees with no breeze, they were finding it impossible to keep cool in either vehicle. We sympathised and poured over maps and books with them, discussing the alternatives, but when we left them two days later they were still not sure which way to go and for all we know they may still be there discussing it. They were yet another pair of middle-aged-gappers, wandering on this not-so-lonely planet.

We knew that we could spare just one more day in Ljubljana, and then we would be heading slightly north to the cooler foothills of the Julian Alps. Catching the bus again next morning we took a closer look at the city and its buildings; an eclectic mixture of light coloured baroque and art nouveau, wide streets and open courtyards, tree shaded promenades and parks. We also wanted to check our emails and as luck would have it, we decided to go to the University Library internet resource to do this. From the outside, this library is an austere looking building with walls of red brick interspersed with random blocks of white, rough-faced, cut stone. Rigidly linear windows seemed at odds with the haphazard stonework. The entrance had heavy closed doors of very solid looking, dark metal, completely unadorned apart from two brass handles, one dull and unused, but the other well-worn and shiny. Both handles were shaped resembling distinctive horses' heads. We levered the shiny one down and pushed open the door, wondering if indeed we were at the right place. This building is another designed by Joze Plecnik, and is an absolute must to visit, if you are in any way interested in architecture.

We stepped through the door and into an interior of solid black and dark grey marble. Stairs, walls, columns, benches and seats were all austere, linear, heavy and dark, and yet it didn't feel sombre or gloomy. The precision of line and minimal decoration, along with the absolute symmetry of this interior, where every doorway and corridor lined up to give you a perfectly proportioned view, made this a very exciting building. I wanted to explore it all. We went up the marble steps, through dark glass doors and into the foyer – an area of grey marble columns, marble walls and dark wood ceilings. Doors of thick, inlaid wood and dark metal, sealed off the further rooms. The library itself can only be accessed by students, or with special permission, which we didn't have. If we had been able to visit this room we would have seen the rows of sleek, wood and marble desks, art nouveau desk lamps and bizarre, cascading, ceiling lights. We explored as much as we could, eventually reaching the internet room where, sitting at smooth-wood, designer desks, we accessed our emails, and then found a small room where we could at least buy some postcards of the building. As usual I got chatting, this time to the young girl selling the cards while Simon and Jack crept off to do some more exploring. She asked me about England, saying that she thought it might not be a very safe place to travel. I assured her that you had to be careful in some areas, but it wasn't that bad, and asked her about Slovenia. She said that she felt safe in Slovenia, she could hitch-hike safely and walk at night safely, but feared how long this would continue to last now that more and more people were going there. I sadly had to agree that this easy going, well organised, attractive country might one day change.

Saying goodbye to our new Dutch friends, (who may still be there trying to decide which way to go next), we left Ljubljana and headed north west to visit the Triglav National Park. This Park, covering 83,807 hectares, in the central region of the Julian Alps, is the largest, and encompasses tree covered gorges, rocky canyons, glacial lakes, gentle alpine meadows and the highest snow-capped mountains in Slovenia. Bled, famous for its picturesque lake and mediaeval castle, sits at the entrance to the park, but we were heading for the 'pearl' of the Alps, namely Lake Bohinj, (pronounced Boheenya).

We travelled along the valley of the crystal clear, Sava River as it threaded its way through green alpine meadows of wild flowers and ever deepening gorges. At Bled we skirted past the lake with its numerous tourist hotels, and took a smaller road into the Bohinj Basin. The flat valley floor was now being squeezed thinner and thinner between the sides of a precipitous tree covered gorge and the Sava was now a smaller river, with bright coloured kayakers bouncing over clear green, frothing mountain water. We entered the Park and continued along the valley road to the far end of Lake Bohinj, pulling up outside the beautifully positioned 'Zlatorog Camping'. Without too much problem, just a little shunting back and forth, we swung through the gates and then proceeded to take up spaces 2,3,and 4 with our ever embarrassing Big American Butt. Without doubt, the largest thing that had ever managed to squeeze itself onto the site, we felt rather like two-headed aliens, plus spaceship, until Simon had tucked us as discreetly as possible under some trees; rather like trying to hide an elephant in a corn field. We heard comments like, 'Oh my God, the Americans have arrived'. So we gave everyone a few minutes to get over our ridiculous size before we got out for a look around.

Zlatorog is a small, friendly campsite which slopes gently down to the shores of Lake Bohinj. Much of the slope is tree covered, so it is a bit of a juggling act to get a position that doesn't have too many tree roots or branches to deal with. However, with luck you can camp right alongside the lake shore. On the far side of the lake, soaring mountains surround the basin, their sheer cliffs reaching right down to the water. As you look down the lake, the valleys unfold into the distance. This campsite has a relaxed atmosphere, with a busy play area for the many children and adequate facilities. There is no disco, loud music or night clubbing but you can spend the evening drinking wine and talking by candle-light under the roof of the simple, open air restaurant. (There is no shop, so take your own food with you). Bright yellow Canadian canoes and wooden rowing boats can be hired – and that's just what we did as soon as we had got set-up. We rowed across the lake as the sun set and the camp lights were coming on. It's another of those great sites that could easily become a home from home.

Professional organisations offer endless choices of sporting activities for you to try in this area. You can hang-glide, raft, canoe, kayak, abseil, climb, pot-hole or take a panoramic flight in a glider. Next day, Simon and Jack were keen to try a few of the river sports, and the choice was between rafting, canyoning and hydro-speeding. I really didn't feel the need to test myself against the elements, but I was being persuaded to try at least one of these, and so that I didn't appear a complete wimp, I said I would go hydro-speeding, which looked like the easiest to me......(.how wrong can you be?) We booked it up for that afternoon. In the meantime, with the Vogel ski centre 1,500 meters up above us, we rode our bikes up to the cable car station and took a long, almost vertical ride up the side of Mount Vogel to the ski slopes. There we had a fantastic birds-eye view of the lake below, the surrounding valleys and far across the tops of the Julian Alps. It was cold on the top of the mountains but the views were staggering. We walked across the empty ski runs, now covered with grass and tiny alpine flowers and stepped around fat, friendly cows who contentedly chewed the cud, their ding-dong cow bells rhythmically sounding out across the valleys with every chomp. I could have happily stayed up on that mountain top for the rest of the day, and later on, I wished I had done – but of course I didn't know what was in store for me that afternoon.

We cycled the three kilometres down to the arranged meeting place and waited for the arrival of our hydro-speeding guide. He squealed up in a well rounded van and leapt out with all the enthusiasm of a fit young puppy, just raring to have some fun. I instantly got the feeling that I had chosen badly and was going to regret thinking that at my age, I still might enjoy dangerous water sports in freezing rivers. Robbie, our bouncy guide, kitted us out with wet suits, flippers and ...crash helmets...(an ominous sign) – before herding us and three other people (all young and fit) onto a small minibus and driving us in a rather hair-raising fashion, to the place where we would enter the river. In all seriousness, it took me a long while to stop having nightmares about this river experience and it put me off any water sports for a long time afterwards.

The first problem was that we had not previously tried on the wet-suits, and when I did eventually get to put it on, I discovered that mine was very, very tight on me. I was more of a size fourteen now, not a size ten, and it was so tight that I found it hard to breathe and could not easily move my arms and legs because my muscles were so constricted. However, we put them on, along with flippers, lifejackets and crash helmets, and Robbie then handed us our 'Boogie-Boards'. These were made of thick plastic, but resembled heavy, lumps of wood with handles to grip at the sides. With these handles you were supposed to steer yourself through the rapids, around the rocks and over the waterfalls! All was now becoming clear. This was not going to be in any way similar to the gentle drift down the sunny Dordogne River that we had enjoyed several years before in France. This was definitely boys stuff as far as I was concerned, even though there was one other female in the group, (young and fit of course).

The river Sava takes on a whole different, ominous look when you're being swept down it at breakneck speed, clinging on to a completely unwieldy boogie-board, being thrown against rocks, slammed into boulders and hurtled over rapids. My squashed muscles and restricted breathing were giving me real problems and I simply had no control over where I was going. The river was full and fast; the boulders big and hard and I absolutely hated it. An adrenalin rush – not really: fun – not at all; this was a sport for twenty year old extreme sport fanatics who had got bored with bungee jumping and free-fall rock climbing! Robbie was out in front in a canoe, guiding us, (as if I could see anything useful from under my large helmet), and Simon was keeping alongside Jack, who seemed to be managing ok, thank goodness. Luckily, a friendly young Slovenian lad took pity on me, and helped me along as best he could, through the terrifyingly fast water. Even so, I was rammed up against huge boulders, lost my board several times and went under the churning waters many times. Three quarters of the way down I was absolutely shattered and really, very scared. There had been no other places where you could get out of the river, but at this point, where the river got even harder to navigate, I could get out and I did. I had the strangest feeling that if I went any further I would not survive. The others continued on down to the finishing point, while I struggled for a long while to simply get out of my restrictive wet suit. I then had to scrabble on hands and knees, dragging my wet suit, life jacket, boogie-board and helmet, up a thirty foot, precipitous, tree-covered river bank until I reached the main road where I could wait to be picked up. There was no way that I would be 'picked-up' by anyone who didn't know me, because by that time I resembled a mud covered river rat – which is probably an insult to river rats everywhere.

All the others finished the course safely, although a little battered, bruised and shaken. When they picked me up on the way back to the camp site, Robbie had an interesting nugget of information to give me. In the previous year a Dutch woman had died at a place just beyond where I had got out. She had been trapped, pushed under a huge rock by the sheer force of the water and drowned before anyone could get to her. I sometimes wish that he had never told me that. Some people may love this kind of sport, but I will never, ever, do it again!

When we arrived back at camp I headed straight for the hot showers. Simon and Jack, being all keyed–up and full of adrenalinski, jumped on their bikes and cycled off in search of the Savica Slap (waterfall), the source of the river, which gushes out from a limestone cave and falls 71 meters, before flowing on down the gorge and into the lake. It was further than they thought and already getting late in the day, but they gamely pushed their bikes up an endless rough track to reach the view point, admired it and then careered back down in almost complete darkness. This reckless behaviour could have had something to do with the large whiskies that Simon and I had downed on our return to camp, just to steady the nerves again and purely for medicinal purposes you realise. You could say that we had overdone it yet again that day, and I think you'd be absolutely right.

Aching and bruised the next morning we compared scars. My hips, bottom and thighs were an interesting shade of black and blue, and the men had elbow and shin bruising. We all felt battered and had stiff joints; and to think that we'd paid for the pleasure - and it was raining again. This was actually a great relief to me because the men had booked to go canyoning that day, but this had now been cancelled due to bad weather and the dangerous state of the river. I wondered how the river could have possibly got any more dangerous and was very relieved. I think that secretly, they were too!

One of the problems of being situated quite high up in the mountains was that the bad weather rolled round and round the valleys for days at a time. But the good news was that it was my birthday (or so I thought). I opened my cards and presents. A bar of chocolate from Jack, (last of the big spenders), and a special silver bracelet of small linked elephants, which I had admired in Varazdin, from Simon. I then went up to the phone box to call my mother so that she could wish me happy birthday and I could catch up on news from home.

"Hi Mum", I said, "I'm just phoning to see how you are, and because it's my birthday today".

"What are you talking about dear", she replied, "Your birthday was yesterday".

So, sometime in the past few weeks I had lost a day, which wouldn't normally worry me, but I'm a bit funny about my birthday. I don't know why but I felt strangely miffed that I had actually missed my own birthday and had even spent most of it almost drowning. Well, there didn't seem much point in celebrating my non-birthday any-more, so I went off to the laundry room, tumble dried our line of soggy washing, and sulked for as long as possible. You see, not every day is so great, when your travelling.

The camp site was quiet that dreary afternoon. Motor-homers sat snugly behind closed doors and damp campers huddled in their tents or sat chatting in the covered restaurant area. All the children seemed to have disappeared except for one little girl, for whom rain was not going to stop play. Fully clad in a bright red, water-proof cape with the hood pulled well up over her blond hair, she splashed her blue Wellington boots at the edge of the lake all afternoon, taking great pleasure in either feeding the ducks or shooing them away. A scruffy little dog, which constantly used his dripping coat like a spray machine, kept her company and enthusiastically joined in her play. The canoes and rowing boats sat idle, now as wet inside as out and the pretty, blue Jays that were usually flying from tree to tree, were no-where to be seen. A certain malaise seemed to hover over us too. Ever since we had started heading north, on our homeward route, it seemed as if our year was almost over. We had been travelling for ten months; we had lived in our motor home for almost a year and we had become very used to all of it. Every day held something new or different, not always good but usu-ally interesting. We had an easy way of living in the Beast; sometimes we needed our own space, but we had also become very close as a family. We knew that before long we would be back in England trying to work out what we would do next, and Jack would be going back to school in September. We talked about all of this and made a conscious decision to make the very most of the remaining time that we had. We would head back through Austria and Switzerland to France where we had arranged to meet up with Simon's family who were sharing a holiday Gite in Burgundy. Later, in August, we would hopefully meet up with my son Peter, when he would be on holiday in Brittany. But, before that, we decided that we would take the opportunity to visit the French Alps and more specifically the famous Chamonix area and Mount Blanc.

Our route from Slovenia to Austria took us through the Karavanke Mountain chain, which at an altitude of 1000 meters above sea level, was stunningly beautiful. Two impressive tunnels, each eight kilometres long, allow the cross border traffic to drive literally through the mountains, emerging briefly amidst misty, snow covered peaks and perpendicular valleys, before starting the long descent into Austria. At the end of that days' driving through spectacular scenery, we found a good lay-by to spend the night. Simon had a shower, I cooked supper, Jack read a few pages of his book and then we shut the blinds, snuggled down and watched one of our favourite George Clooney movies on the DVD player. We certainly had the best of all worlds.

Back to France

The trouble with trying to drive from Slovenia to Chamonix (in France), is that there is an uncompromising range of awesome mountains in the way, namely – The Alps. You can either go round the bottom of them, straight across northern Italy which we had already done when going to Monza and back, or around the top of them making a wide sweep up towards Zurich and then down to Bern and Geneva. There are smaller roads, suitable for cars, but with time and size against us we decided to use the A roads through southern Austria until we could join the motorway east of Innsbruck and stick with it all the way to Geneva. We could hardly complain at having to drive through such fantastic scenery though.

This is the largest mountain chain in Europe; sweeping in an impressive arc from Mediterranean France to middle Austria and varying from 60 to 120 miles wide in places, with several peaks rising to over 4000 meters. It was caused by the convergence of the African and Eurasian plates which began around 90 million years ago. The major period of mountain building took place around 20 million years ago and the landscape which you see today is the result of glaciations during the last two million years. This vast time scale rather puts into perspective our own brief appearance on the planet. 'U'-shaped hanging valleys, and lakes such as Como and Garda, which were naturally dammed by glacial moraines, provide excellent visual proof of the power of glaciers. Retreating glaciers allow specialized plants to colonise the newly exposed rocky slopes and here alpine flowers and grasses thrive. Snow is evident on the higher slopes all year round and in summer the lower slopes are covered with alpine meadows. We were heading for Mont Blanc, the highest mountain (4,807 meters) in the range, although the Matterhorn and the Eiger come a close second and third. We also wanted to visit the Mer de Glace (Sea of Ice) which is close by. This is the second largest glacier in the Alps being seven kilometres long, 1,950 meters across at its widest point and up to a staggering 400 meters deep. Jack was getting a 'hands on' geography lesson as we drove through this region, when glacial moraines and hanging valleys would 'get real'.

Working our way across the southern Austrian Alps, stopping frequently by tumbling mountain streams to enjoy the impressive scenery, we passed Grosglockner, Austria's highest mountain, which we had been told to look out for by the Austrian family who had befriended us at Moravski Spa. Unfortunately it was shrouded in heavy mist, so we only glimpsed its lower slopes. That evening we wild camped in a lay-by close to a small village. A convenient hole in the hedge at the back of the lay-by allowed us to walk through onto a cycle path which took us on a pleasant evening stroll around the streets. In full view, behind the village, a range of snow capped mountains provided a fabulous back drop equal to anything from The Sound of Music.

The roads climbed and dropped, climbed and dropped, weaving their way through southern Austria towards Switzerland on a circuitous but scenic route. That day, heavy clouds and persistent rain prevented us from seeing the best views and made driving all the more laborious. We hadn't got off to an early start anyway, due to some late night phone calls to family back in England, plus we had wasted time trying to recover money from our Austrian 'Go' box. This was an electronic monitoring box which we had to buy in order to drive on Austrian motorways. You had to buy a minimum 50 euros worth of credit at a time and we were leaving the country with about 30 euros worth still unused. However, despite our best attempts we were unable to recover the money. We then had to buy special road tax for use on the Swiss roads. We felt as if we were being inexorably dragged back into the expensive, northern European lifestyle and felt desperately like taking the next road south and just 'going round' for another year. Responsibility and reality were creeping ever nearer. We pulled into another lay-by early that afternoon and gave up on the day. We were in a wide Swiss valley of agricultural fields and small neat villages, all backed by craggy grey mountains. A dark moody sky allowed shafts of sunlight to spotlight green swathes in the fertile valley, iridescent against the black, sombre mountains, and two red kites entertained us with acrobatic flight as we ate our meal and tried to adopt a more positive attitude to our future.

Switzerland's excellent motorway network now took us speedily, if not a little boringly, around the great blocks of mountain which make up so much of that country. Around Bern, the misty skies cleared to allow the sun to shine once more and as we crossed the flat open plain between Bern and Lausanne, the white peaks of the French Alps, dazzling against the clear sky, enticed us towards them. Skirting around Geneva, (which we decided to view better at a later date), we entered France again, for the third time on our trip. A useful picnic 'aire', (yes, we were back to those wonderful aires again), had motor home facilities, so before we headed on we were able to unload our grey waste tanks and fill up with fresh water. With a full pantry under the bed, and a well stocked fridge, we were ready to spend a few days at Chamonix. We were going to be lucky with the weather now, because grey skies had given way to blue, and wall to wall sunshine shone again as we finally entered the deep, winding valley of the River Arve.

Tumbling, crystal clear, ice cold mountain water flows right through the centre of Chamonix, but you could be forgiven for not noticing the river as you will spend most of your time gazing upwards at the magnificent scenery. Mont Blanc is just one of many mountains which tower over the town; soaring, snow covered and utterly awesome. Wisps of white, ghost-cloud drift through the peaks and the arcing sun makes solid rock faces shift in ever-changing shapes. We arrived on the only road into town and quickly spotted a huge car park where we could park up and stay for a few days. There were many motor-homes there already, with some almost as big as ours, but we still managed to struggle while getting through the entrance barriers. They were really designed for cars and were fairly narrow. We squeezed up to the entrance where we had to insert our ready bought ticket, but for some reason the barrier wouldn't go up. We tried and tried and tried but with no luck, so now, holding everyone else up as usual, I ran over to the phone which was available for summoning the attendant. In garbled French I explained our problem and after an embarrassingly long time, a small van squealed into the car park. The disgruntled attendant did a double-take of the Beast and came to the front of the barrier. Then, signalling for us to pull forward just a few inches, he put our ticket in the machine and hey presto, the barrier opened. So, if you are ever at Chamonix and have this problem, just make sure that you are close enough to the barrier and you're ticket will work! I hoped that everyone around was too busy looking at the amazing scenery to notice our farcical entrance, and we quickly parked up alongside the biggest motor-home that we could see; which happened to be German.

This is a great place to park-up as it is literally five minutes walk from the town centre and ski lifts. Jack had a shower and then took over the kitchen, cooking us a great chilli-con-carne for supper, while Simon and I walked to the tourist centre and bought our lift passes for the following morning. In peak season queues for tickets can be long, especially early in the morning when climbers and walkers are waiting to head off and it helps if you can buy your ticket and boarding passes the day before – and don't forget that if you miss your ride you may forfeit your ticket.

Next morning we entered the 8.0 am cable car, which would take us in two separate stages up to 3,842 meters above sea level, to the Aiguille du Midi - the solitary spire of rock situated just eight kilometres from the summit of Mont Blanc. The early morning air was clear and fresh and our long, green valley was still in cool shade, waiting for the sun to climb above the peaks to warm the land. The lift-car rose from the valley floor, passing over forest and hill, gently ascending, while the town, river, road and people rapidly diminished below us and the whole valley came into view. We were soon looking out across the granite peaks of lower mountain ranges and Chamonix now resembled a tiny village in miniature. Ten breathtaking minutes later we arrived at the Plan de L'Aiguille, the half way point. We then had to board the second cable car, which would take us on another ten minute ride up to the top, the Aiguille du Midi. So, with slightly sweaty hands, I gripped the hand rails inside the cable car on a fairly scary, almost vertical ride up the side of the mountain over jagged, snow covered rock. The drop below us was staggering and the cable wires which held us aloft looked ridiculously undersized. Finally, we soared almost vertically upwards into the thin blue atmosphere of the snow covered summit.

We now looked down on granite mountain tops and across the peaks of endless mountain ranges into the blue, blue yonder. Here, Simon helped me to disengage my locked fingers, and we disembarked onto the terraces of the restaurant and café complex where we strolled and enjoyed the breathtaking views around us. How anyone had managed to build anything onto that jagged pinnacle, at such a height, I could not imagine. The terraces were hammered into the rock and decorated with thick, year round, permanent icicles of grand proportion. We walked all around the pinnacle, taking in the complete vista; a panorama of the main French, Swiss and Italian summits from about seven mountain ranges. It was truly beautiful. Up there, where even on a summer's day the temperature would normally be down to minus ten degrees, the air was raw. We huddled in our warmest coats while a fellow tourist took a group photo of us three, with the blue sky and dazzling white peak of Mont Blanc just behind us.

Jack and Simon now ascended to the final, topmost part of the Aiguille. To do this they entered a small lift which held just eight people at a time. This went up the inside of the rock and came out on a small terrace at the very pinnacle. They said that it was fantastic, and I happily took their word for it, content to stay where I was. More tourists were now arriving on the lifts and well-equipped climbers, clanking around in their cumbersome kit, were preparing to leave the snug security of the buildings to head out onto the mountain. They followed their guide in single file, out along a narrow ridge of dazzling, frozen snow, and soon disappeared into the distance becoming a line of tiny black dots in a dramatic white landscape. There is something quite ethereal about being amongst mountain tops. An absolute serenity and peacefulness seems to hang in the thin cool air. They are so vast, so awesome, so uncompromising and so marvellously untouched by man.

A massive sky, streaked by thin white clouds, stretched forever over summits and peaks which rolled one after the other, as far as the eye could see. Like the deserts and the oceans, they seemed immortal.

Before long, we heard the excited chatter of those ever-present stampeding Japanese tourists and we decided to take the lift back down to the middle landing stage. There we would get off and start our walk across to the glacier. This well-worn trail is just below the snow line and takes two to three hours to complete - depending on how fit you feel. You do need comfortable shoes and some of it is quite sheer, although it is all very safe and well marked. This was a glorious walk across steep hillsides, covered with alpine flowers, with wonderful views all around us. Snowy peaks were just above and the green, green valley was way below. As far as the eye could see was blue sky and mountains. It was hot now, so our coats were in our back packs and our jumpers were tied around our waists. Jack leapt onward like a youthful mountain goat, while I dragged behind admiring stunted rhododendron bushes or minute forget-me-nots of deepest blue with pure yellow centres. Simon enjoyed the peace and kept us moving onward when we dawdled at the many cairns of stone, trying to add just three more to the very top of each cairn.

At last we reached the final climb which led us to a viewpoint. There we joined fellow walkers who had sat down to rest and study the glacier which filled the valley below us. At first I wondered what all the fuss was about. To me it simply looked like a valley of dirty grey and white snow, but when I took the binoculars and studied it more closely I realised the magnitude of this enormous sheet of ice. The Mer de Glace is so called because it resembles a sea of frozen waves, with distinct alternating lines of light and dark ice on its surface. These are caused by variations of dust and debris which collects in the ice. From a distance, the surface appears cracked by hundreds of thin lines, but when you look through binoculars you realise that these are actually huge crevasses. In one area, I could see a long line of small dark spots and when I focused on them I saw that they were in fact walkers, roped together. They looked absolutely miniscule on the surface of the glacier that stretches back up into the winding valley, a seven kilometre, solid, block which creeps forward 90 meters a year.

At the mouth of the glacier, a deep grotto has been tunnelled into the ice, enabling you to see it from the inside. We started down the steep, zig-zag path which would take us to the mountain railway station and the ice cave. Unfortunately, this is where you descend back into tourism and it does get very busy. An old mountain train brings carriages of people up from Chamonix to visit the glacier, cafes, restaurants and souvenir shops, which all ply for the custom of a steady torrent of tourists. We grabbed some filled rolls for a late lunch and then crammed into one of the small, gondola-type cable cars. Down to the face of the glacier we went, having just a short walk along metal ramps to reach the entrance to the ice grotto. Because the glacier is in perpetual motion, the ice grotto has been freshly cut each year for the last fifty years. The lofty face of the glacier was a dirty grey colour, not really resembling ice at all, but when we entered the dripping passageway and walked into the depths of the tunnel, we were transported into a world of sapphire blue. This is a strange phenomenon of dense glacial ice, which due to its crystalline structure, absorbs all except the shortest and bluest wavelengths of visible light. Trooping through the carved rooms, in a moving sea of tourists, we duly admired ice sculptures while a steady drip, drip of freezing water dropped onto our heads, reminding us that we were standing underneath thousands of tones of ice. It was an excellent way of appreciating just how big the whole thing was.

Pottering around Chamonix and walking quietly in the lower hills was all that we could manage the next day. Hang gliders in all colours of the rainbow, drifted down into the valley from far up high, playing on the updrafts like floating feathers. Red-socked walking tours marched briskly up into the mountains, only to straggle slowly back that evening, slightly bent and weak at the knees. We relaxed and enjoyed the ambiance, knowing that we would be moving-on the following day. Squeezing out between the heavy concrete barriers was even harder than squeezing in. With literally only half an inch to spare in all directions and a serious problem with the length,

Simon had a nightmare time getting us through the exit and we would have happily paid more than the ten euros it had cost us for the two days, if only it had been a little easier. However, before long we were rolling back down the Arve Valley on our way to Burgundy.

Getting sidetracked is one of the pleasanter inevitabilities of motor homing. If you can pull up and explore an unscheduled but interesting find, then why not? So, on our way to Burgundy, that's exactly what we did. It didn't take much of our time, only about five hours, and it turned into one of those unforgettable moments. We hadn't been driving long, but after the difficulties of extracting ourselves from the Chamonix parking area, we soon felt like stopping for a cup of coffee. We were skirting around the bottom of Geneva, heading for Macon, when we pulled into a large car park alongside the motorway. I put the kettle on and Simon and Jack got out for a wander around and to stretch their legs. We all noticed a rather strange building in the corner of the car park and on further inspection discovered that it was an extremely neat and well organised cable car station, or as the French called it, a 'Telepherique'. The attendant told us that we were at the base of Mont Saleve, a ridge which rose almost vertically to 1,380 meters and that from the top of the ridge we would be able to get amazing views down onto Geneva and across to the Alps. The telepherique was designed to take bicycles too, and he assured us that at the top it was only a short, flat ride to the view point.

So, despite all agreeing earlier that we were going to take it very easy that day, we finished our coffee, un-hitched the bikes from the back of the Beast and rode across the car park to the cable car station. The green painted, glass sided cars ran every twelve minutes and would easily hold about nine people and their bikes. It was very quiet and the only other occupants of our car were a very smartly dressed French grandmother and her small grandson. Once again, this was a vertical ride which soared up the side of the ridge, to a height of 1,100 meters. The land rapidly fell away from us and the motorway, our car park and motor home began to look more like a Scalectrix set. When we reached the top we were so high that we couldn't spot the Beast at all. We pushed our bikes off and rode up to the nearby restaurant. Once again, a massive view of France and Switzerland spread out before us, while far below lay the whole of Geneva and the massive lake with its spouting water fountain. From where we stood, the Jet d'eau particularly caught our attention. Well, it's pretty un-missable really as it spouts 16 tons of water, 140 meters up into the sky at about 120 miles per hour and just along from where we were standing more hang-gliding enthusiasts took running jumps off the cliff top, to soar and glide like colourful, oversized birds out over the plains.

Geneva sits at the extreme south-west of Switzerland, between the Alps and the Jura mountains. It has made the most of its geographical position, being just one hours plane ride from Paris or Milan and two hours from London, Rome and Madrid. It has become an international meeting place attracting thousands of people each year to conferences and exhibitions, and hosts the headquarters of the United Nations and the

International Red Cross. The lake, fountain, many parks and surrounding mountains, add that natural ingredient which makes a city extra special. But be warned, you will pay extra special prices there too.

In order to see the mountain ranges on the other side of the Saleve Ridge, we now had to take a short bike ride across this flat plateau. One hour later, and sweating like french onions under a blistering sun, we puffed our way up the final incline to find the plateau. Only mad dogs and Englishmen go out in the mid-day sun, and we now qualified for both of these. That telepherique attendant must have had a wild imagination if he thought the Saleve was flat. But, the 'Panorama de la Chaine du Mont Blanc' seen from the final view point, was well worth the effort. We spent a long while admiring it, and then turned and free-wheeled at top speed, all the way back down the spiralling road to the telepherique, just in time to catch the next ride down to the car park. It had been an unforgettable side-track but it was now four o'clock, the day was disappearing just like our year and we had to get going for Macon.

Peter was going to get a lift over with his friends the following day and I just couldn't wait to see him. I spent most of the next morning hopping up and down like a flea on a dog's back, watching the gate for their car to arrive. Then there was Peter, looking good, although still suffering from the effects of his accident back in February. He stayed with us for a few days and we hired another car so that we could all explore the area together. The coastline was pleasant, with sandy coves and low coastal paths but everywhere was getting busy now, with the holiday season in full swing. The roads were packed with trippers and it was also incredibly hot. It was wonderful to spend time with Peter and we knew that we would be seeing much more of him when we all got back to England; that was one of the things that we were looking forward to most when we returned – and our return seemed absolutely inevitable now.

We passed the days; day tripping to St Nazaire to visit its famous ship yards, and canoeing on a pea green river that was as thick as soup. We barbecued in the evenings, and even met up with our old friend Lizzie whom we had first met in Oliva in Spain – but our ticket on the ferry was now booked. Stark reality was just around the corner and it was too late to turn back. We would have liked to programme a few extra destinations into Maisy; like Morocco or Greece or Timbuktu, but that would be totally irresponsible. So we said our goodbyes to Peter and his friends, arranging to see them back in England, and headed on up through Brittany. That night we wild camped in a car park next to the sea; one of the last that we would have. We were now on the northern coast of France, back where we had started almost a year ago, in the bay of Le Mont St Michel. We had found a quiet road which hugged the coast and had pulled into the car park after spotting a roadside cafe selling fresh mussels and oysters. What better reason could we have for stopping?

This bay had extensive mud-flats and flat marshy grass areas, and beyond that were the mussel and oyster beds. Down at the café, huge pans of water were kept perpetually boiling while endless buckets of absolutely fresh mussels and oysters were cooked. It was extremely basic, just wooden tables and chairs, and a stall next door selling bottles of excellent, cheap, local wine. This was almost our last night and I'm afraid that we overdid it one last time. The fresh sea food was absolutely delicious, served simply with soft hunks of bread and a light local wine, and we sat there for most of the evening eating and drinking as if we'd never see another mussel again. Jack had his fair share too and then wandered back to the motor home to watch a movie, leaving us to weave our own way back along the beach. Much later, in the moonlight, we walked home along the sandy path to the Beast. The tide was now in, which gave us a perfect excuse for skimming pebbles, and for Simon to lay down, fully clothed in the surf and declare that he was never going to leave France. Jack pointed the way to bed, and we eventually obeyed like two truculent teenagers.

We awoke next morning with a slight hangover, a strong taste of mussels and a great view of sky and sea across the bay. We would be catching our ferry the next day and, besides feeling absolutely dismal about the whole thing, we also had a complete panic attack when we realised that we hadn't bought a single present for anyone back home. Le Mont St Michel was on our route back to Caen, so with some misgivings we called in there. We were almost back full circle; eleven months ago we had been there before, just setting out on our wonderful journey. Le Mont in winter had been terrific, but now, in peak season, it was Le Mont St Hell. Cars queued in an endless line just to get to the car park, which was heaving with families coming and going to the town. Jack and I fought our way, like invading barbarians, up the ramparts and into the tourists shops to grab a few mementoes for his closest friends and then fought our way out again. English caravans, cars and motor homes sped past us heading south and for once we were glad to be heading in the other direction.

At Ouistreham, we had our last night in France. Maybe they knew we were leaving or maybe it was a special Saints day, but that night a long firework display illuminated the harbour. We three led on the bed in the back of the motor home and watched it from our back window. Then, at around mid-night we called it a day and went to sleep. At dawn next morning we made our last U turn and headed for the ferry terminal.

One kilometre from the boat, an English removal van came hurtling towards us and smashed to pieces one of our large and essential wing mirrors. It was almost like an omen. We had travelled all round Europe for almost a year without one accident and there we were ten minutes from the ferry and an English van hits us. They didn't stop of course, so with two small, square, bathroom mirrors taped onto the remaining arm we boarded the ferry. We were going home..... ahhh, come to think of it, we didn't have a home to go to!

Of all the people on that boat, I think that we probably looked the most sombre. Sat on the deck, watching the land recede, we would have given anything to be back on a scary cable-car ride, or climbing a gorge, or skimming through blue seas in a boat, or riding our bikes along a sunny, empty promenade by a sandy beach, or skiing down a mountain, or sleeping in a car park or driving over precipitous peaks or climbing a bell tower, or eating fresh mussels with a chilled local wine or laughing together over some crazy thing or other. It was hard not to be sad that it was all over.

It wasn't that we didn't want to go back and see our family and friends. One of the many things that I learned during our trip was just how important those people are to me. How easy it is to let friends drift away from you if you don't take the time to call them, meet up with them and be there for them. My children and grandchildren of course, mean everything to me. It had been the icing and the cherry on the cake that we should experience all that we did with one of our children – I only wished we could have done it with them all. We had travelled out of season, seen countries at their best and worst, met strangers who had immediately become friends, had good times, bad times and just a few ugly times; that's what its like to travel. At the end of it all you will have a million memories; your world will have grown and your life will change. So if you have a dream, don't wait for it to come true – follow it now.

Because if you don't................... you may one day wish that you had.

One year on.........

It took us a few months to settle down again. Not because everything had changed, but more because we had changed. The first few weeks were hectic. We spent a frantic fortnight catching up with family and friends and then took some time deciding what to do next. Our dear old neighbours, Gerry and Steve, had arranged for us to park up at the local airfield for as long as we wanted, so we were able to live in the motor home while we looked for a house to rent on the Welsh borders, which was where Jack's school was. Jack settled the easiest; slotting into school as if he had never been away. His friends accepted him straight back, he very quickly caught up with missed work and has just attained good pass marks in his mock GCSE's. His horizons have broadened and his confidence has grown.

We had to find a way to re-fill the coffers, so we bought an old house, and while Simon fell back on his skills as a brilliant renovator of property, I satisfied my other lifelong ambition. I had always had another dream which had to be followed ......which was to write a book. So, in between all of life's other demands, I got my head down and did it. For me it was a double pleasure to re-live each day of our travels; just talking about it meant that we could enjoy it all over again. A double-whammy if you like. And tomorrow, well who knows. We will have to go travelling again; it's in the blood now and cannot be denied. But when that will be, we do not know. That's for our next adventure; our next dream.

Where it will lead us who can tell, but wherever it goes, we shall surely have to follow.

<u>Campsites we used and would recommend</u>

France
Normandy - Camping de la Gerfleur, 50270 Barneville Carteret.
Tel (+33) (0) 2-3304 3841 email alabouriau@aol.com

Languedoc, Roussillon – Camping la Nautique 11100 Narbonne.
Tel (+33) (0) 4 – 68904819 email info@campinglanautique.com
Aquitaine – Public car parking amongst pine trees at Pyla sur Mer, Les Dunes du Pyla.
(with toilet blocks and water)

Loire Atlantique – Camping l'Hermitage, 36, Avenue de Paradis, 44290 Gueneme
Penfao. Tel (+33) (0) 2-40792348 email conatact@campingl'hermitage.com

Spain
Catalonia – Camping Vilanova 08800 Vilanova y la Geltru
(for Barcelona). Tel (+34) 93-8933402 email info@vilanovapark.es

Valencia – Kiko Park, 46780 Oliva/ Valencia. Tel (+34) 96-2850905
Email kikopark@kikopark.com

Murcia – Caravaning La Manga 30370 La Manga del Mar Menor
Tel (+34)968-563019 email lamanga@caravaning.es

Andalucia – Camping Mar Azul 04711, Almerimar, Almeria.
Tel (+34) 950-497589 email info@campingmarazul.com

Granada (Andalucia) – Camping- Motel Sierra Nevada, Avd. Madrid 107. 18014
Granada. Tel (+34) 958-150062 email campingmotel@terra.es

Ronda (Andalucia) – Camping El Sur, Ctra Algerciras km2.8, 29400 Ronda. Tel (+34)
95-2875939 email info@campingelsur.com

Tarifa (Andalucia) – Camping Tarifa, km 78.87, 11380 Tarifa (Cadiz) Tel (+34) 956
684778

El Puerto de Santa Maria, (Andalucia) – Camping Playa Dunas, 11500 El Puerto.
Tel (+34) 956 872210 email campinglasdunas@terra.es

Portugal
Olhao (Algarve) – Parque de Campismo 8700-912 Olhao.
Tel (+35) 289700300 email sbsicamping@mail.telepac.pt

Italy
Tuscany (for Florence) – Campeggio Il Poggetto 50010 Troghi, Firenze.
Tel (+39) 055-8307323 eamil poggetto@tin.it

Lazio (for Rome) – Campeggio Porticciolo 00062 Bracciano. Tel(+39) 06-99803060 email info@porticciolo.it

Campania (for Pompeii /Naples)- Campeggio Zeus, 80045 Pompeii (next door to ruins) Tel (+39) 081-8615320 email info@campingzeus.it

Sicily (for Lipari Islands) – Campeggio Villaggio Marinello, 98060 Oliveri, Sicily. Tel(+39) 0941-313000 email marinello@camping.it

Sicily (South Coast) – Scarabeo Camping, 97017 Punta Bracetto, Sicily. Tel (+39) 0932-918096 email info@scarabeocamping.it

Taormina (Sicily) – Campeggio La Forcetta Sicula, 98030 S.'Alessio Siculo Tel (+39) 0942-751657 email lafocetta@camping.it

Venice – Campeggio Marina di Venezia, 30010 Cavallino / Treporti, Punta Sabbioni. Tel (+39) 041 5302511 email camping@marinadivenezia.it

Croatia
Rovinj – Campingplatz Polari, 52210 Rovinj, Istria Tel (+385) (0) 52-801501 email polari@jadran.tdr.hr

Paklenika – Campingplatz Paklenika, 23244 Starigrad/Paklenika, Zadar/Knin. Tel (+385) (0) 23- 369236 email alan@zadar.net

Dubrovnik - Campingplatz Autocamp Solitudo, 2000 Dubrovnik Tel(+385) (0) 20-448686 email sales.department@babinkuk.com

Plitvicka – Autocamp Korana 47246 Plitvicka/ Jezera (Karlovak)
Tel (+385) (0) 53-751888 email info@np-plitvice.com

Slovenia
Campingplatz Moravske Toplice Spa, 9226 Moravske Toplice.
Tel(+386) (0) 2-5121200 email receptija.camp2@terme3000.si

Ljubljiana – Campingplatz Jezica, Dunajska 270, 113 Ljubljana Tel (+386) (0) 1-5683913 email acjezica@gp.net

Printed in the United Kingdom
by Lightning Source UK Ltd.
121477UK00001B/158/A

TAILS
I LOSE

JUSTYN REES LARCOMBE

L I O N

Published by Lion Books
an imprint of
Lion Hudson plc
Wilkinson House, Jordan Hill Road,
Oxford OX2 8DR, England
www.lionhudson.com/lion

ISBN 978 0 7459 5647 3
e-ISBN 978 0 7459 5648 0

First edition 2014

Acknowledgments
The Twelve Steps of Alcoholics Anonymous adapted with
permission of Alcoholics Anonymous World Services, Inc.
("AAWS") Permission to adapt the Twelve Steps does not
mean that AAWS has reviewed or approved the contents of
this publication, or that AAWS necessarily agrees with the
views expressed herein. A.A. is a program of recovery from
alcoholism only - use of the Twelve Steps in connection
with programs and activities which are patterned after A.A.,
but which address other problems, or in any other non-A.A.
context, does not imply otherwise.

A catalogue record for this book is available from the British
Library

Cover photo © Justyn Rees Larcombe

Printed and bound in Great Britain by
Marston Book Services Ltd, Oxfordshire